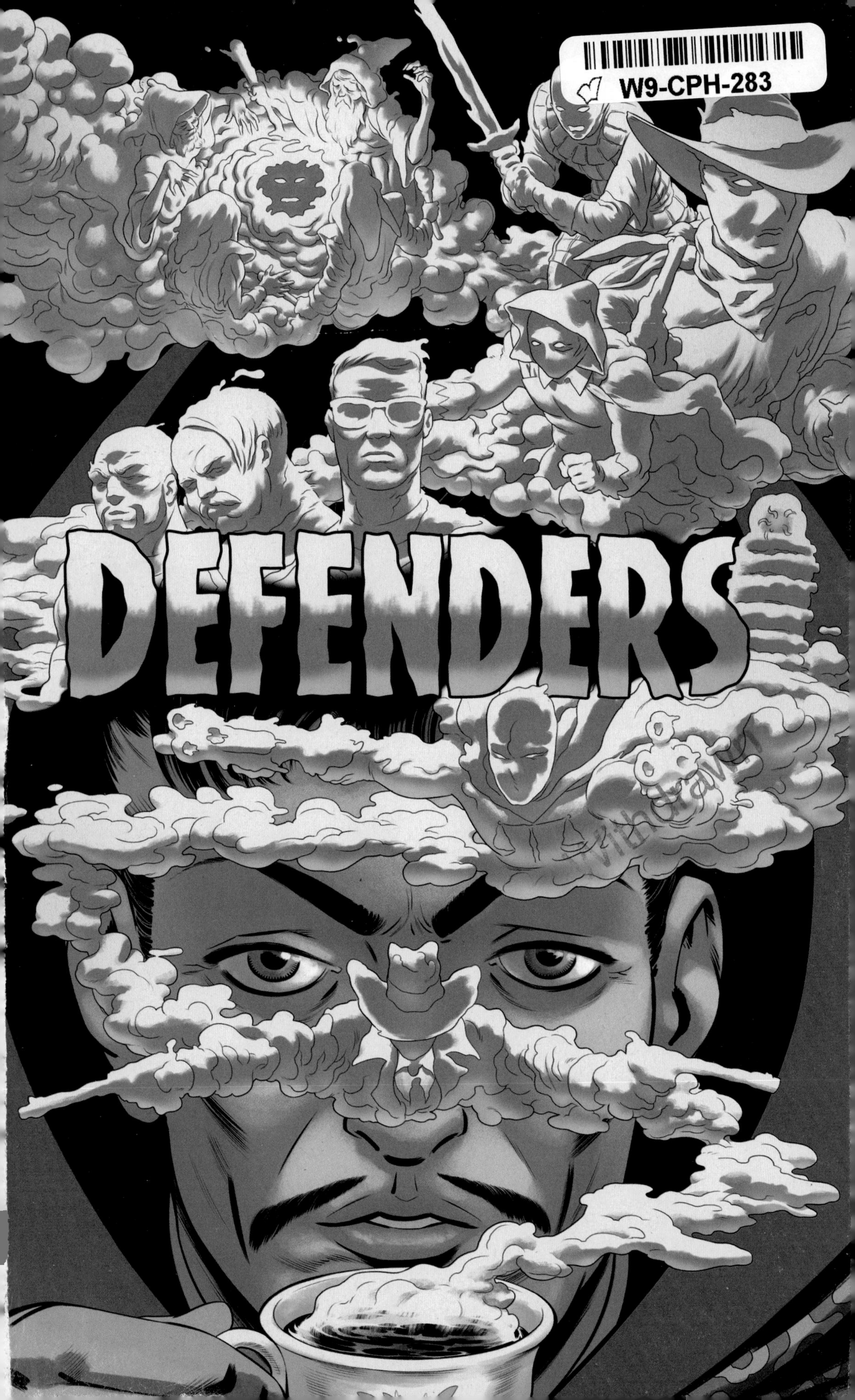
DEFENDERS

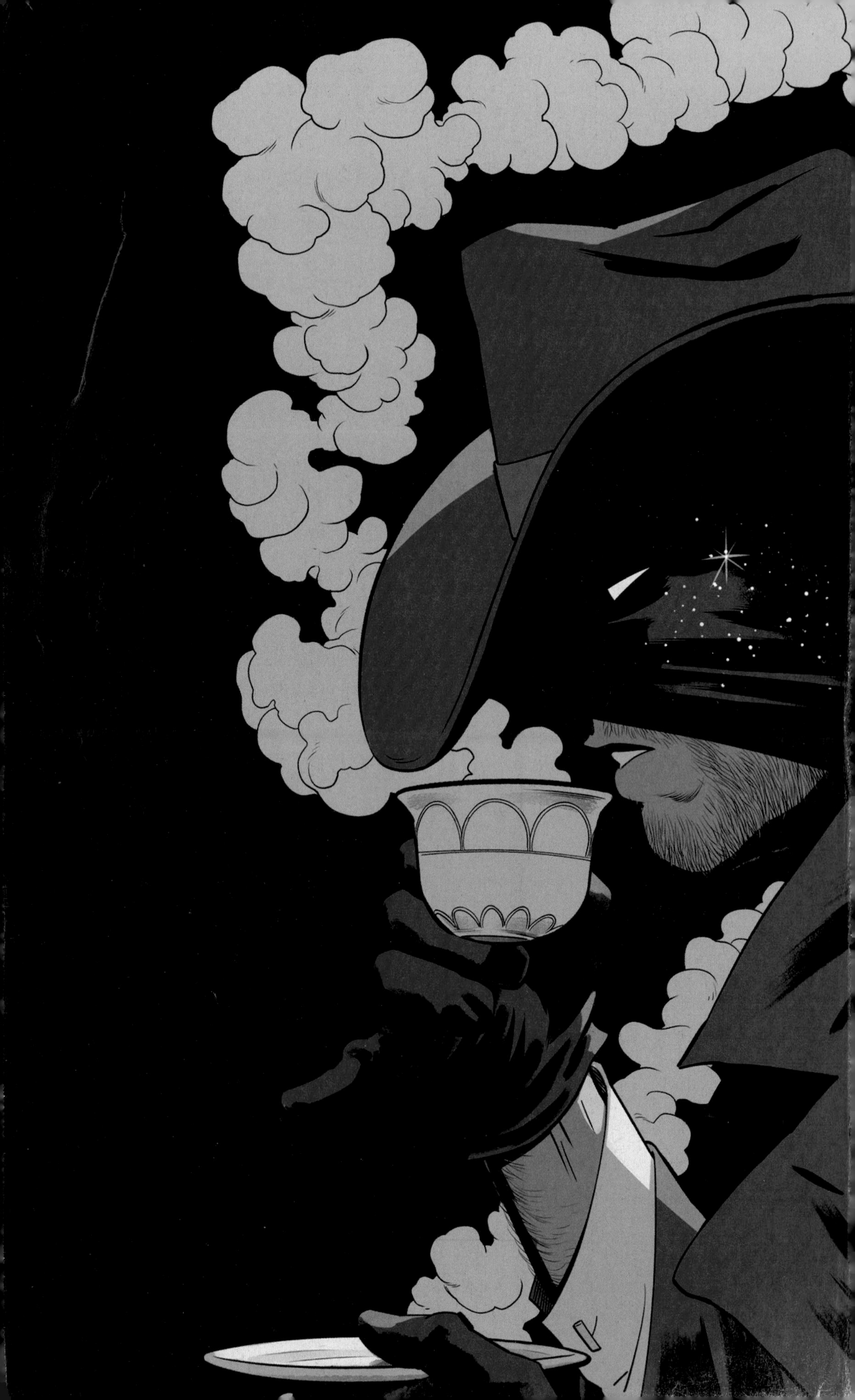

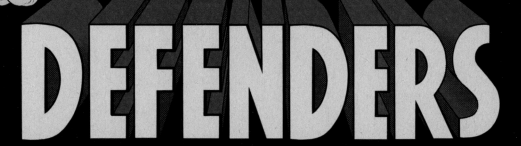

DEFENDERS

THERE ARE NO RULES

STORYTELLERS
AL EWING & JAVIER RODRÍGUEZ

INKERS
JAVIER RODRÍGUEZ
WITH **ÁLVARO LÓPEZ** (#1)

LETTERER
VC's **JOE CARAMAGNA**

COVER ART
JAVIER RODRÍGUEZ

ASSISTANT EDITOR
KAITLYN LINDTVEDT

ASSOCIATE EDITOR
ALANNA SMITH

EDITORS
WIL MOSS & SARAH BRUNSTAD

COLLECTION EDITOR **DANIEL KIRCHHOFFER**
ASSISTANT MANAGING EDITOR **MAIA LOY**
ASSOCIATE MANAGER, TALENT RELATIONS **LISA MONTALBANO**
DIRECTOR, PRODUCTION & SPECIAL PROJECTS **JENNIFER GRÜNWALD**
VP PRODUCTION & SPECIAL PROJECTS **JEFF YOUNGQUIST**
BOOK DESIGNER **ADAM DEL RE**
SVP PRINT, SALES & MARKETING **DAVID GABRIEL**
EDITOR IN CHIEF **C.B. CEBULSKI**

DEFENDERS: THERE ARE NO RULES. Contains material originally published in magazine form as DEFENDERS (2021) #1-5 and MARVEL COMICS (2019) #1000-1001. First printing 2022. ISBN 978-1-302-92472-0. Published by MARVEL WORLDWIDE, INC., a subsidiary of MARVEL ENTERTAINMENT, LLC. OFFICE OF PUBLICATION: 1290 Avenue of the Americas, New York, NY 10104. **Printed in Canada.** KEVIN FEIGE, Chief Creative Officer; DAN BUCKLEY, President, Marvel Entertainment; JOE QUESADA, EVP & Creative Director; DAVID BOGART, Associate Publisher & SVP of Talent Affairs; TOM BREVOORT, VP, Executive Editor; NICK LOWE, Executive Editor, VP of Content, Digital Publishing; DAVID GABRIEL, VP of Print & Digital Publishing; MARK ANNUNZIATO, VP of Planning & Forecasting; JEFF YOUNGQUIST, VP of Production & Special Projects; ALEX MORALES, Director of Publishing Operations; DAN EDINGTON, Director of Editorial Operations; RICKEY PURDIN, Director of Talent Relations; JENNIFER GRÜNWALD, Director of Production & Special Projects; SUSAN CRESPI, Production Manager; STAN LEE, Chairman Emeritus. For information regarding advertising in Marvel Comics or on Marvel.com, please contact Vit DeBellis, Custom Solutions & Integrated Advertising Manager, at vdebellis@marvel.com. For Marvel subscription inquiries, please call 888-511-5480. **Manufactured between 2/18/2022 and 3/22/2022 by SOLISCO PRINTERS, SCOTT, QC, CANADA.**

10 9 8 7 6 5 4 3 2 1

I

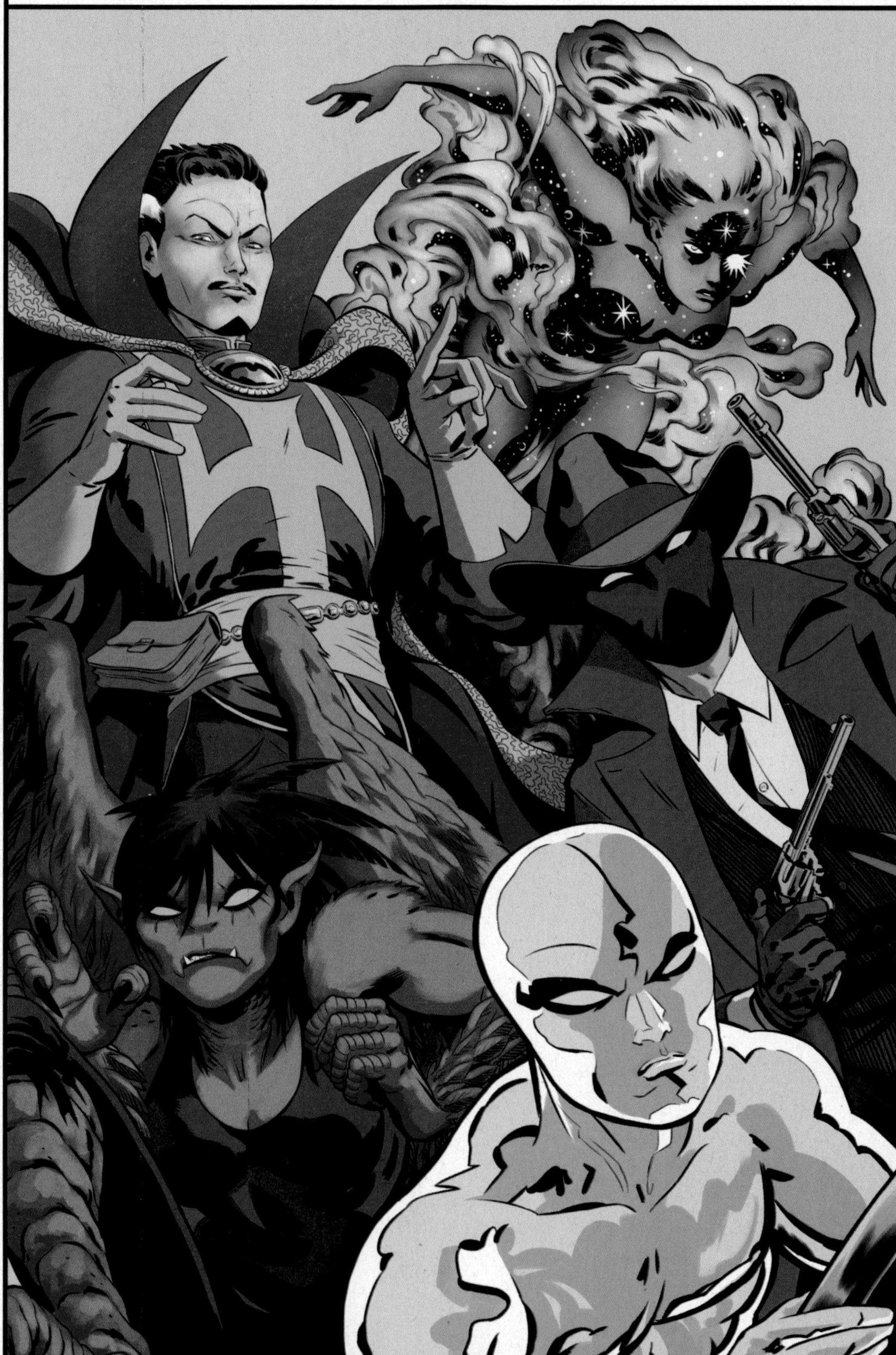

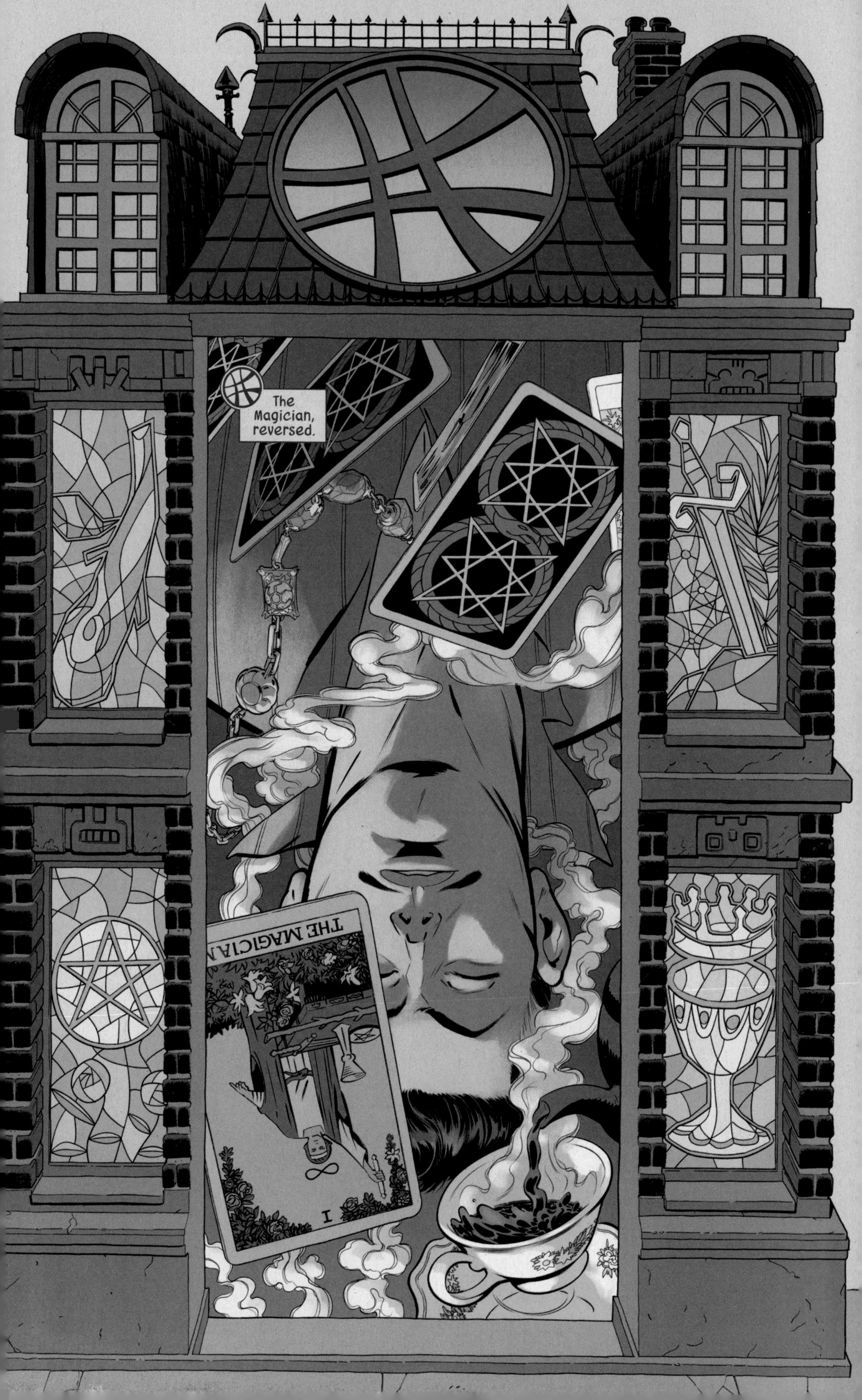
The Magician, reversed.
THE MAGICIAN
I

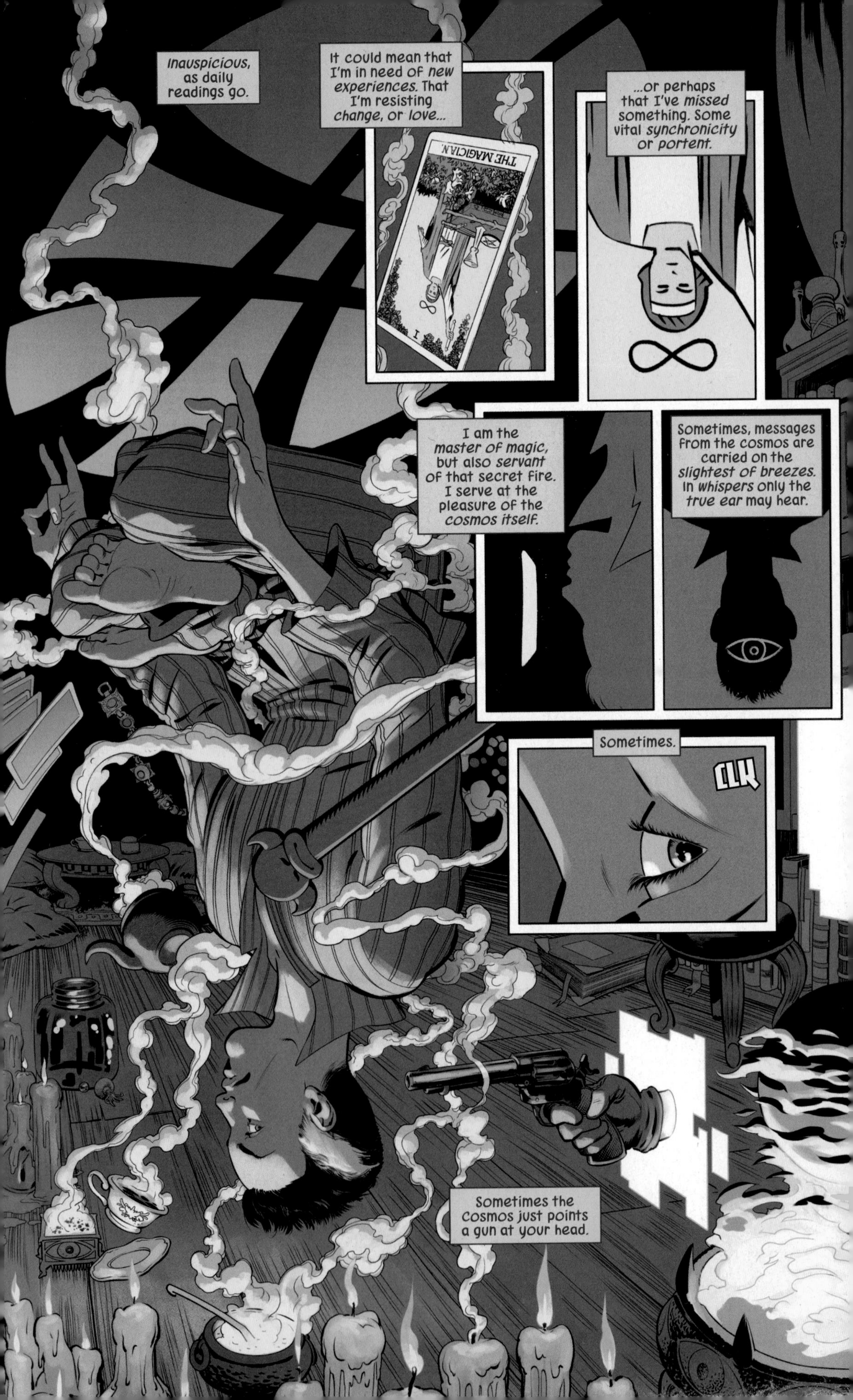
Inauspicious, as daily readings go.
It could mean that I'm in need of new experiences. That I'm resisting change, or love...
THE MAGICIAN.
I
...or perhaps that I've missed something. Some vital synchronicity or portent.
I am the master of magic, but also servant of that secret fire. I serve at the pleasure of the cosmos itself.
Sometimes, messages from the cosmos are carried on the slightest of breezes. In whispers only the true ear may hear.
Sometimes.
CLK
Sometimes the cosmos just points a gun at your head.

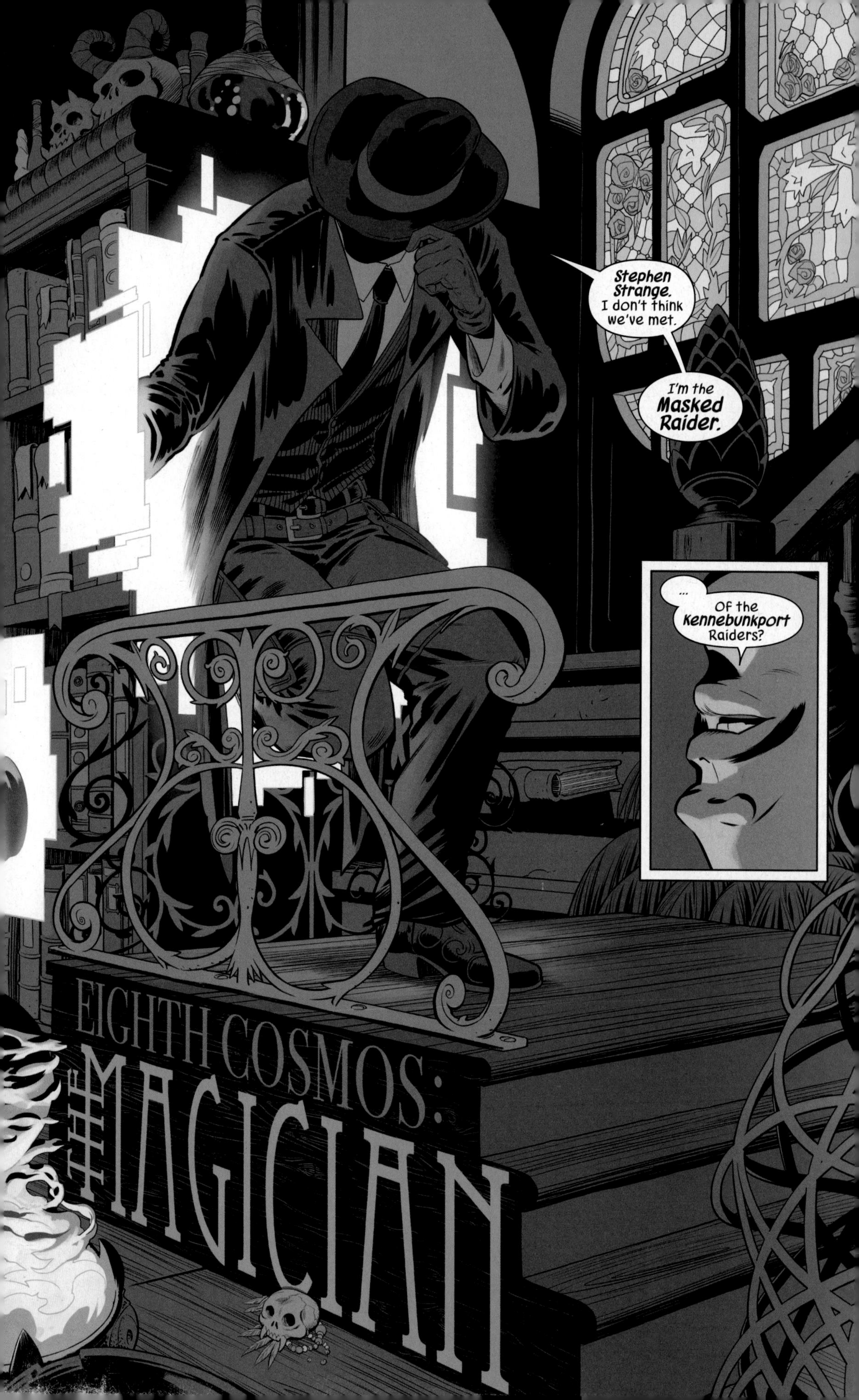
Stephen Strange. I don't think we've met.
I'm the Masked Raider.
... Of the Kennebunkport Raiders?
EIGHTH COSMOS:
THE MAGICIAN

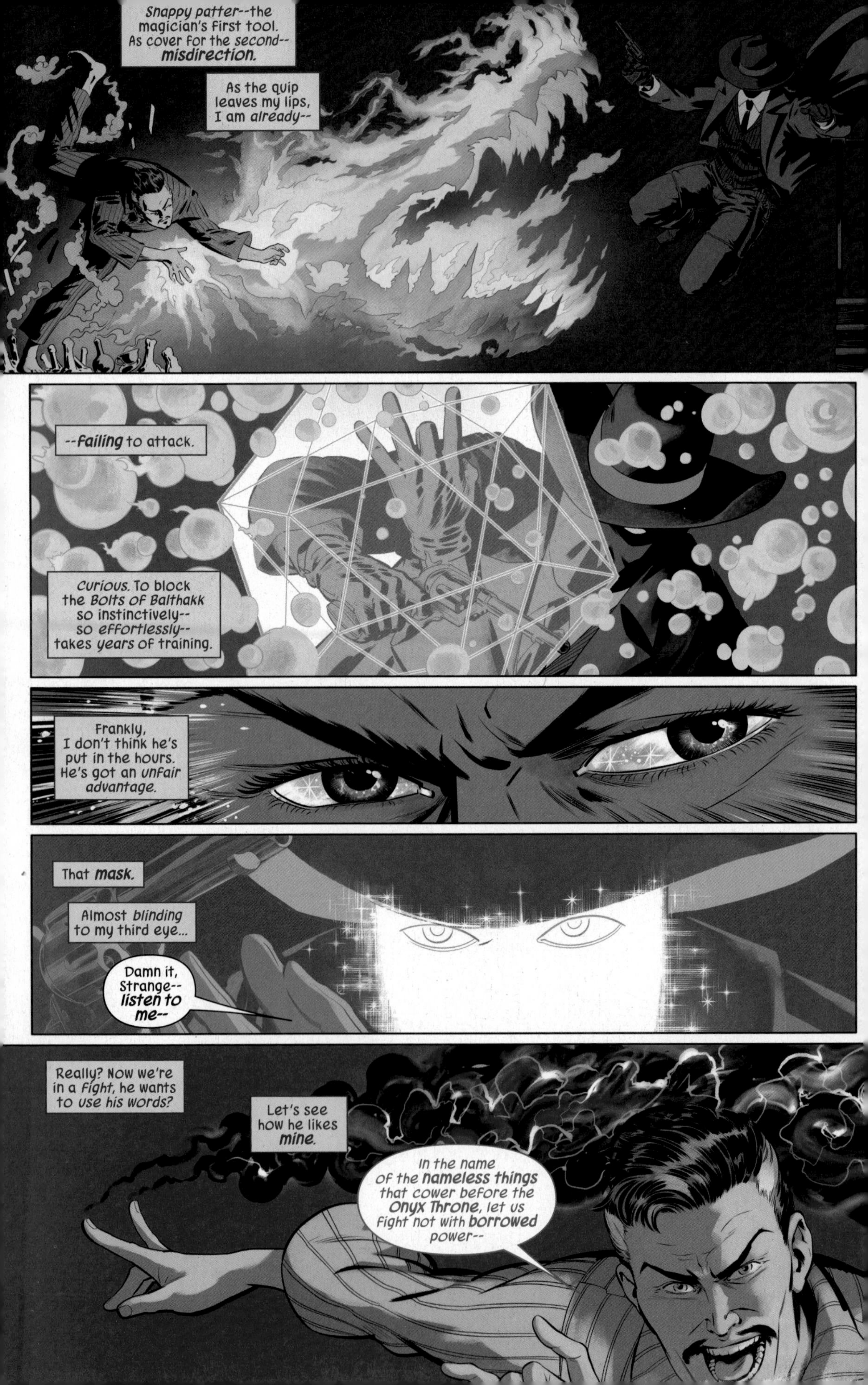

Snappy patter--the magician's first tool. As cover for the second--misdirection.
As the quip leaves my lips, I am already--
--failing to attack.
Curious. To block the Bolts of Balthakk so instinctively--so effortlessly--takes years of training.
Frankly, I don't think he's put in the hours. He's got an unfair advantage.
That mask.
Almost blinding to my third eye...
Damn it, Strange--listen to me--
Really? Now we're in a fight, he wants to use his words?
Let's see how he likes mine.
In the name of the nameless things that cower before the Onyx Throne, let us fight not with borrowed power--

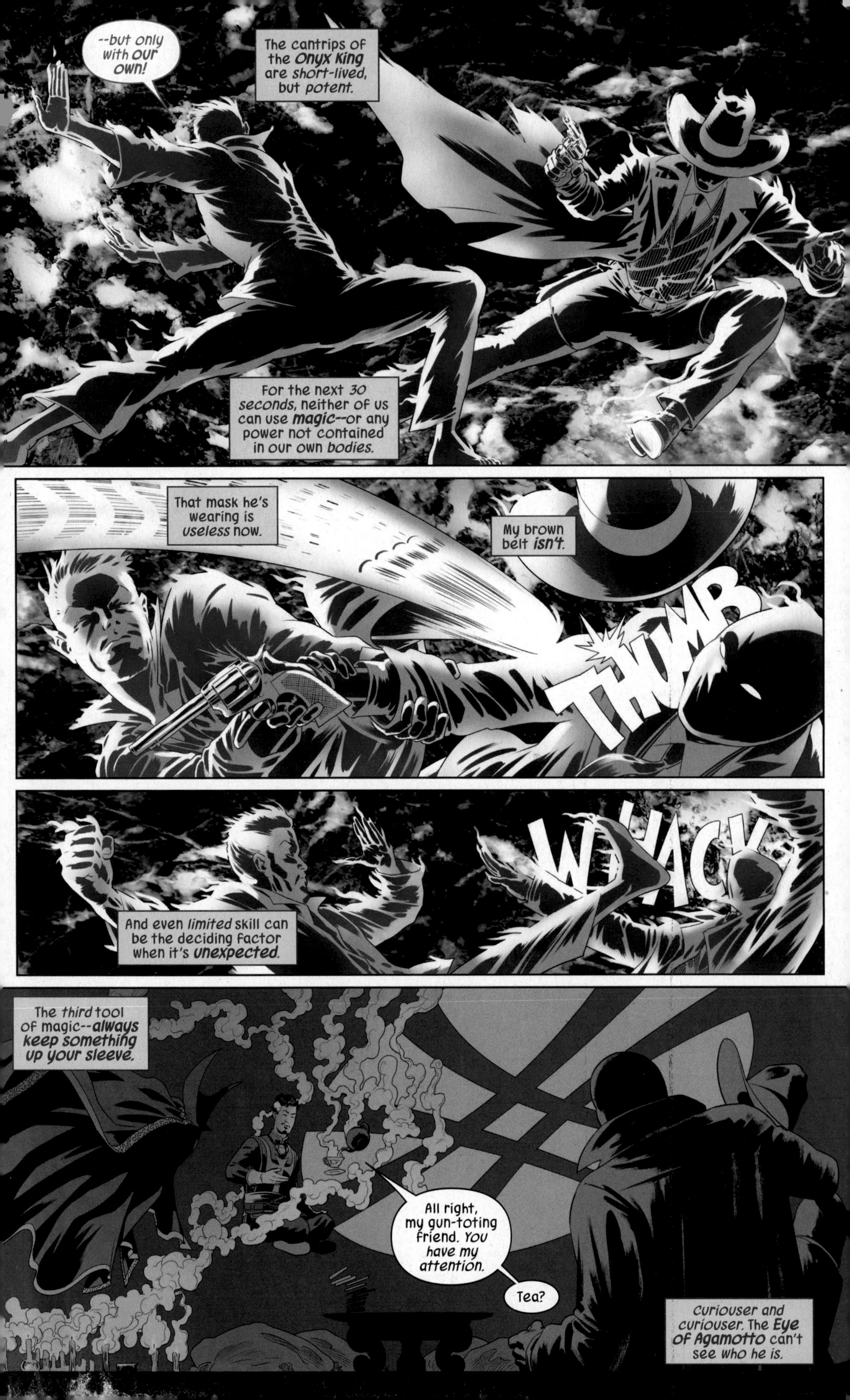
--but only with our own!
The cantrips of the Onyx King are short-lived, but potent.
For the next 30 seconds, neither of us can use magic--or any power not contained in our own bodies.
That mask he's wearing is useless now.
My brown belt isn't.
THMB
WHACK
And even limited skill can be the deciding factor when it's unexpected.
The third tool of magic--always keep something up your sleeve.
All right, my gun-toting friend. You have my attention.
Tea?
Curiouser and curiouser. The Eye of Agamotto can't see who he is.

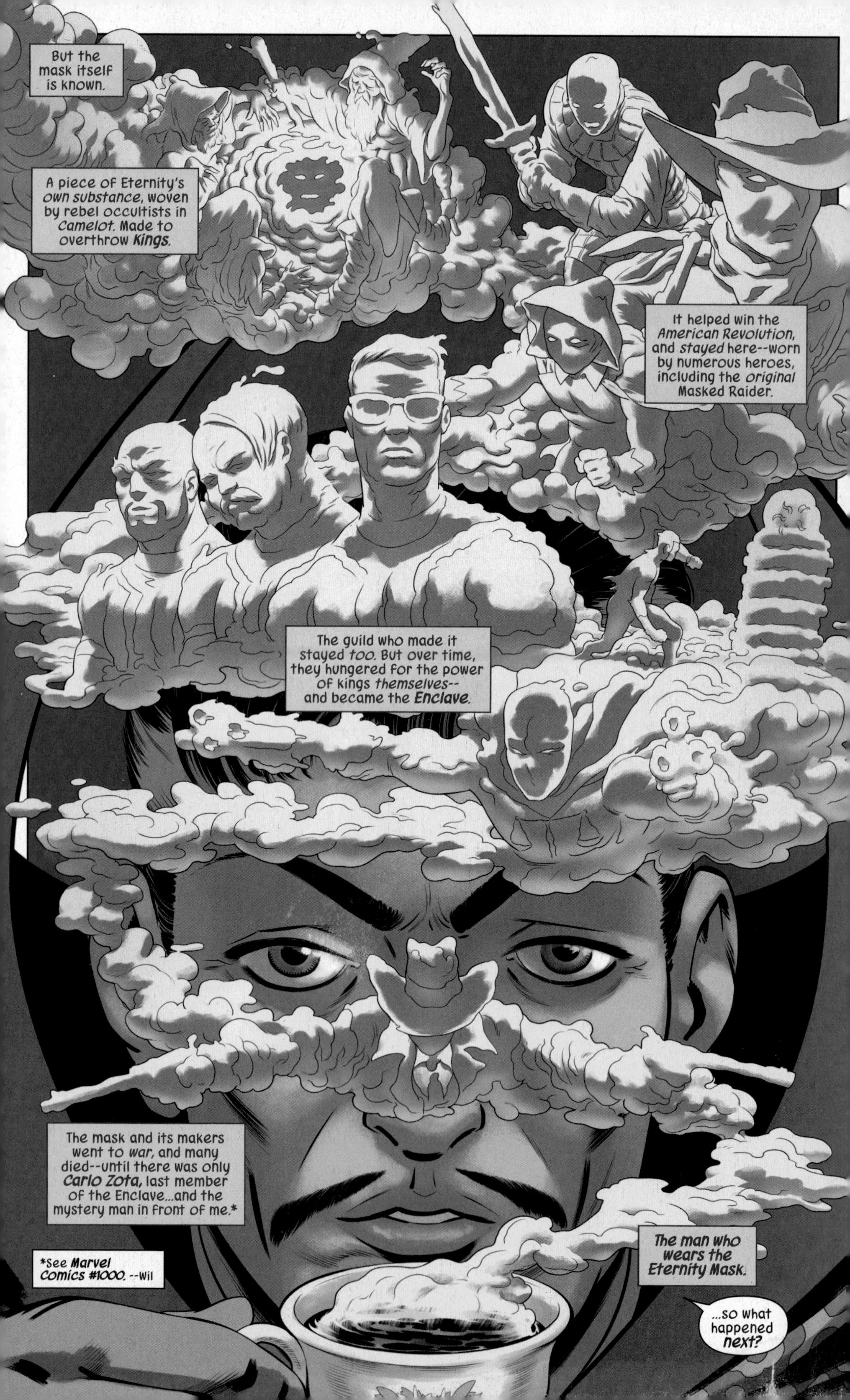

But the mask itself is known.
A piece of Eternity's own substance, woven by rebel occultists in Camelot. Made to overthrow Kings.
It helped win the American Revolution, and stayed here--worn by numerous heroes, including the original Masked Raider.
The guild who made it stayed too. But over time, they hungered for the power of kings themselves--and became the Enclave.
The mask and its makers went to war, and many died--until there was only Carlo Zota, last member of the Enclave...and the mystery man in front of me.*
*See Marvel Comics #1000. --Wil
The man who wears the Eternity Mask.
...so what happened next?

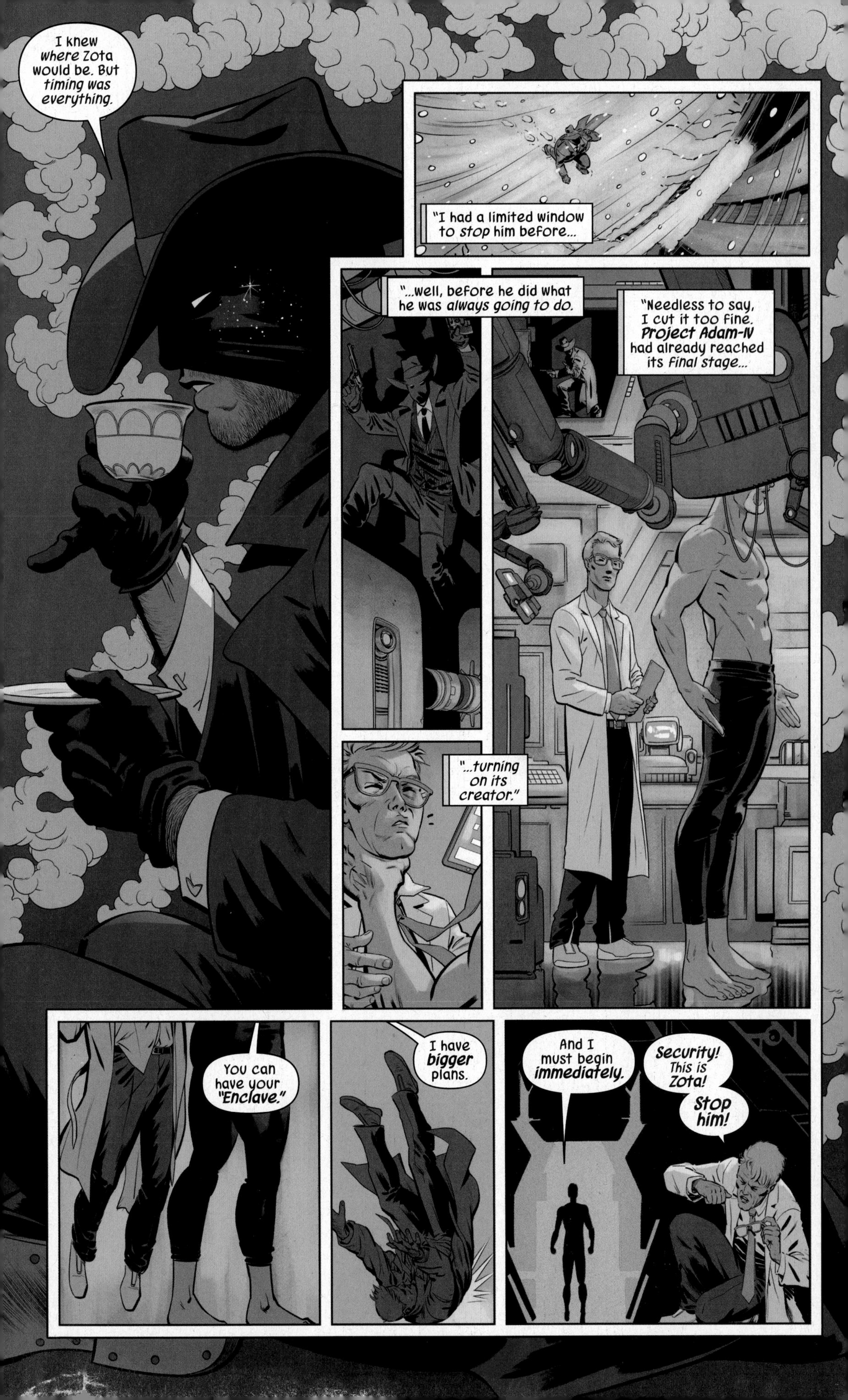
I knew where Zota would be. But timing was everything.
"I had a limited window to stop him before...
"...well, before he did what he was always going to do.
"Needless to say, I cut it too fine. Project Adam-IV had already reached its final stage...
"...turning on its creator."
You can have your "Enclave."
I have bigger plans.
And I must begin immediately.
Security! This is Zota!
Stop him!

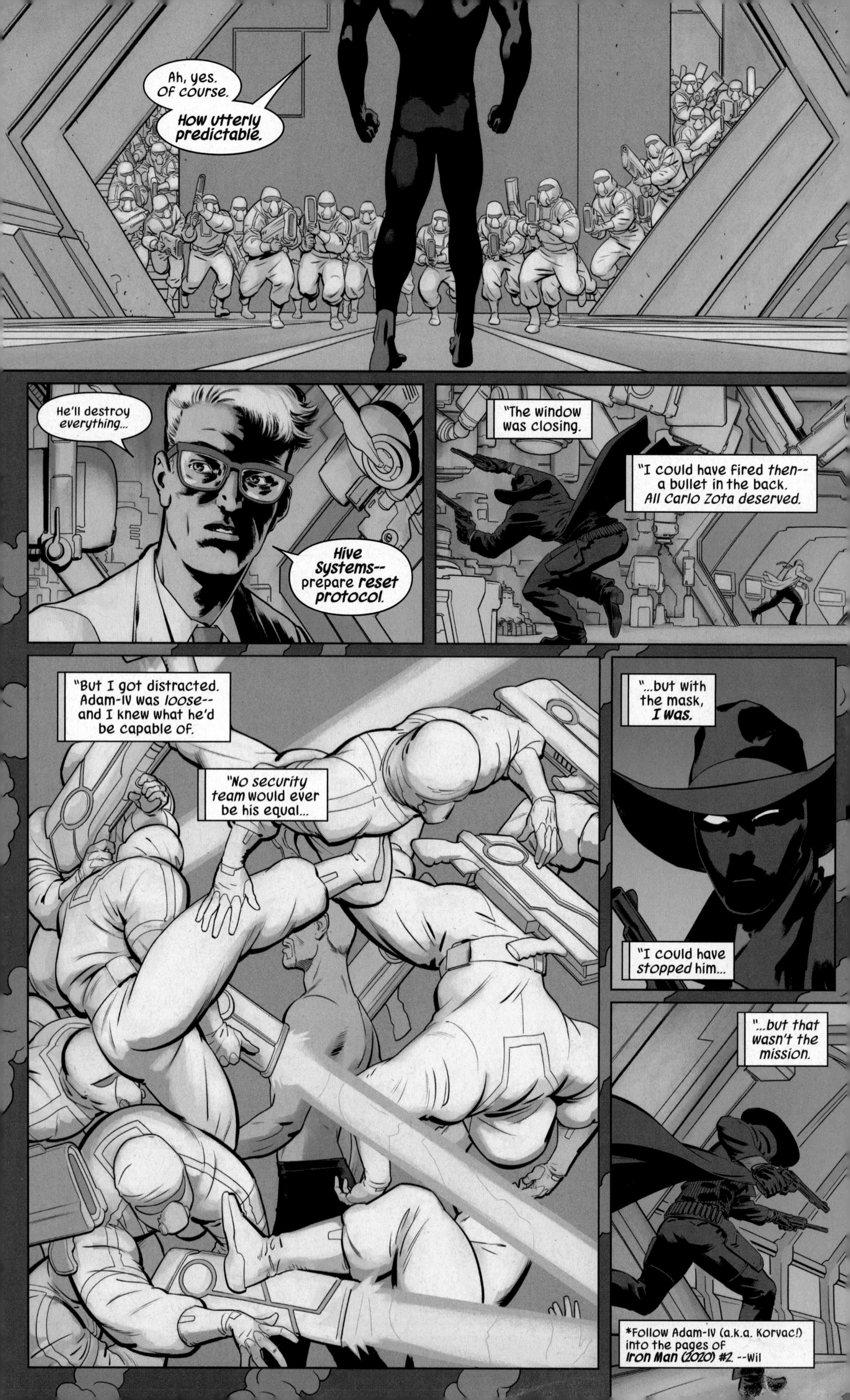

Ah, yes. Of course.
How utterly predictable.
He'll destroy everything...
Hive Systems-- prepare reset protocol.
"The window was closing.
"I could have fired then-- a bullet in the back. All Carlo Zota deserved.
"But I got distracted. Adam-IV was loose-- and I knew what he'd be capable of.
"No security team would ever be his equal...
"...but with the mask, I was.
"I could have stopped him...
"...but that wasn't the mission.
*Follow Adam-IV (a.k.a. Korvac!) into the pages of Iron Man (2020) #2. --Wil

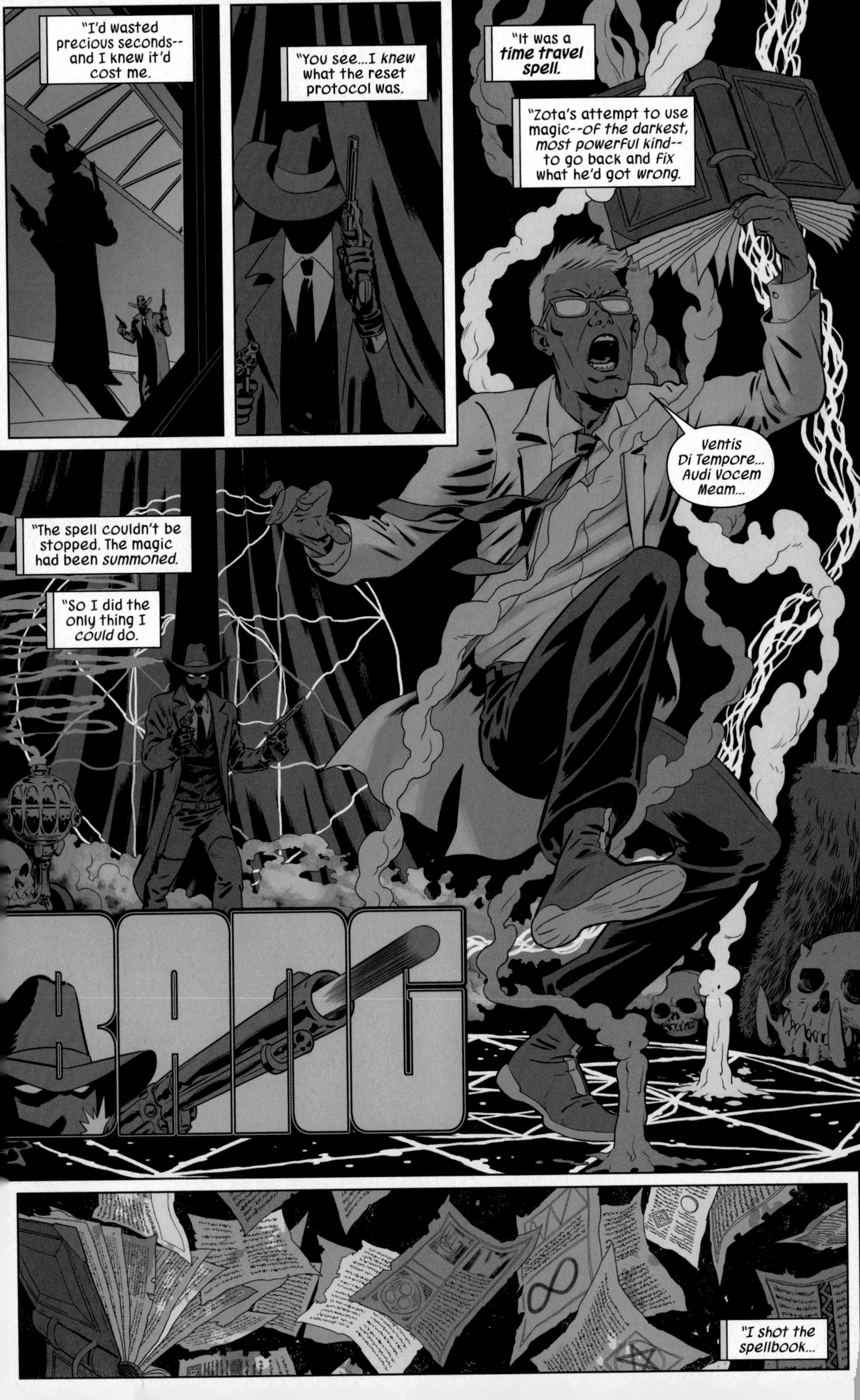
"I'd wasted precious seconds--and I knew it'd cost me.
"You see...I knew what the reset protocol was.
"It was a time travel spell.
"Zota's attempt to use magic--of the darkest, most powerful kind--to go back and fix what he'd got wrong.
Ventis Di Tempore... Audi Vocem Meam...
"The spell couldn't be stopped. The magic had been summoned.
"So I did the only thing I could do.
BANG
"I shot the spellbook...

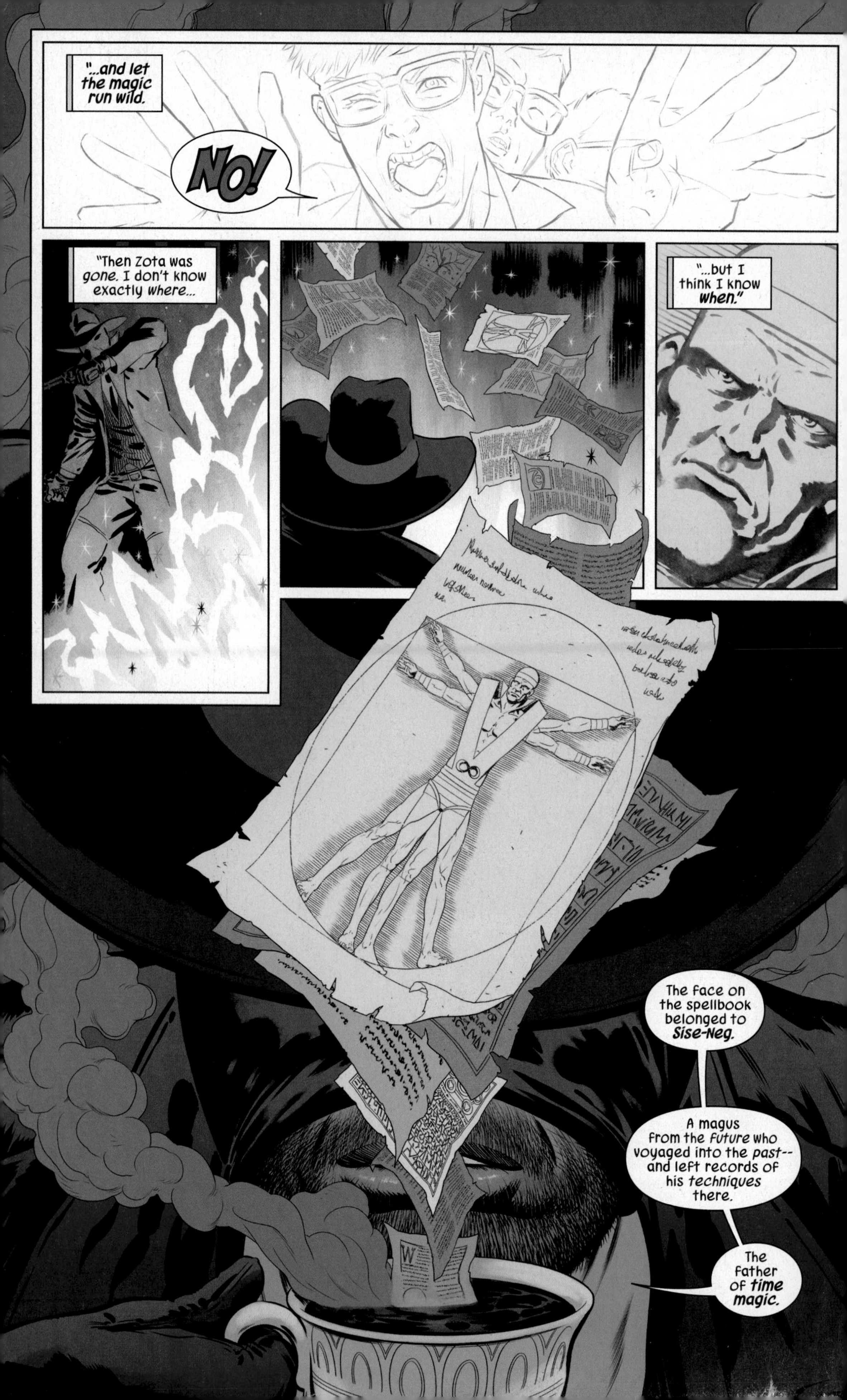
"...and let the magic run wild.
NO!
"Then Zota was gone. I don't know exactly where...
"...but I think I know when."
The face on the spellbook belonged to Sise-Neg.
A magus from the future who voyaged into the past-- and left records of his techniques there.
The father of time magic.

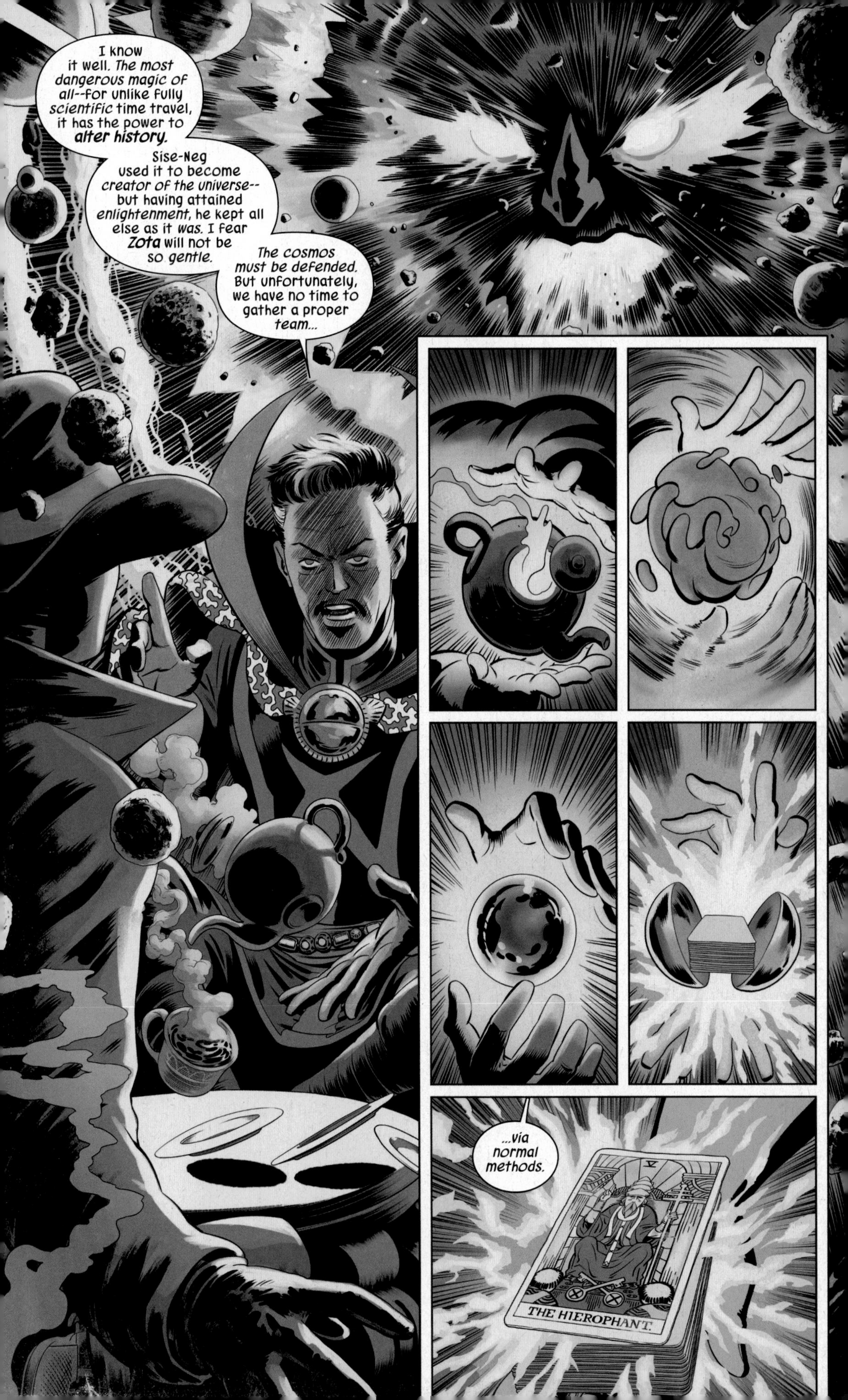
I know it well. The most dangerous magic of all--for unlike fully scientific time travel, it has the power to alter history.
Sise-Neg used it to become creator of the universe--but having attained enlightenment, he kept all else as it was. I fear Zota will not be so gentle.
The cosmos must be defended. But unfortunately, we have no time to gather a proper team...
...via normal methods.
V
THE HIEROPHANT.

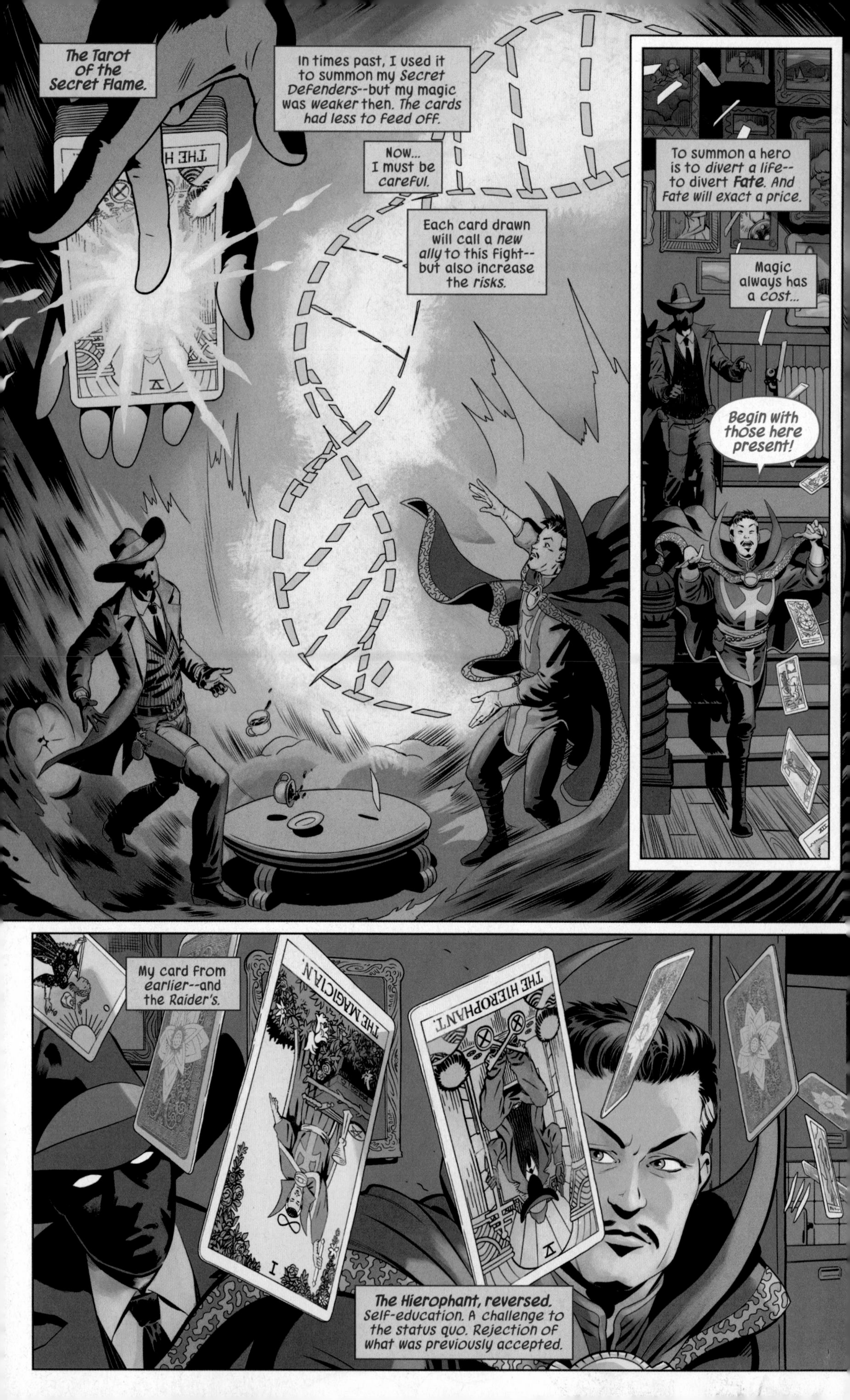
The Tarot Of the Secret Flame.
In times past, I used it to summon my Secret Defenders--but my magic was weaker then. The cards had less to feed off.
Now... I must be careful.
Each card drawn will call a new ally to this fight--but also increase the risks.
To summon a hero is to divert a life--to divert Fate. And Fate will exact a price.
Magic always has a cost...
Begin with those here present!
My card from earlier--and the Raider's.
THE MAGICIAN.
THE HIEROPHANT.
The Hierophant, reversed. Self-education. A challenge to the status quo. Rejection of what was previously accepted.

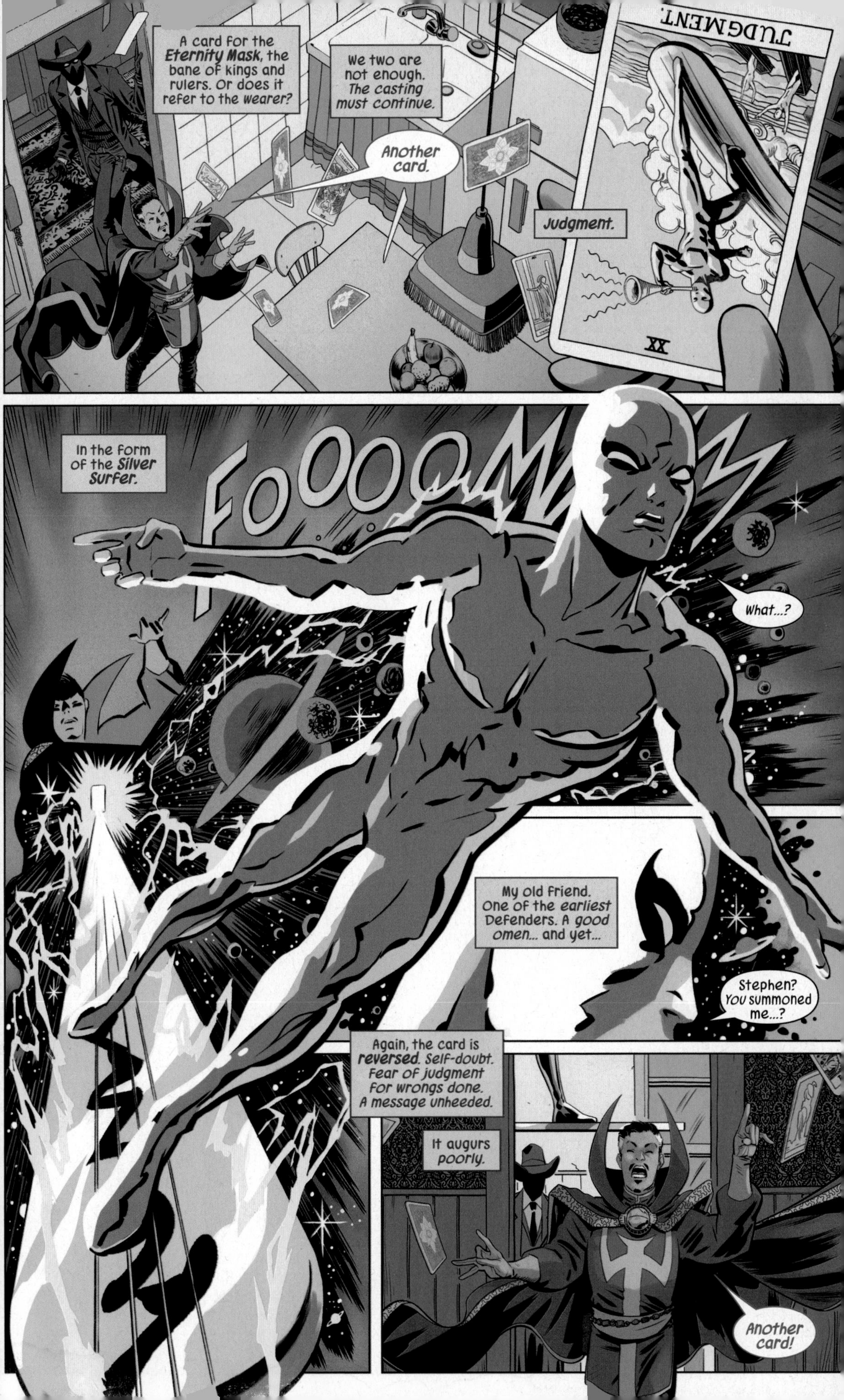
A card for the Eternity Mask, the bane of kings and rulers. Or does it refer to the wearer?
We two are not enough. The casting must continue.
Another card.
JUDGMENT
XX
Judgment.
In the form of the Silver Surfer.
FOOOOMMM
What...?
My old friend. One of the earliest Defenders. A good omen... and yet...
Stephen? You summoned me...?
Again, the card is reversed. Self-doubt. Fear of judgment for wrongs done. A message unheeded.
It augurs poorly.
Another card!

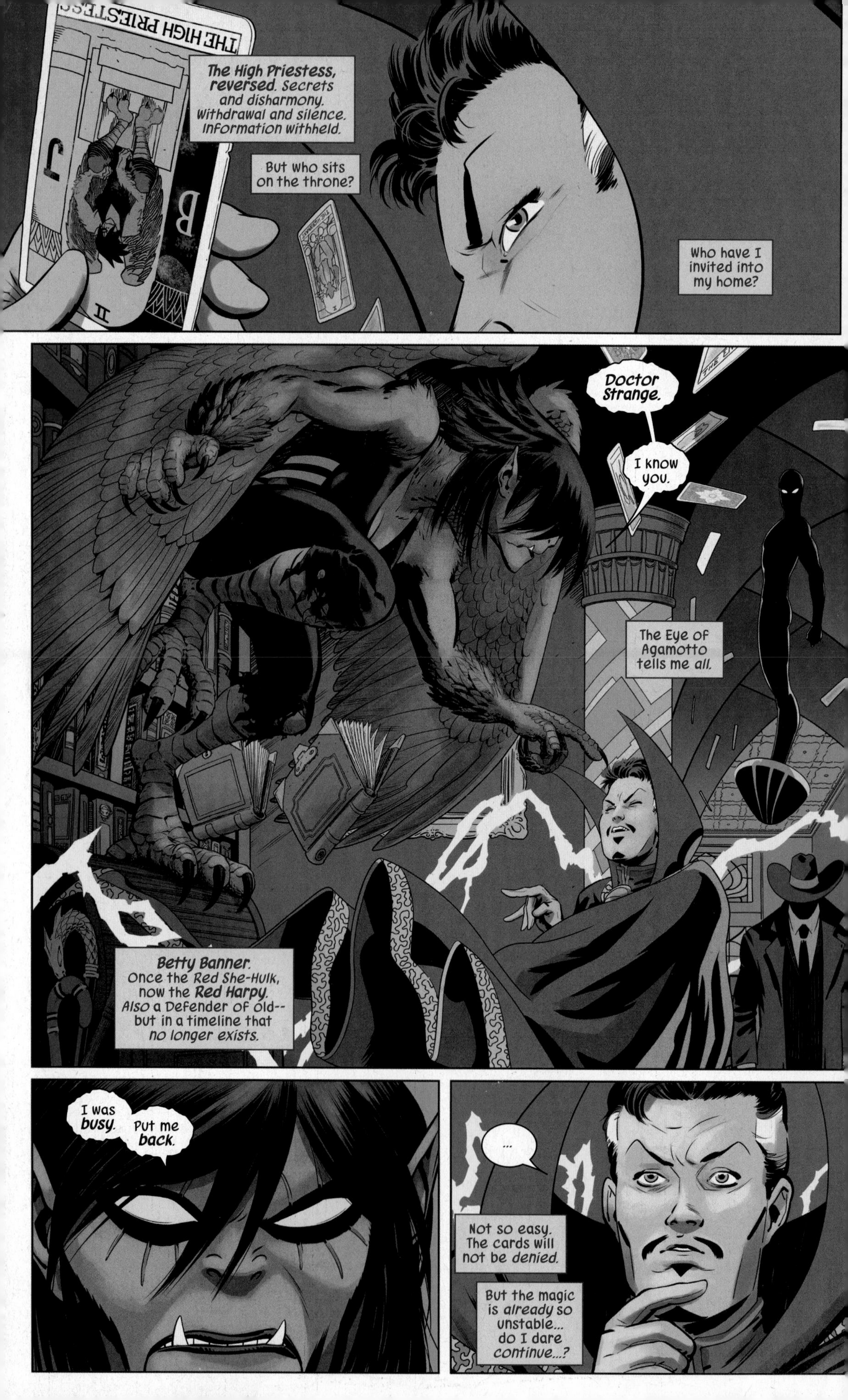
THE HIGH PRIESTESS
The High Priestess, reversed. Secrets and disharmony. Withdrawal and silence. Information withheld.
But who sits on the throne?
Who have I invited into my home?
Doctor Strange.
I know you.
The Eye of Agamotto tells me all.
Betty Banner. Once the Red She-Hulk, now the Red Harpy. Also a Defender of old--but in a timeline that no longer exists.
I was busy.
Put me back.
...
Not so easy. The cards will not be denied.
But the magic is already so unstable... do I dare continue...?

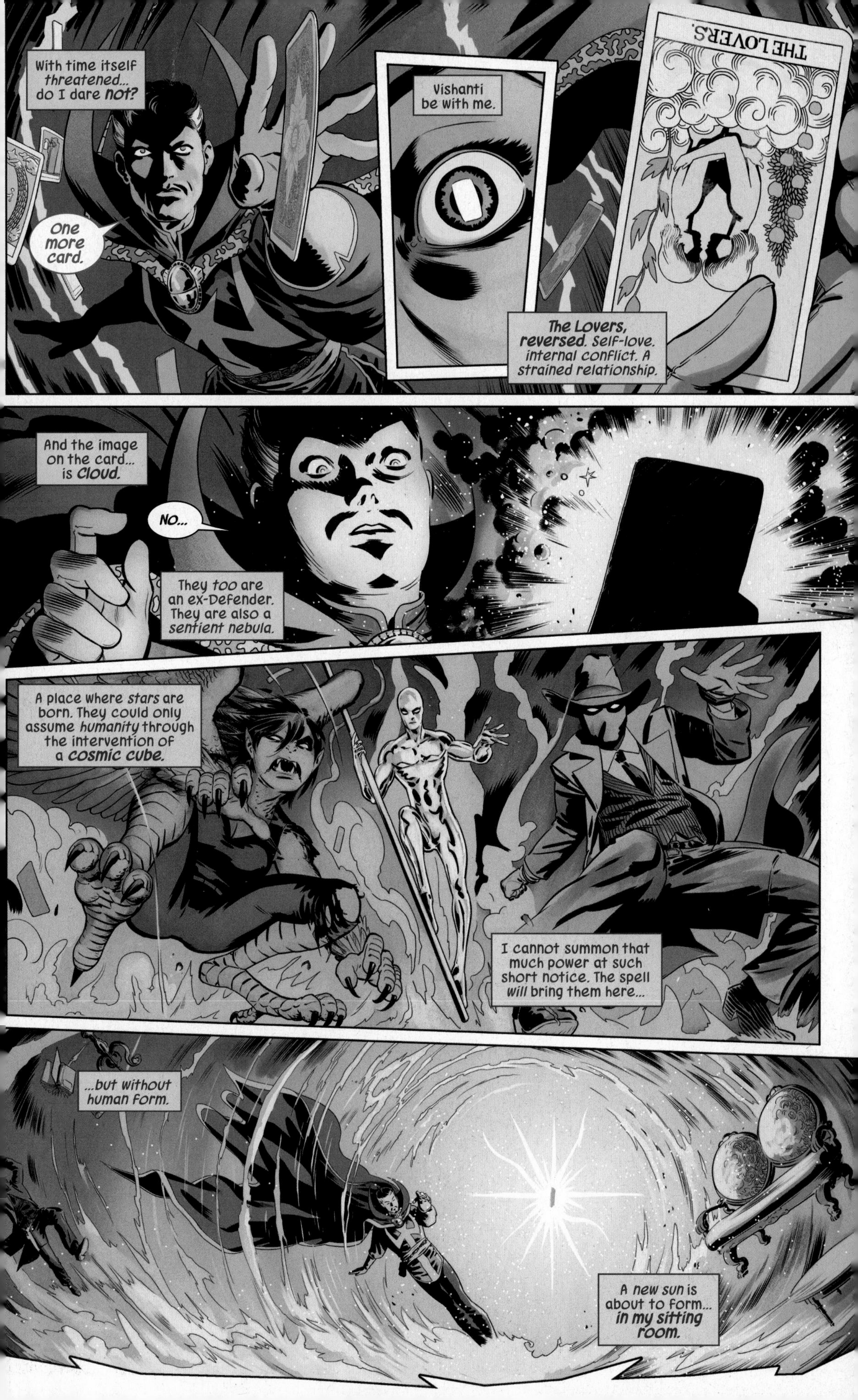

With time itself threatened... do I dare not?
One more card.
Vishanti be with me.
THE LOVERS.
The Lovers, reversed. Self-love. internal conflict. A strained relationship.
And the image on the card... is Cloud.
NO...
They too are an ex-Defender. They are also a sentient nebula.
A place where stars are born. They could only assume humanity through the intervention of a cosmic cube.
I cannot summon that much power at such short notice. The spell will bring them here...
...but without human form.
A new sun is about to form... in my sitting room.

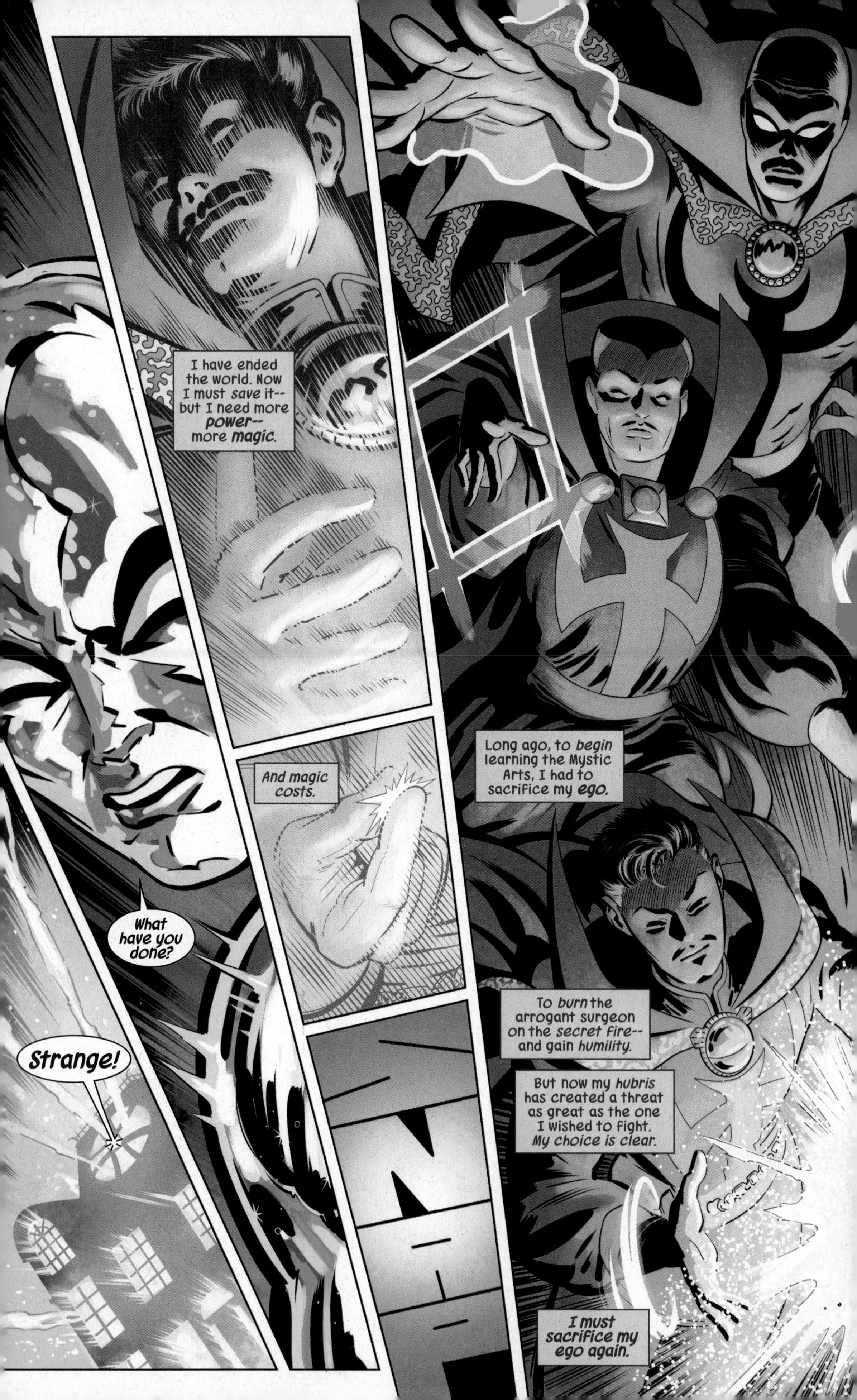
I have ended the world. Now I must save it-- but I need more power-- more magic.
And magic costs.
What have you done?
Strange!
Long ago, to begin learning the Mystic Arts, I had to sacrifice my ego.
To burn the arrogant surgeon on the secret fire-- and gain humility.
But now my hubris has created a threat as great as the one I wished to fight. My choice is clear.
I must sacrifice my ego again.

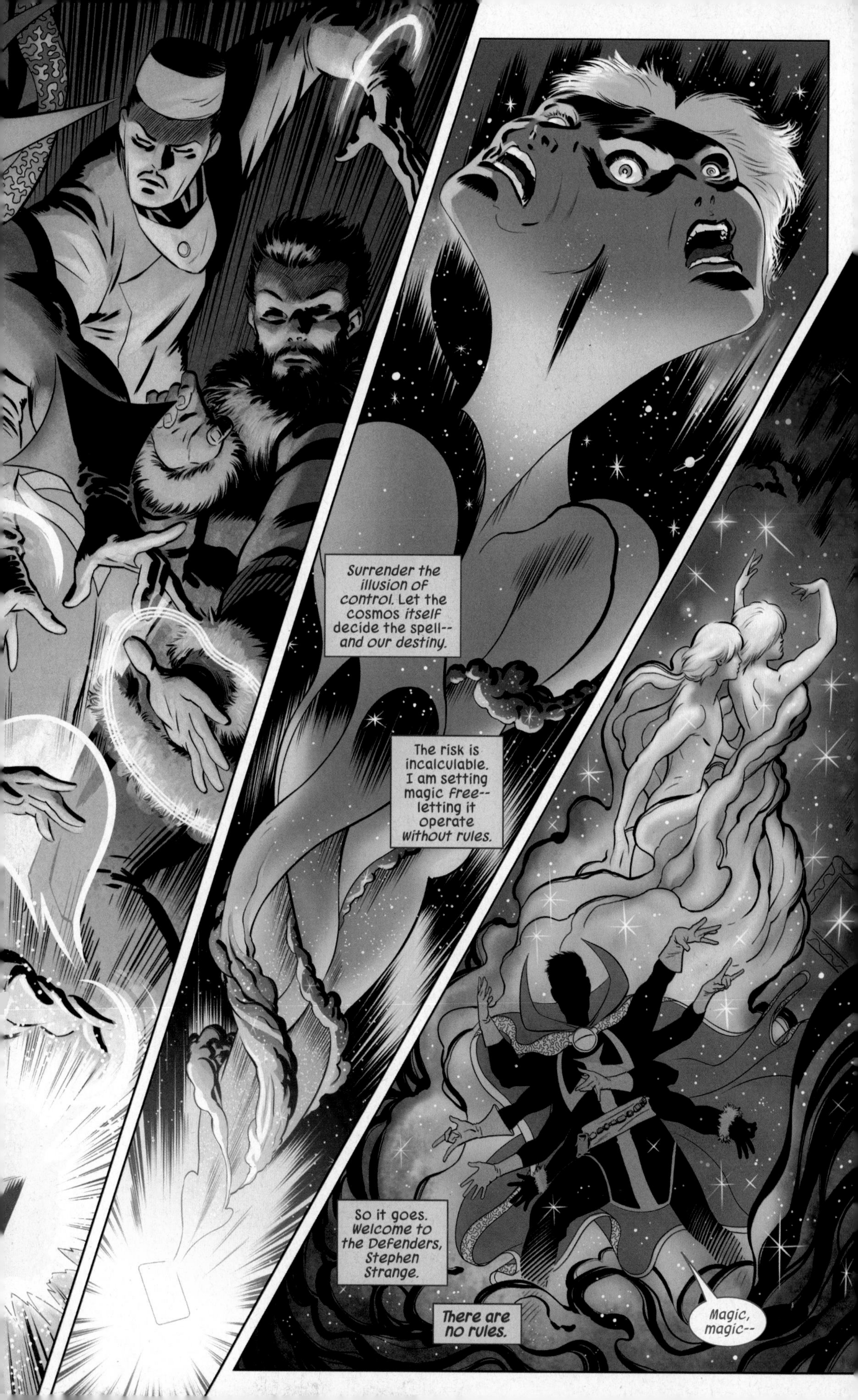
Surrender the illusion of control. Let the cosmos *itself* decide the spell-- and our destiny.
The risk is incalculable. I am setting magic *free*-- letting it operate *without rules.*
So it goes. Welcome to the Defenders, Stephen Strange.
There are no rules.
Magic, magic--

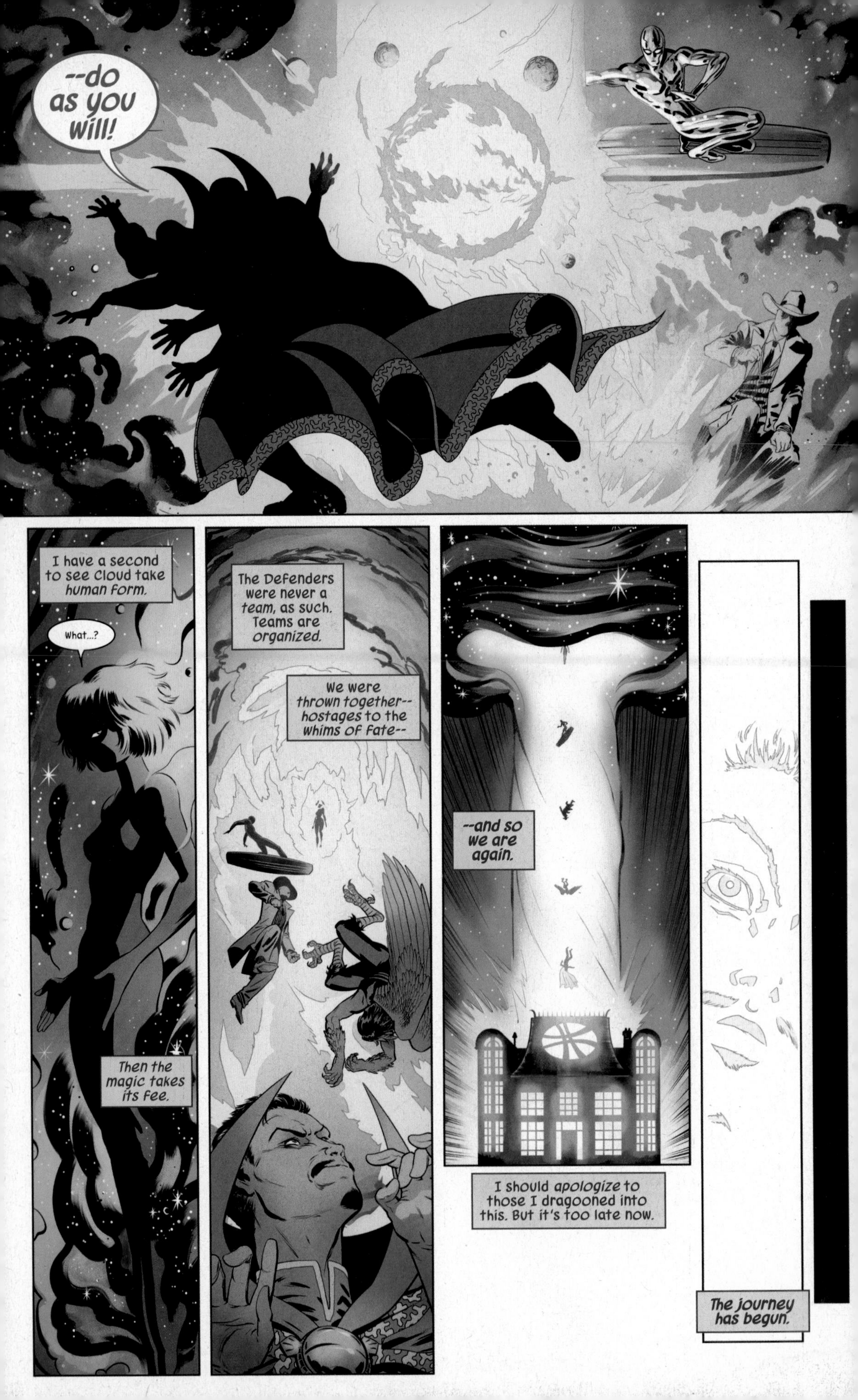
--do as you will!
I have a second to see Cloud take human form.
What...?
Then the magic takes its fee.
The Defenders were never a team, as such. Teams are organized.
We were thrown together--hostages to the whims of fate--
--and so we are again.
I should apologize to those I dragooned into this. But it's too late now.
The journey has begun.

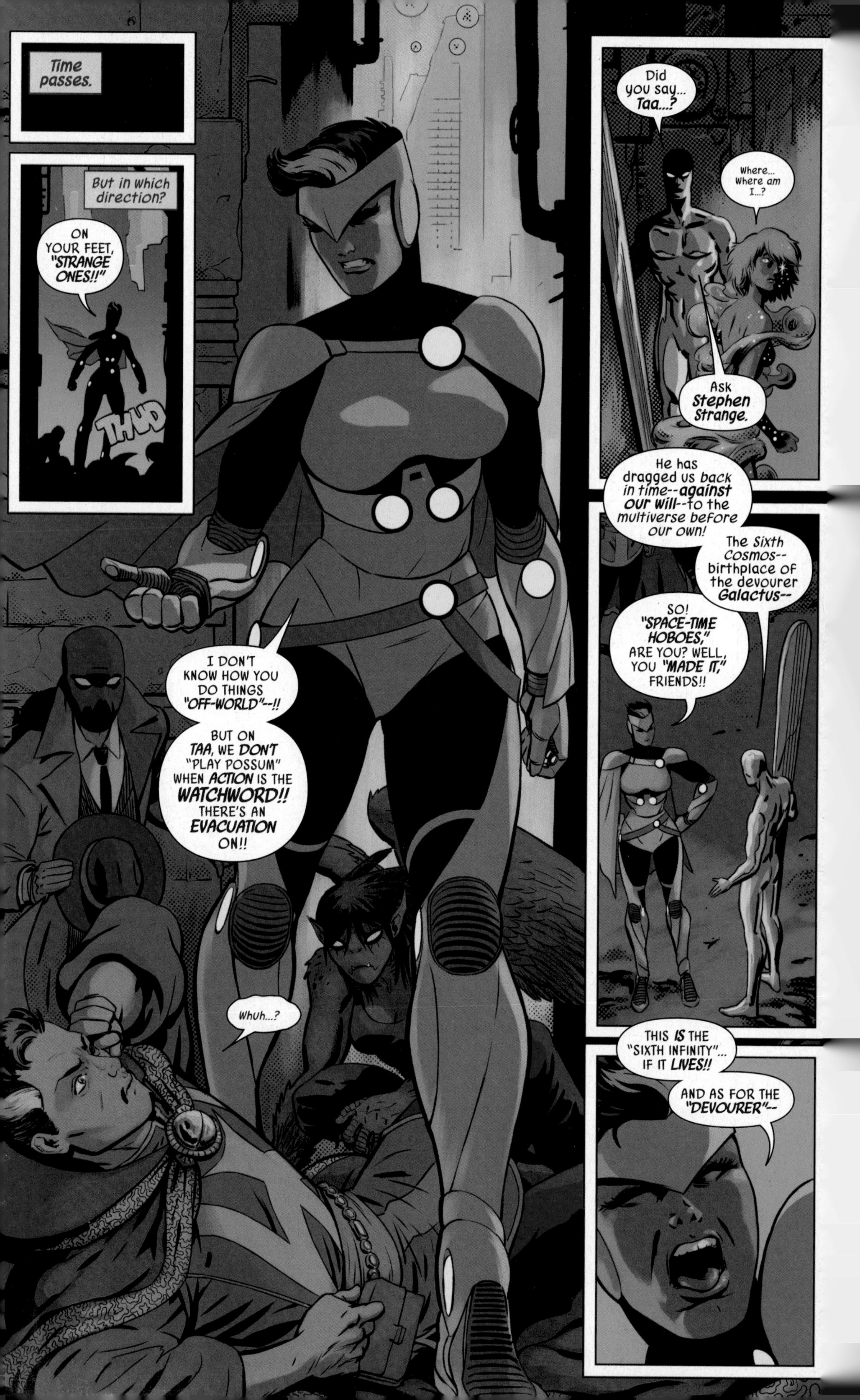
Time passes.
But in which direction?
ON YOUR FEET, "STRANGE ONES!!"
THUD
I DON'T KNOW HOW YOU DO THINGS "OFF-WORLD"--!!
BUT ON TAA, WE DON'T "PLAY POSSUM" WHEN ACTION IS THE WATCHWORD!! THERE'S AN EVACUATION ON!!
Whuh...?
Did you say... Taa...?
Where... Where am I...?
Ask Stephen Strange.
He has dragged us back in time--against our will--to the multiverse before our own!
The Sixth Cosmos--birthplace of the devourer Galactus--
SO! "SPACE-TIME HOBOES," ARE YOU? WELL, YOU "MADE IT," FRIENDS!!
THIS IS THE "SIXTH INFINITY"... IF IT LIVES!!
AND AS FOR THE "DEVOURER"--

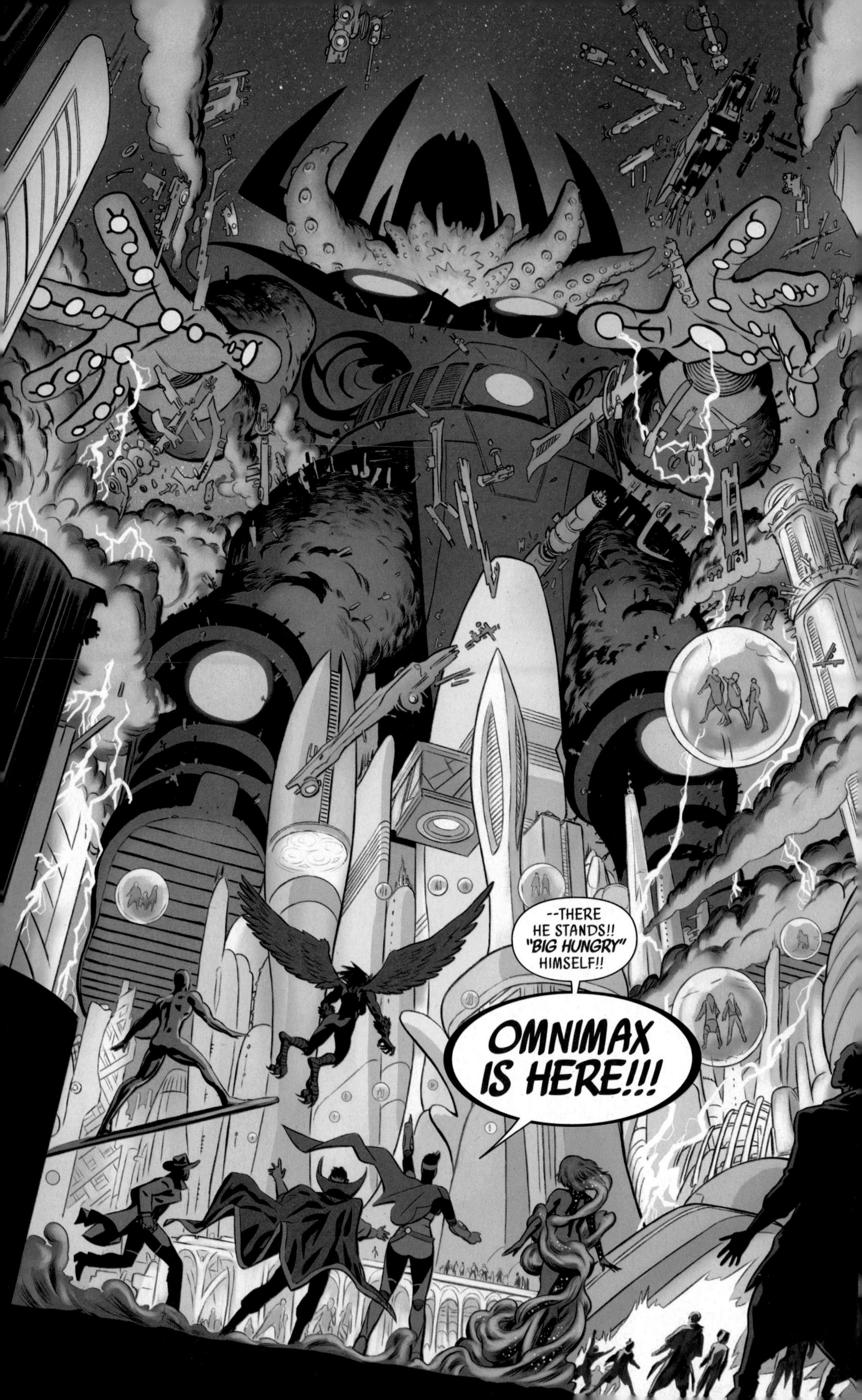
--THERE HE STANDS!! "BIG HUNGRY" HIMSELF!!
OMNIMAX IS HERE!!!

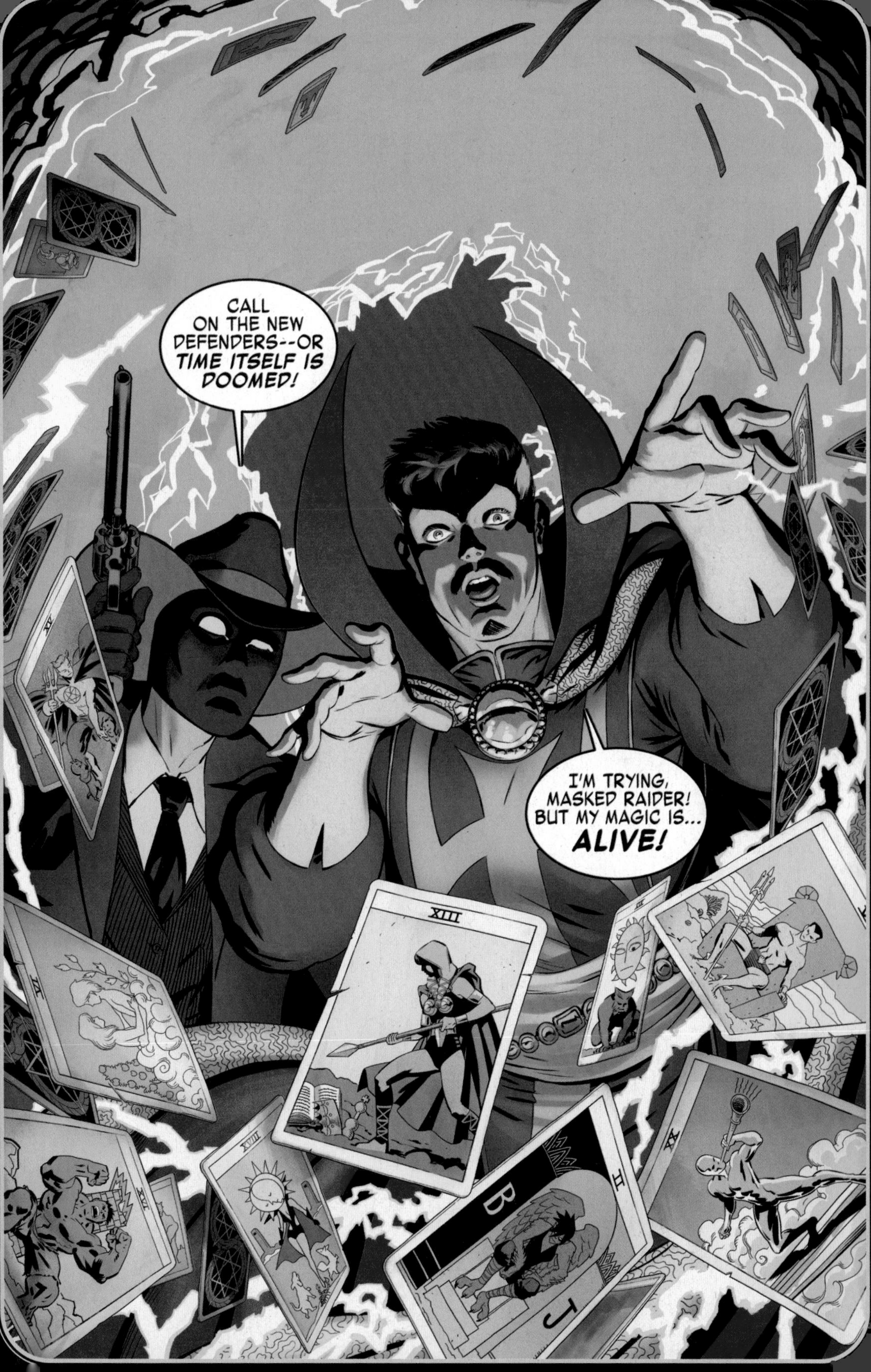
CALL ON THE NEW DEFENDERS--OR TIME ITSELF IS DOOMED!
I'M TRYING, MASKED RAIDER! BUT MY MAGIC IS... ALIVE!

II

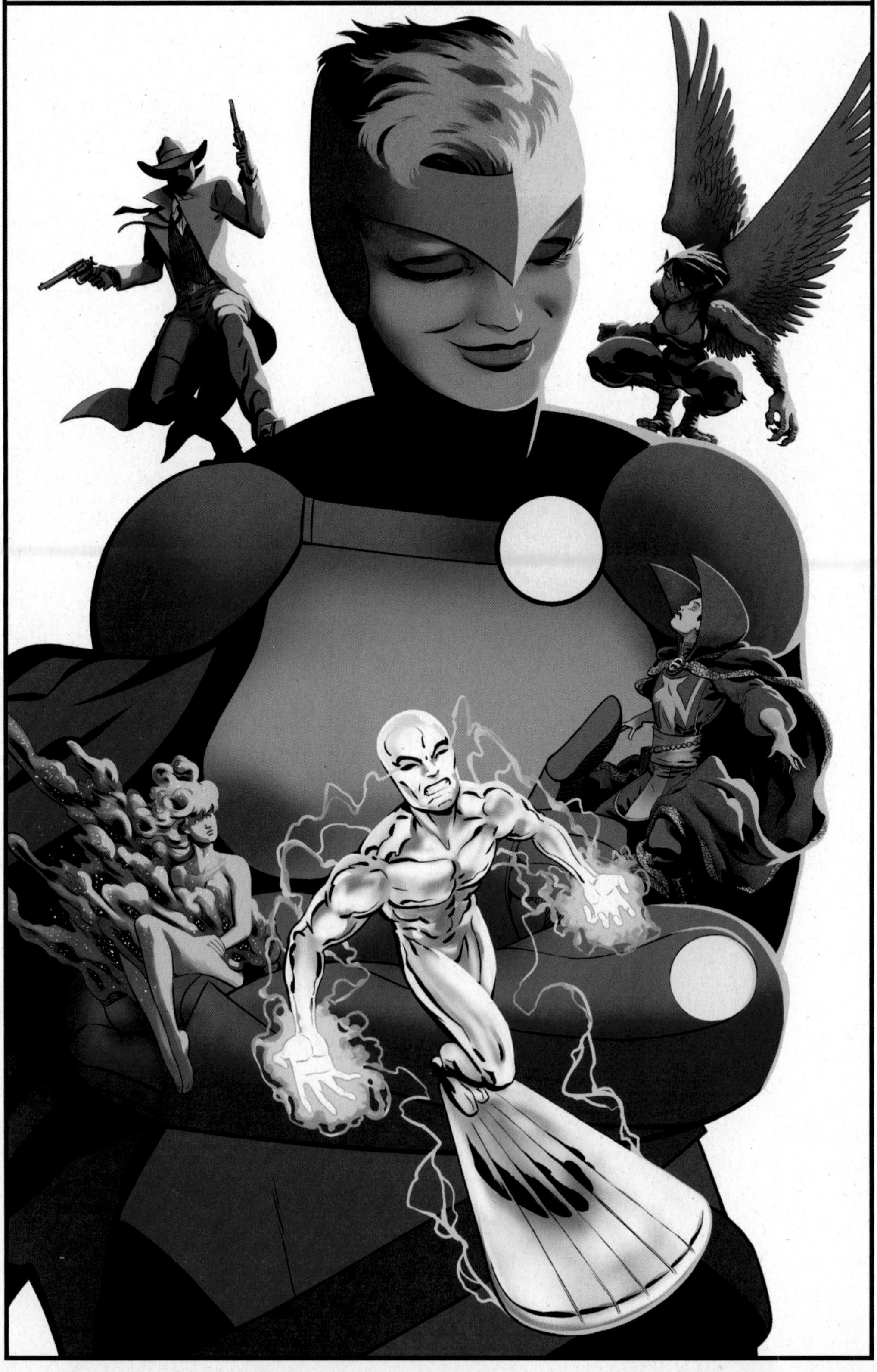

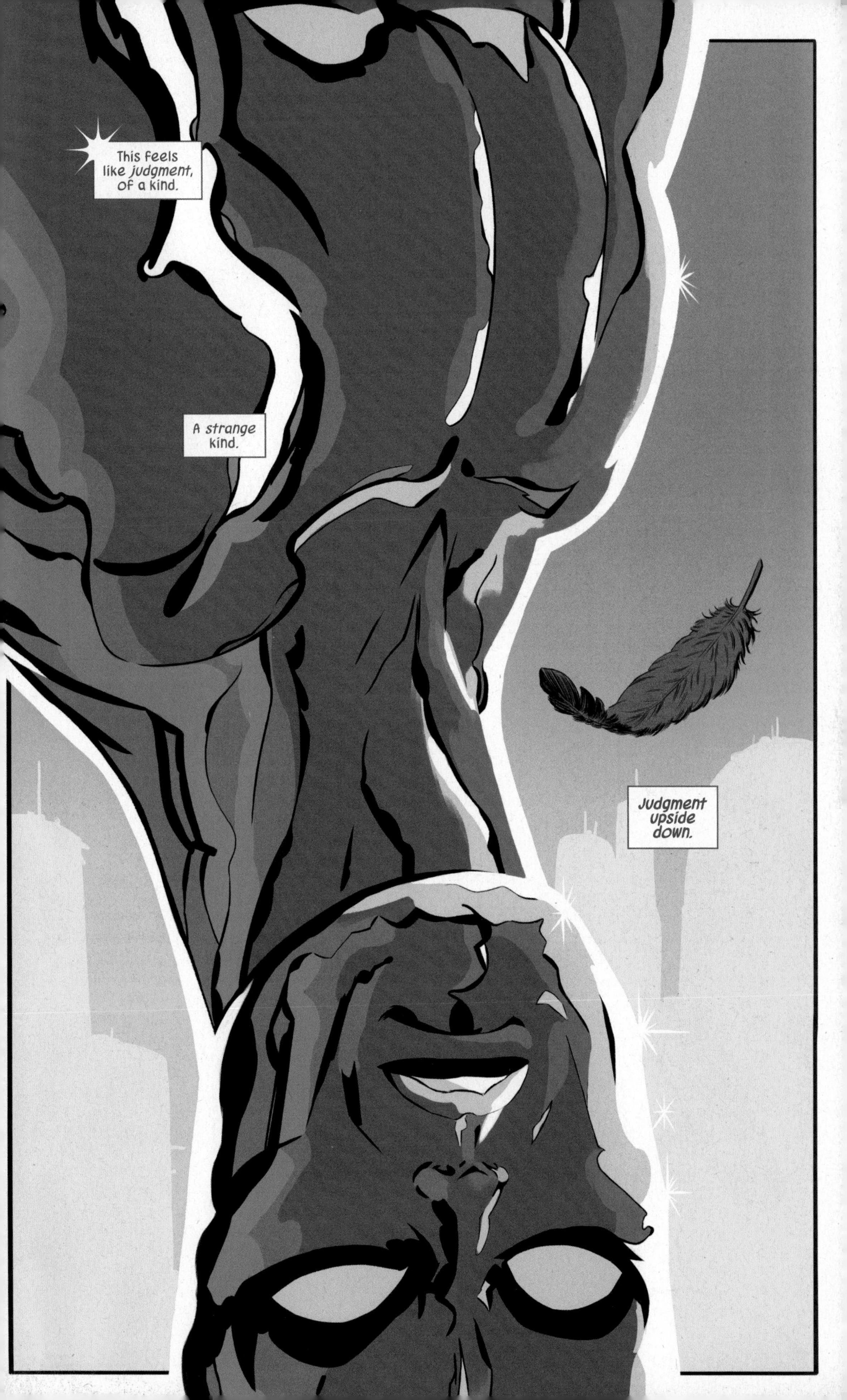
This feels like *judgment*, of a kind.
A *strange* kind.
Judgment upside down.

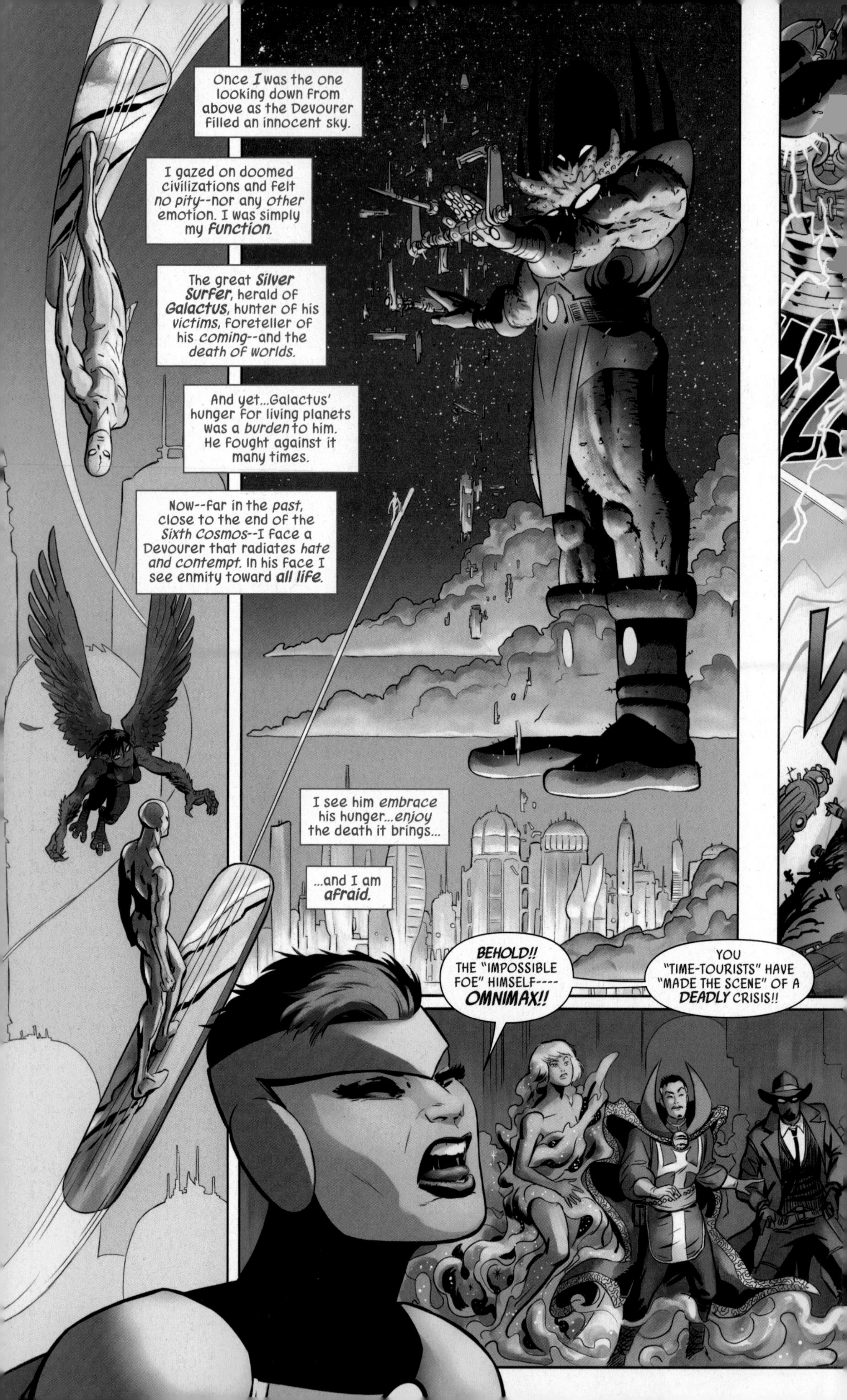
Once *I* was the one looking down from above as the Devourer filled an innocent sky.
I gazed on doomed civilizations and felt *no pity*--nor any *other* emotion. I was simply my ***function***.
The great ***Silver Surfer***, herald of ***Galactus***, hunter of his *victims*, foreteller of his *coming*--and the *death of worlds*.
And yet...Galactus' hunger for living planets was a *burden* to him. He fought against it many times.
Now--far in the *past*, close to the end of the *Sixth Cosmos*--I face a Devourer that radiates *hate and contempt*. In his face I see enmity toward ***all life***.
I see him *embrace* his hunger...*enjoy* the death it brings...
...and I am ***afraid.***
BEHOLD!! THE "IMPOSSIBLE FOE" HIMSELF---- ***OMNIMAX!!***
YOU "TIME-TOURISTS" HAVE "MADE THE SCENE" OF A ***DEADLY*** CRISIS!!

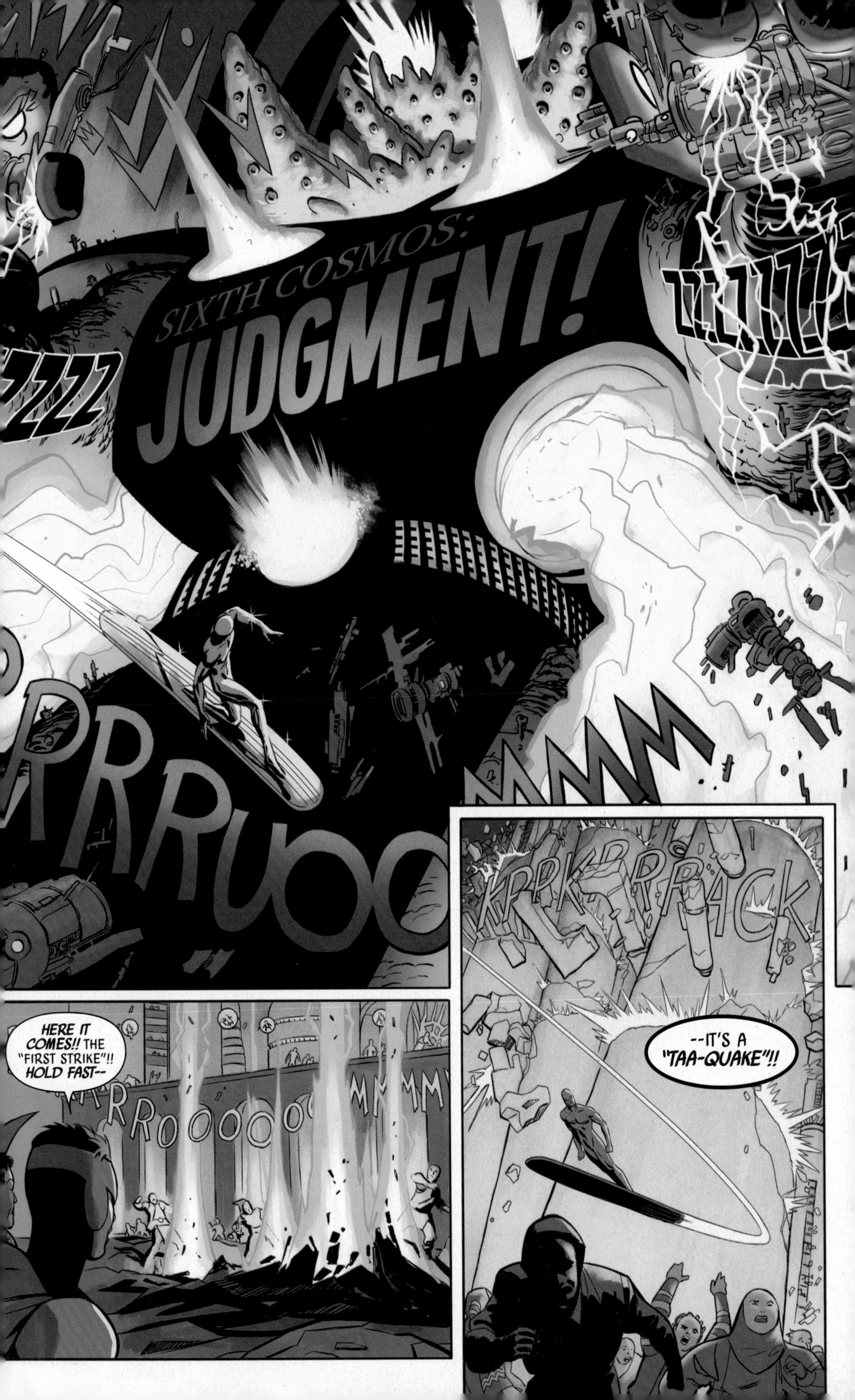
SIXTH COSMOS:
JUDGMENT!
HERE IT COMES!! THE "FIRST STRIKE"!! HOLD FAST--
--IT'S A "TAA-QUAKE"!!

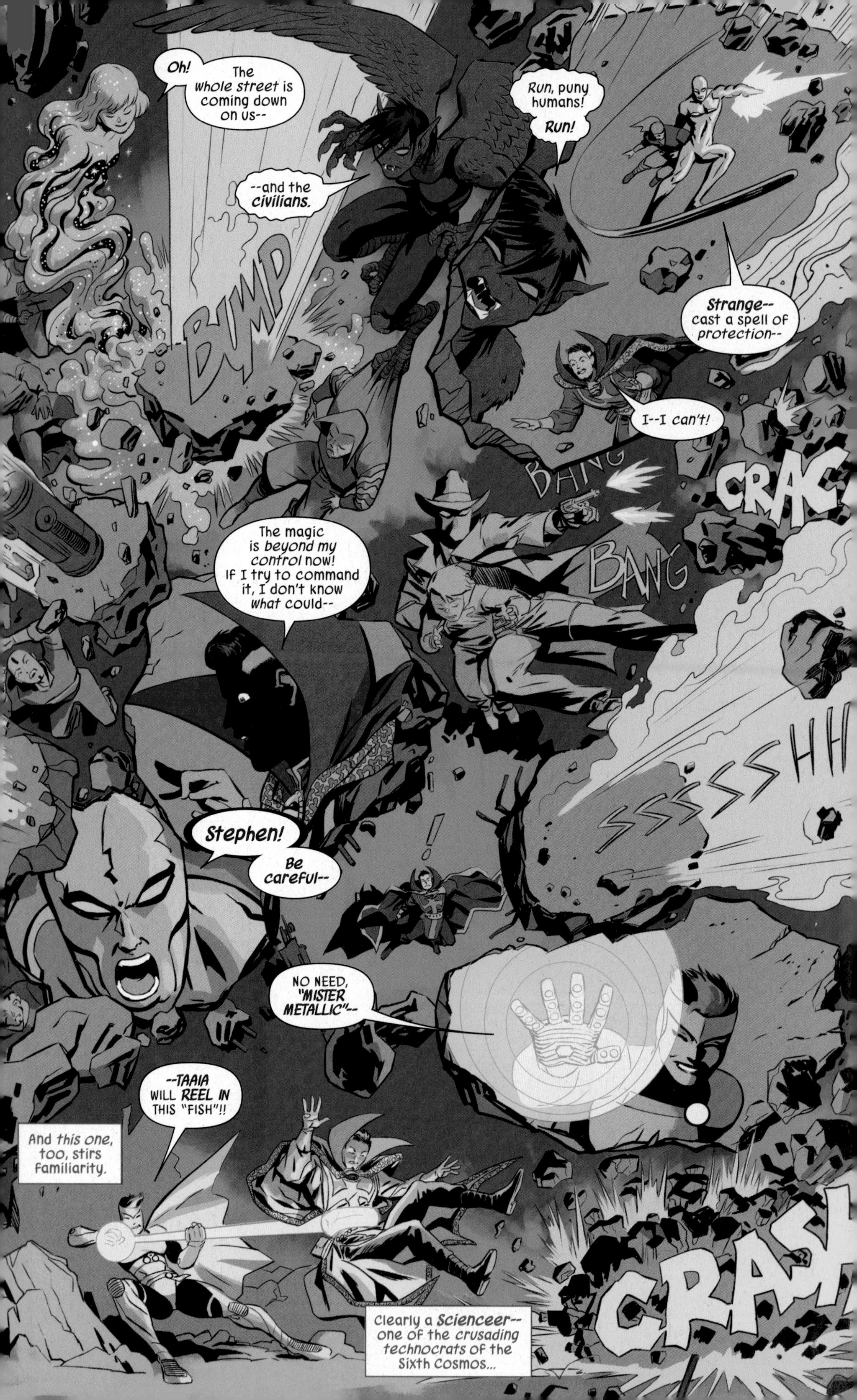

Oh! The whole street is coming down on us--
--and the civilians.
Run, puny humans! Run!
BUMP
Strange-- cast a spell of protection--
I--I can't!
BANG
BANG
CRAC
The magic is beyond my control now! If I try to command it, I don't know what could--
SSSSSSHH
Stephen!
Be careful--
!
NO NEED, "MISTER METALLIC"--
--TAAIA WILL REEL IN THIS "FISH"!!
And this one, too, stirs familiarity.
Clearly a Scienceer-- one of the crusading technocrats of the Sixth Cosmos...
CRASH

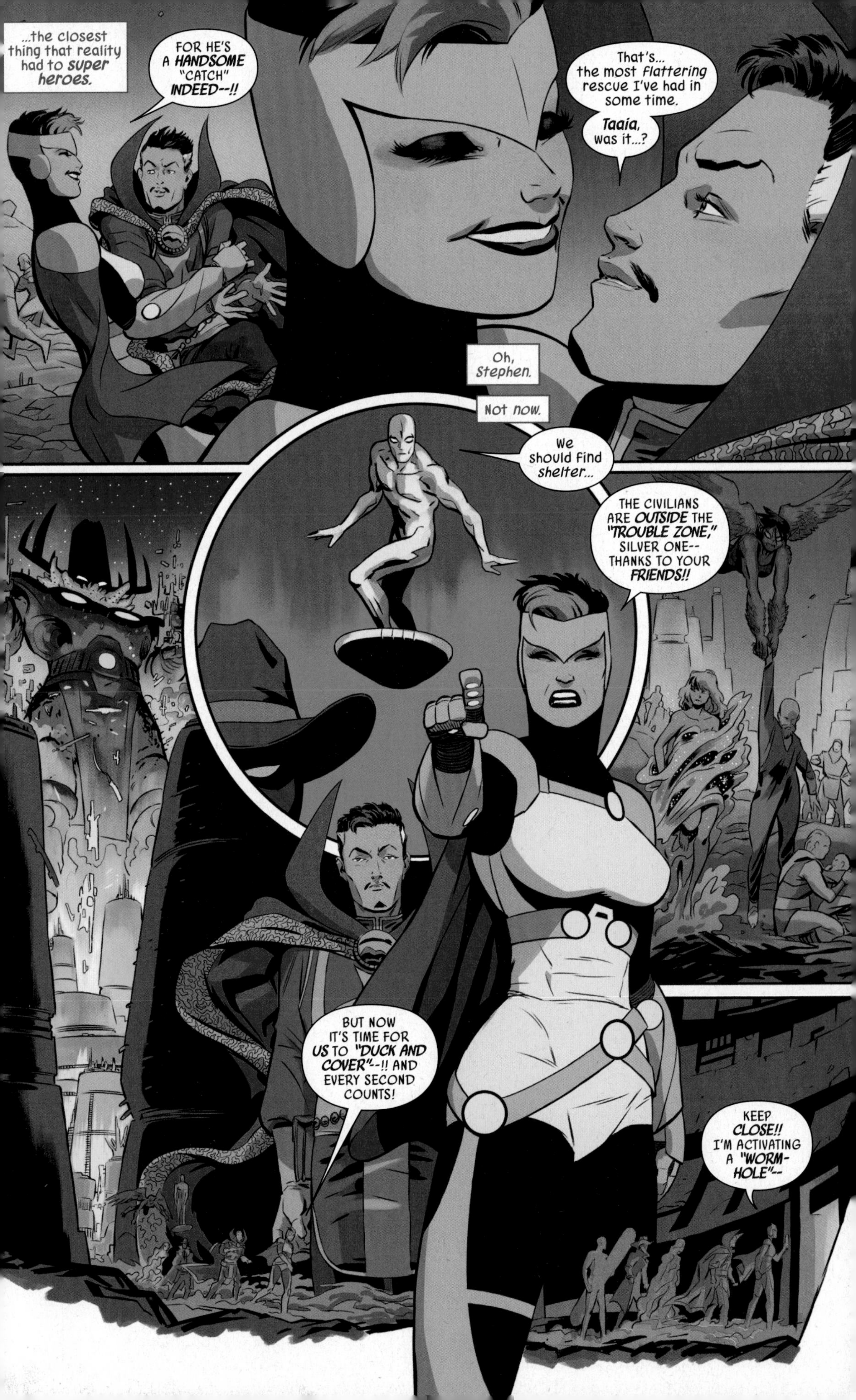
...the closest thing that reality had to super heroes.
FOR HE'S A HANDSOME "CATCH" INDEED--!!
That's... the most flattering rescue I've had in some time.
Taaia, was it...?
Oh, Stephen.
Not now.
We should find shelter...
THE CIVILIANS ARE OUTSIDE THE "TROUBLE ZONE," SILVER ONE-- THANKS TO YOUR FRIENDS!!
BUT NOW IT'S TIME FOR US TO "DUCK AND COVER"--!! AND EVERY SECOND COUNTS!
KEEP CLOSE!! I'M ACTIVATING A "WORM-HOLE"--

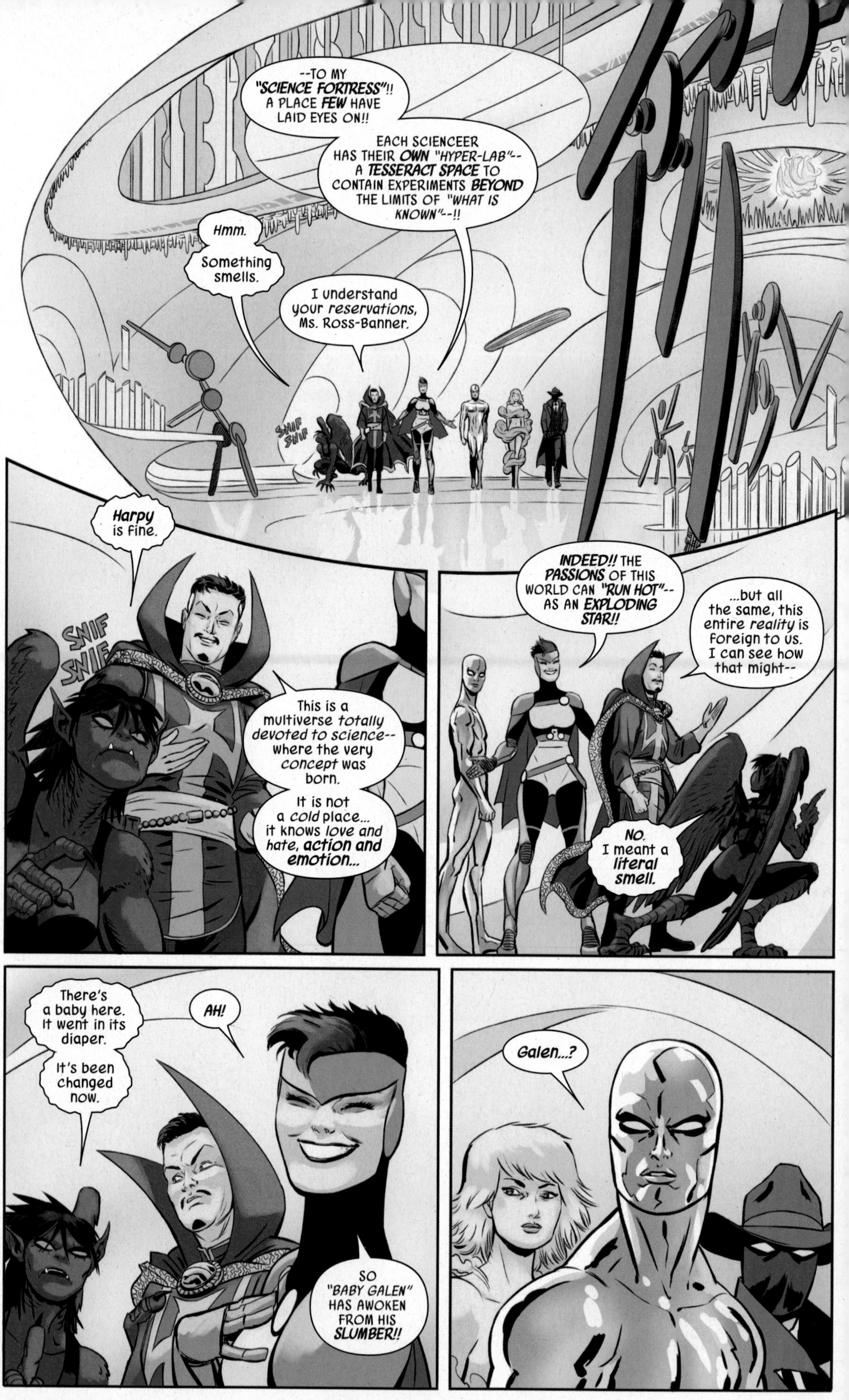
--TO MY "SCIENCE FORTRESS"!! A PLACE FEW HAVE LAID EYES ON!!
EACH SCIENCEER HAS THEIR OWN "HYPER-LAB"-- A TESSERACT SPACE TO CONTAIN EXPERIMENTS BEYOND THE LIMITS OF "WHAT IS KNOWN"--!!
Hmm.
Something smells.
I understand your reservations, Ms. Ross-Banner.
SNIF SNIF
Harpy is fine.
SNIF SNIF
This is a multiverse totally devoted to science-- where the very concept was born.
It is not a cold place... it knows love and hate, action and emotion...
INDEED!! THE PASSIONS OF THIS WORLD CAN "RUN HOT"-- AS AN EXPLODING STAR!!
...but all the same, this entire reality is foreign to us. I can see how that might--
NO. I meant a literal smell.
There's a baby here. It went in its diaper.
It's been changed now.
AH!
SO "BABY GALEN" HAS AWOKEN FROM HIS SLUMBER!!
Galen...?

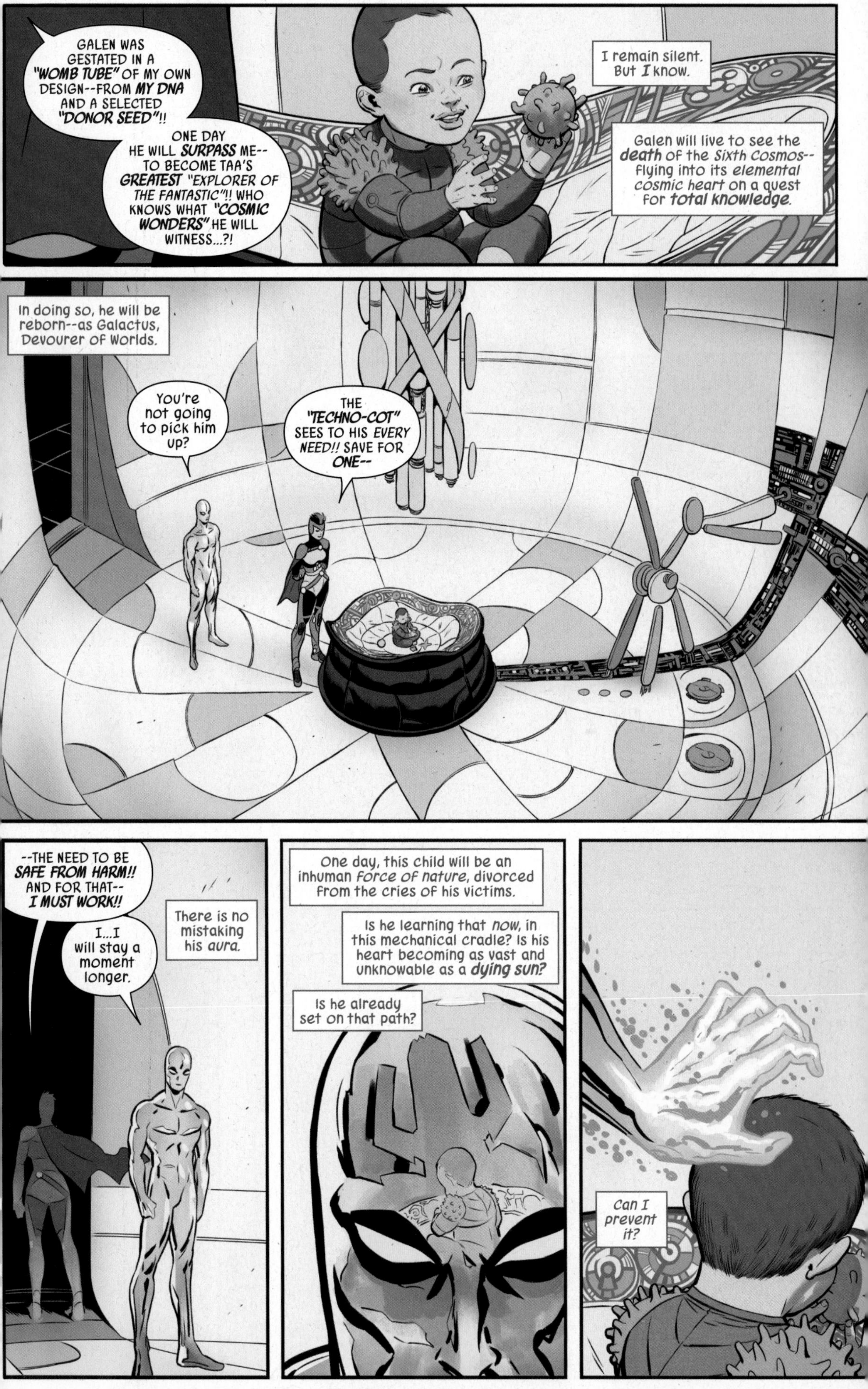
GALEN WAS GESTATED IN A "WOMB TUBE" OF MY OWN DESIGN--FROM MY DNA AND A SELECTED "DONOR SEED"!!
ONE DAY HE WILL SURPASS ME--TO BECOME TAA'S GREATEST "EXPLORER OF THE FANTASTIC"!! WHO KNOWS WHAT "COSMIC WONDERS" HE WILL WITNESS...?!
I remain silent. But I know.
Galen will live to see the death of the Sixth Cosmos--flying into its elemental cosmic heart on a quest for total knowledge.
In doing so, he will be reborn--as Galactus, Devourer of Worlds.
You're not going to pick him up?
THE "TECHNO-COT" SEES TO HIS EVERY NEED!! SAVE FOR ONE--
--THE NEED TO BE SAFE FROM HARM!! AND FOR THAT--I MUST WORK!!
I...I will stay a moment longer.
There is no mistaking his aura.
One day, this child will be an inhuman force of nature, divorced from the cries of his victims.
Is he learning that now, in this mechanical cradle? Is his heart becoming as vast and unknowable as a dying sun?
Is he already set on that path?
Can I prevent it?

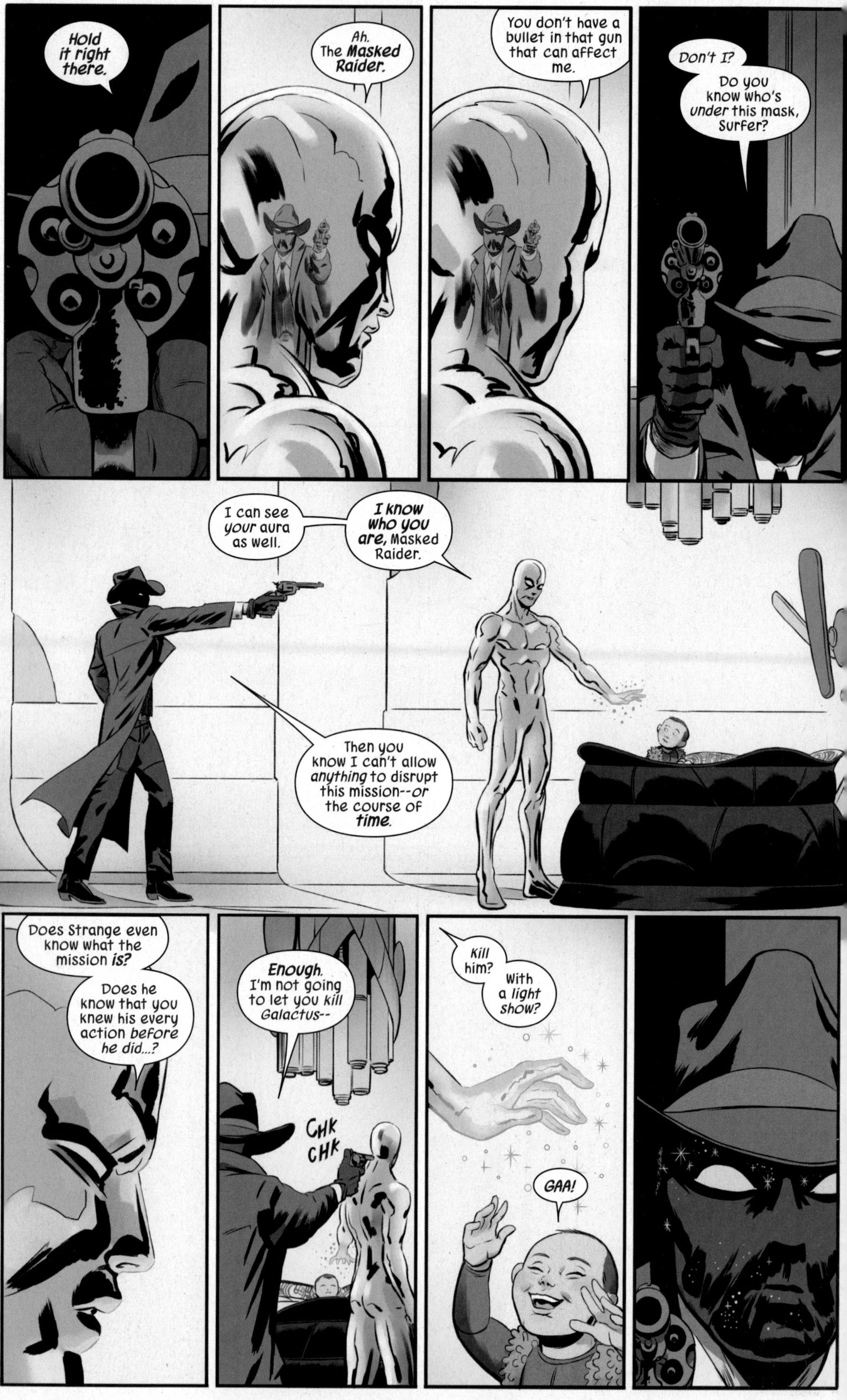
Hold it right there.
Ah. The Masked Raider.
You don't have a bullet in that gun that can affect me.
Don't I?
Do you know who's under this mask, Surfer?
I can see your aura as well.
I know who you are, Masked Raider.
Then you know I can't allow anything to disrupt this mission--or the course of time.
Does Strange even know what the mission is?
Does he know that you knew his every action before he did...?
Enough. I'm not going to let you kill Galactus--
CHK CHK
Kill him? With a light show?
GAA!

It might not match the techno-cot, but it got his attention.

Come here, little one.

You don't want to...?

Are you shocked? Should I desire judgment?

I cannot change what *created* me, Raider. But perhaps there *is* a destiny at work here. A *gift* I can give.

So here is knowledge, Galen. Of the reality to come--in all its *beauty* and *sorrow* and *joy*. Bury it deep within.

It will drive you on. And in time, it will *arm* you--for the long fight *against* your hunger.

It would be *easier* for you to be a force of nature, Galen of Taa...

...but I have taken that from you.

And *that* is my judgment.

But now... I wonder.

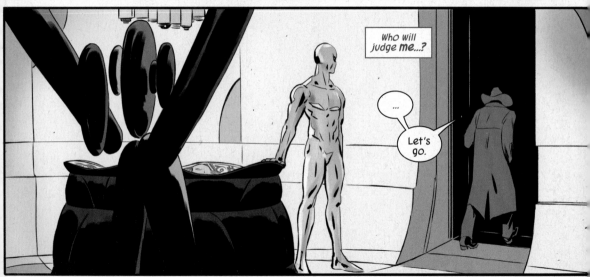

Who will judge *me*...?

...

Let's go.

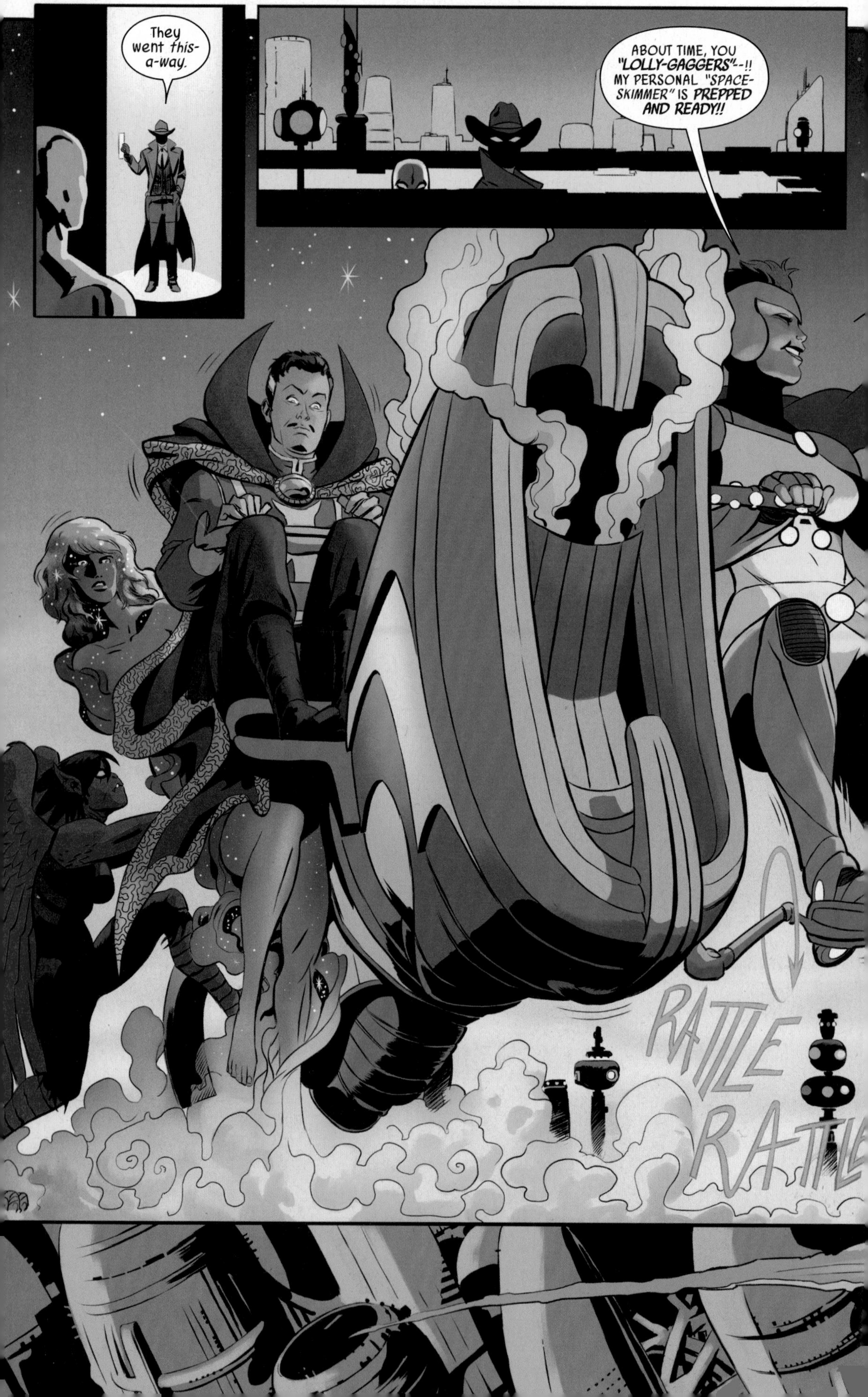
They went this-a-way.
ABOUT TIME, YOU "LOLLY-GAGGERS"--!! MY PERSONAL "SPACE-SKIMMER" IS PREPPED AND READY!!
RATTLE
RATTLE

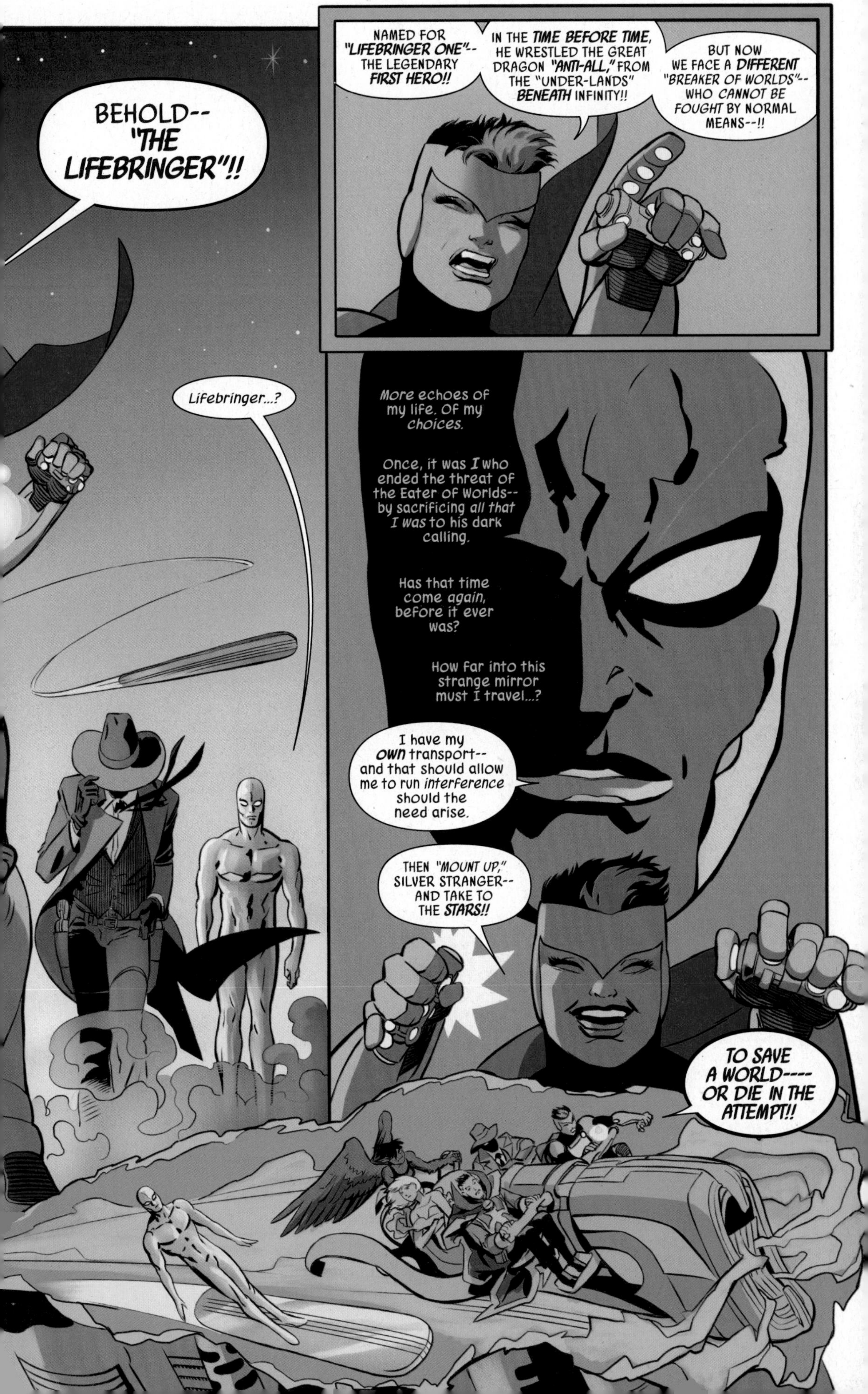
BEHOLD-- "THE LIFEBRINGER"!!
NAMED FOR "LIFEBRINGER ONE"-- THE LEGENDARY FIRST HERO!!
IN THE TIME BEFORE TIME, HE WRESTLED THE GREAT DRAGON "ANTI-ALL," FROM THE "UNDER-LANDS" BENEATH INFINITY!!
BUT NOW WE FACE A DIFFERENT "BREAKER OF WORLDS"-- WHO CANNOT BE FOUGHT BY NORMAL MEANS--!!
Lifebringer...?
More echoes of my life. Of my choices.
Once, it was I who ended the threat of the Eater of Worlds-- by sacrificing all that I was to his dark calling.
Has that time come again, before it ever was?
How far into this strange mirror must I travel...?
I have my own transport-- and that should allow me to run interference should the need arise.
THEN "MOUNT UP," SILVER STRANGER-- AND TAKE TO THE STARS!!
TO SAVE A WORLD---- OR DIE IN THE ATTEMPT!!

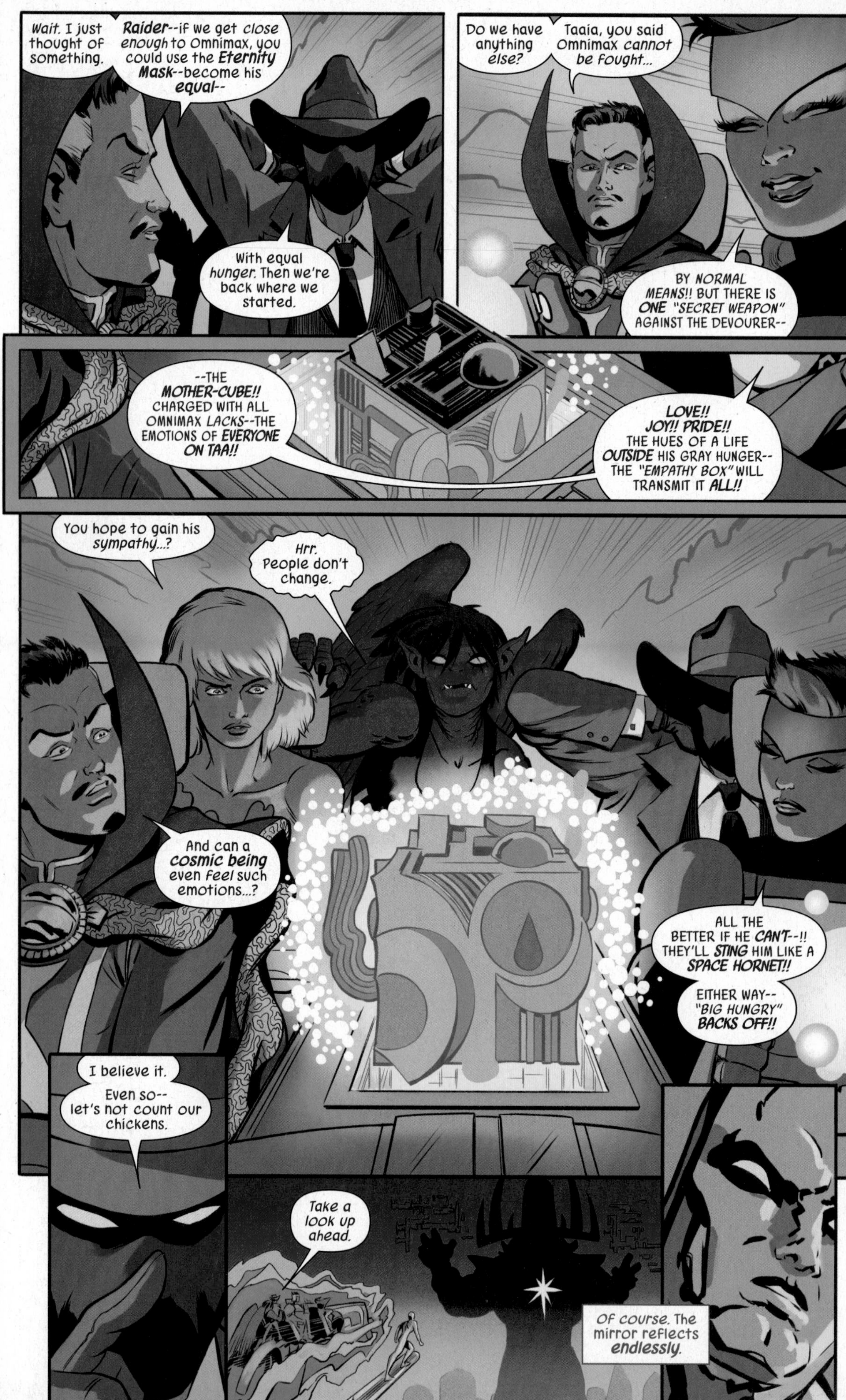
Wait. I just thought of something.
Raider--if we get close enough to Omnimax, you could use the Eternity Mask--become his equal--
With equal hunger. Then we're back where we started.
Do we have anything else?
Taaia, you said Omnimax cannot be fought...
BY NORMAL MEANS!! BUT THERE IS ONE "SECRET WEAPON" AGAINST THE DEVOURER--
--THE MOTHER-CUBE!! CHARGED WITH ALL OMNIMAX LACKS--THE EMOTIONS OF EVERYONE ON TAA!!
LOVE!! JOY!! PRIDE!! THE HUES OF A LIFE OUTSIDE HIS GRAY HUNGER-- THE "EMPATHY BOX" WILL TRANSMIT IT ALL!!
You hope to gain his sympathy...?
Hrr. People don't change.
And can a cosmic being even feel such emotions...?
ALL THE BETTER IF HE CAN'T--!! THEY'LL STING HIM LIKE A SPACE HORNET!!
EITHER WAY-- "BIG HUNGRY" BACKS OFF!!
I believe it.
Even so-- let's not count our chickens.
Take a look up ahead.
Of course. The mirror reflects endlessly.

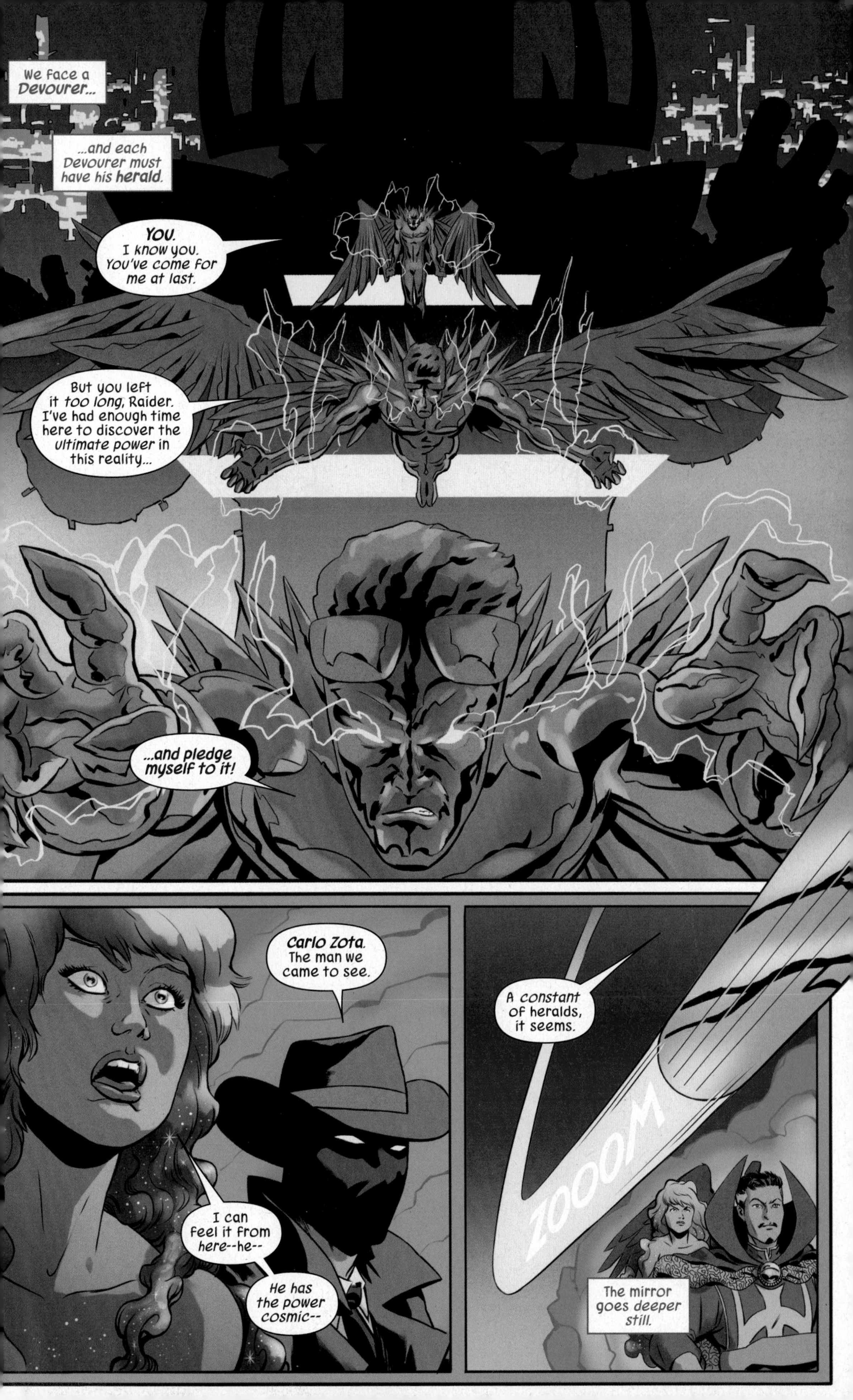

We face a Devourer...
...and each Devourer must have his herald.
YOU. I know you. You've come for me at last.
But you left it too long, Raider. I've had enough time here to discover the ultimate power in this reality...
...and pledge myself to it!
Carlo Zota. The man we came to see.
I can feel it from here--he--
He has the power cosmic--
A constant of heralds, it seems.
ZOOOM
The mirror goes deeper still.

And in it, I see myself-- or what I *might* have been. We are reflected in each other.

Equal forces, equally matched... *almost.*

KATHOOOOOOOOMM

He has *attuned* himself to this era-- become a part of it. And *I...*

...I am beginning to feel the tug of *millennia,* calling me back to a later time. As I use *my* power, it purges Strange's magic from me.

I fear I do not have *long* here...

CLOUD!! IT'S *YOUR* TURN AT THIS *DEADLY* GAMBIT!!

WITH YOUR POWER, YOU CAN *FEED* THE DEVOURER'S HUNGER--

--WITH AN "ENERGY *SNACK*" OF YOUR *OWN!*

To get his attention...?

I--I'll do my best-- There!

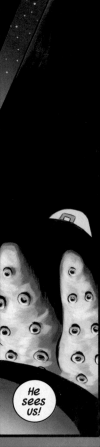

He sees us!

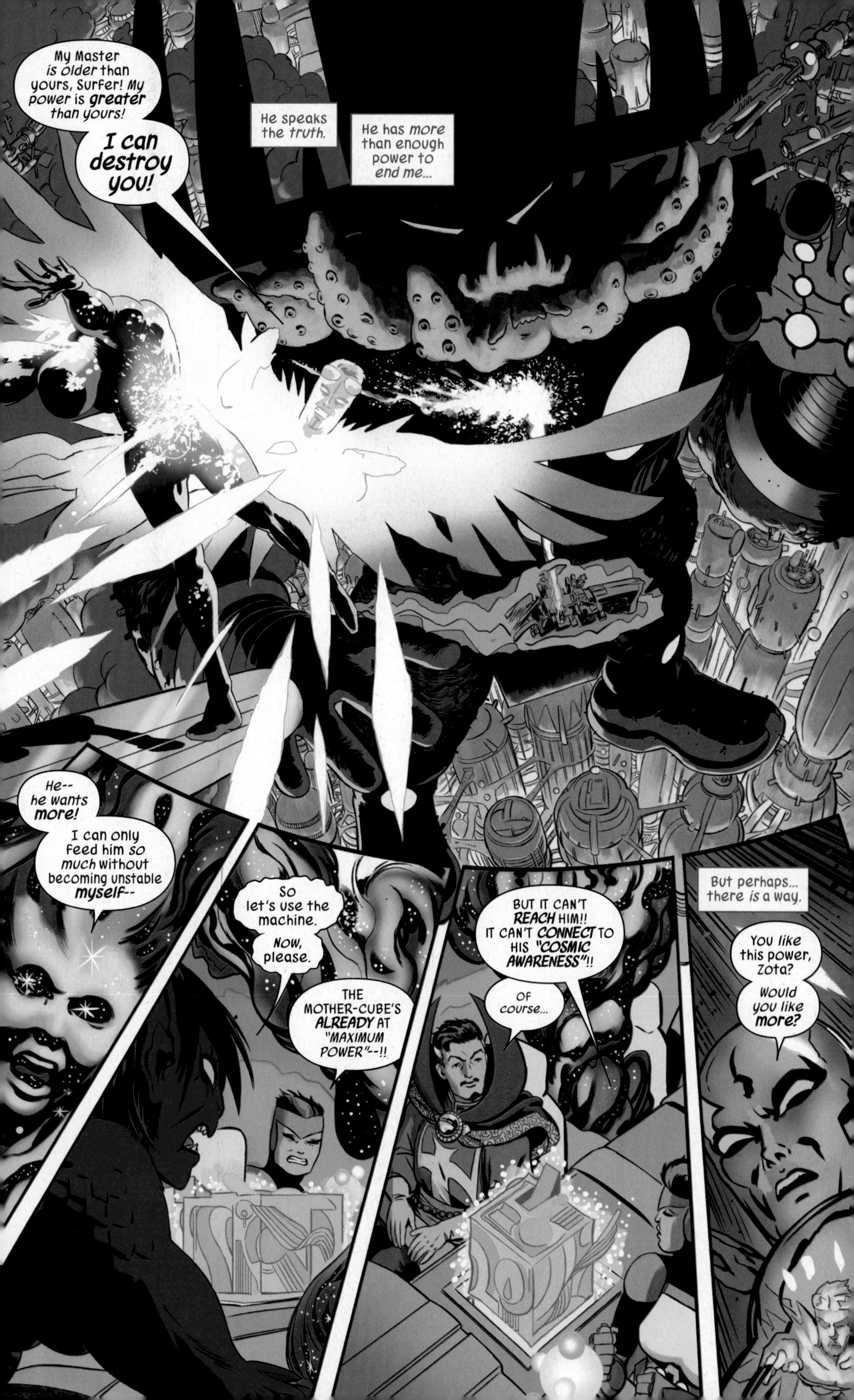
My Master is older than yours, Surfer! My power is greater than yours!
I can destroy you!
He speaks the truth.
He has more than enough power to end me...
He-- he wants more!
I can only feed him so much without becoming unstable myself--
So let's use the machine.
Now, please.
THE MOTHER-CUBE'S ALREADY AT "MAXIMUM POWER"--!!
BUT IT CAN'T REACH HIM!! IT CAN'T CONNECT TO HIS "COSMIC AWARENESS"!!
Of course...
But perhaps... there is a way.
You like this power, Zota?
Would you like more?

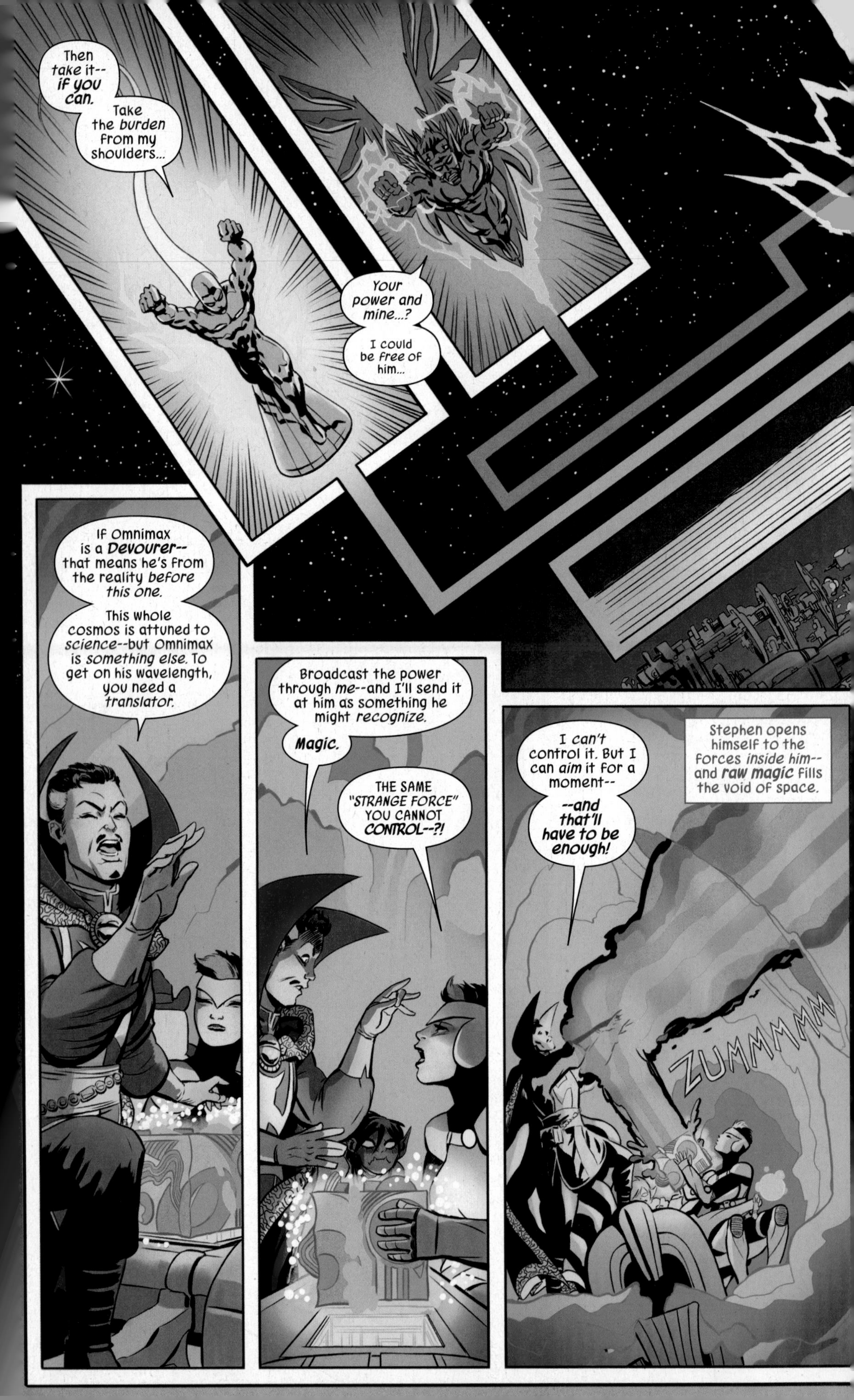

Then take it-- if you can.
Take the burden from my shoulders...
Your power and mine...?
I could be free of him...
If Omnimax is a Devourer-- that means he's from the reality before this one.
This whole cosmos is attuned to science--but Omnimax is something else. To get on his wavelength, you need a translator.
Broadcast the power through me--and I'll send it at him as something he might recognize.
Magic.
THE SAME "STRANGE FORCE" YOU CANNOT CONTROL--?!
I can't control it. But I can aim it for a moment--
--and that'll have to be enough!
Stephen opens himself to the forces inside him--and raw magic fills the void of space.
ZUMMMMM

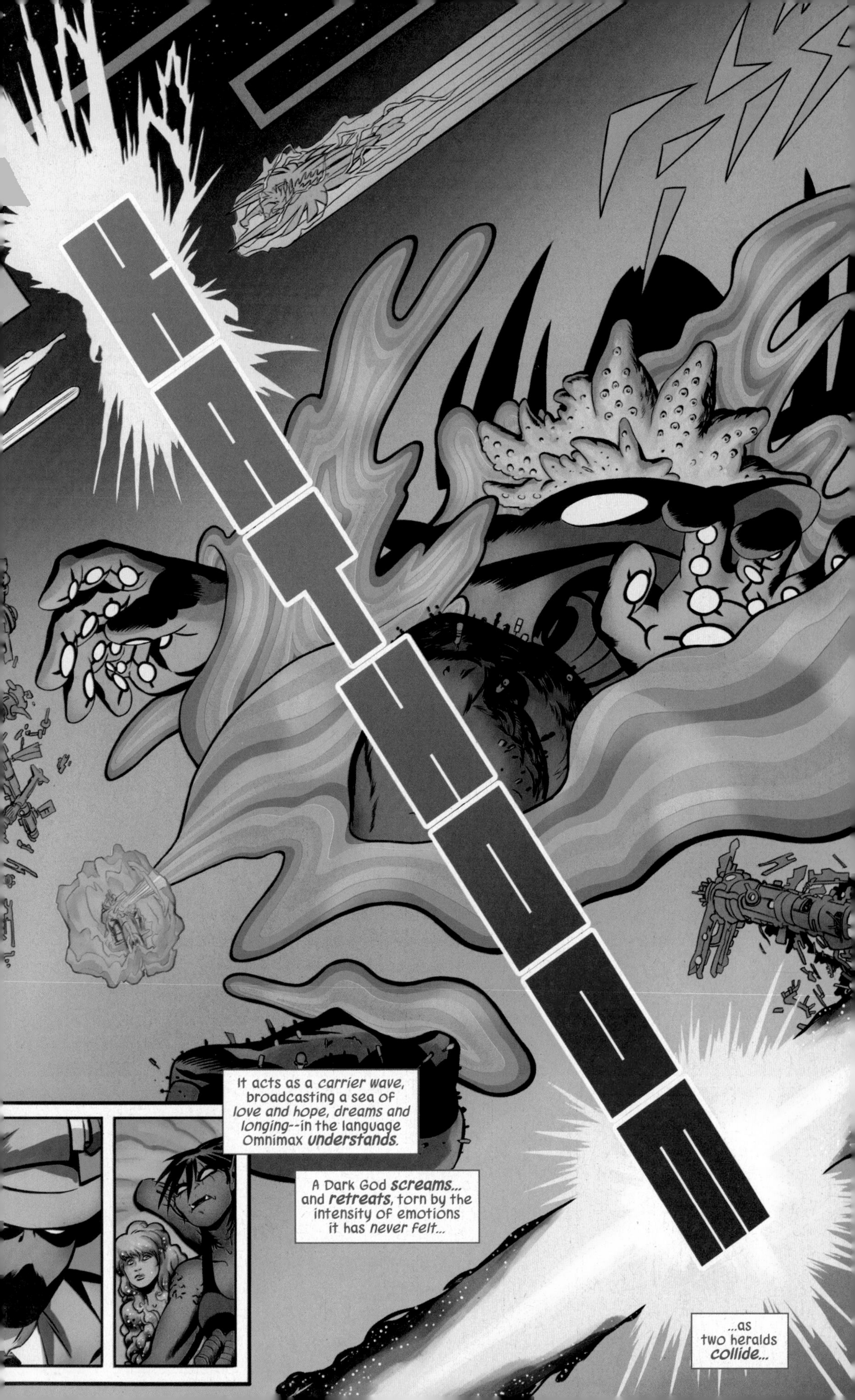
It acts as a carrier wave, broadcasting a sea of love and hope, dreams and longing--in the language Omnimax understands.
A Dark God screams... and retreats, torn by the intensity of emotions it has never felt...
...as two heralds collide...

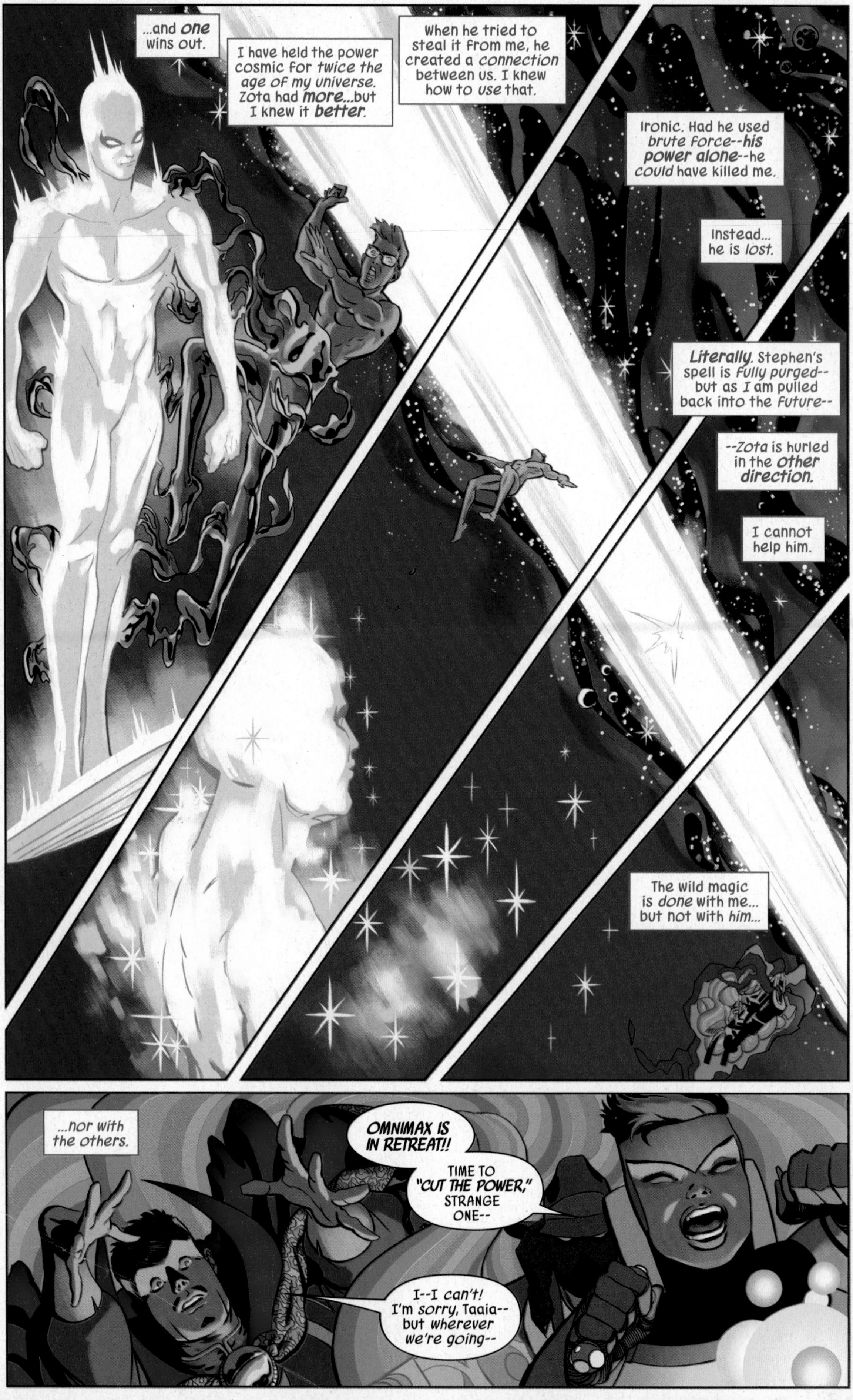
...and one wins out.
I have held the power cosmic for twice the age of my universe. Zota had more...but I knew it better.
When he tried to steal it from me, he created a connection between us. I knew how to use that.
Ironic. Had he used brute force--his power alone--he could have killed me.
Instead... he is lost.
Literally. Stephen's spell is fully purged--but as I am pulled back into the future--
--Zota is hurled in the other direction.
I cannot help him.
The wild magic is done with me... but not with him...
...nor with the others.
OMNIMAX IS IN RETREAT!!
TIME TO "CUT THE POWER," STRANGE ONE--
I--I can't! I'm sorry, Taaia--but wherever we're going--

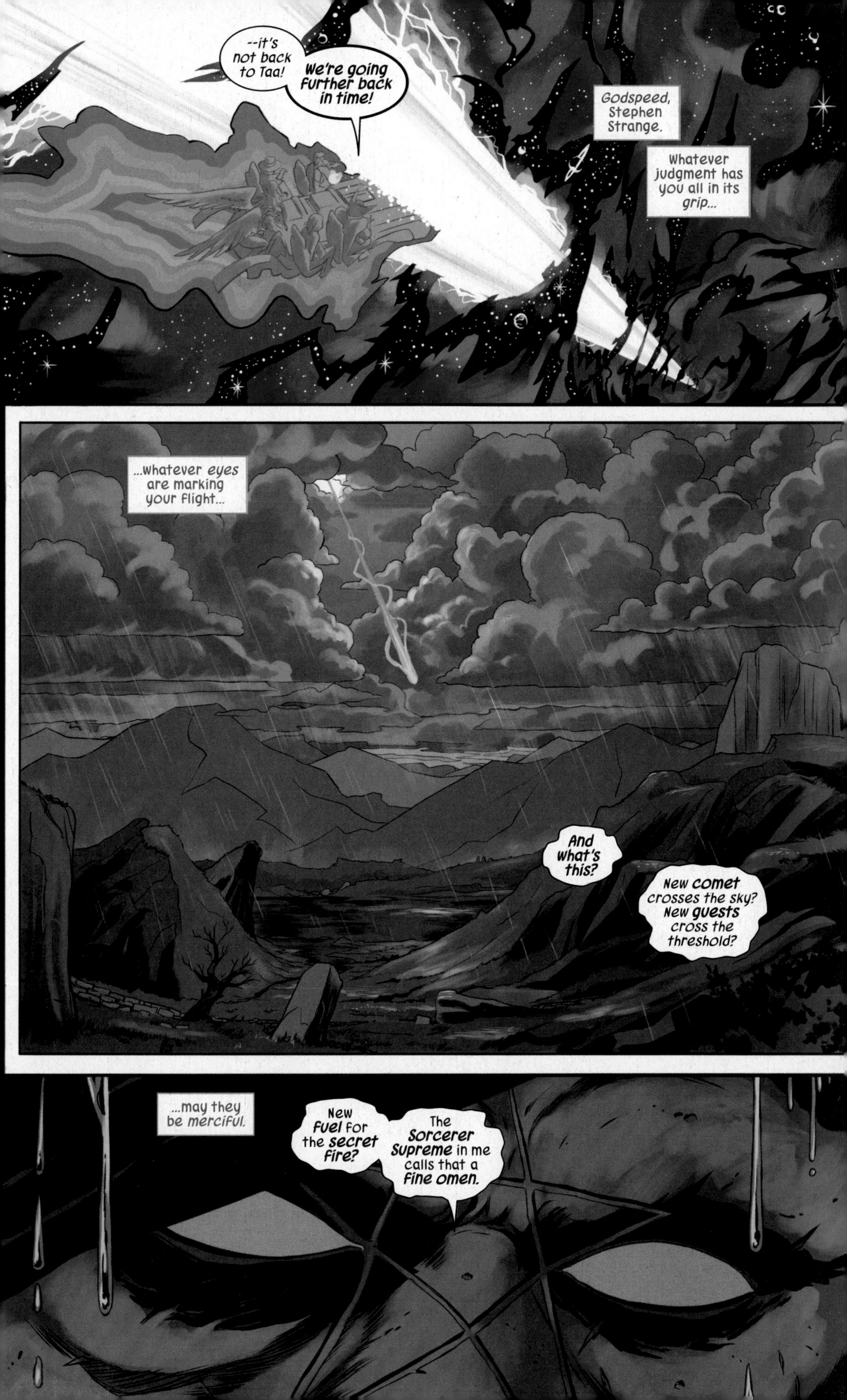
--it's not back to Taa!
We're going further back in time!
Godspeed, Stephen Strange.
Whatever judgment has you all in its grip...
...whatever eyes are marking your flight...
And what's this?
New comet crosses the sky? New guests cross the threshold?
...may they be merciful.
New fuel for the secret fire?
The Sorcerer Supreme in me calls that a fine omen.

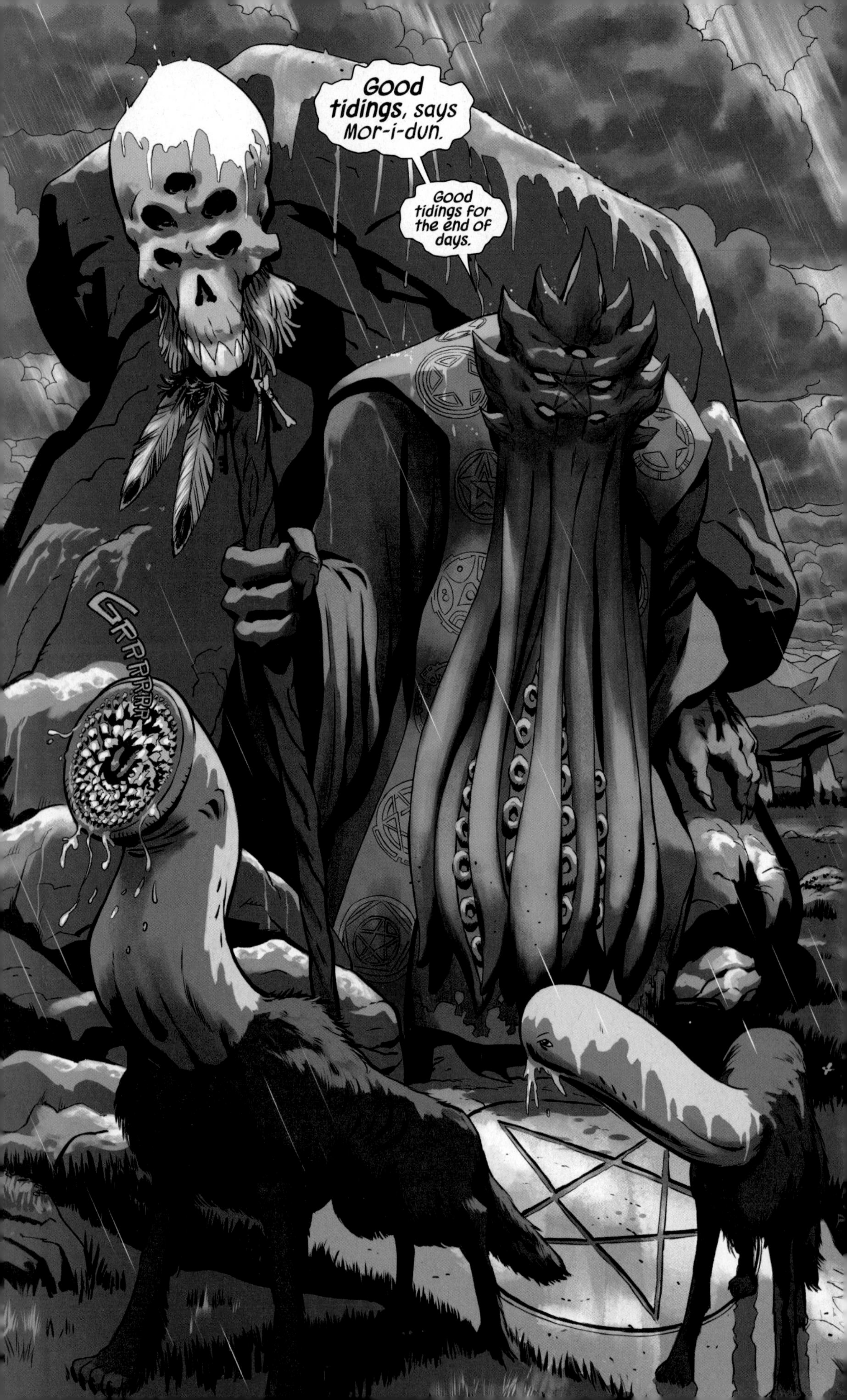
Good tidings, says Mor-i-dun.
Good tidings for the end of days.
GRRRRRR

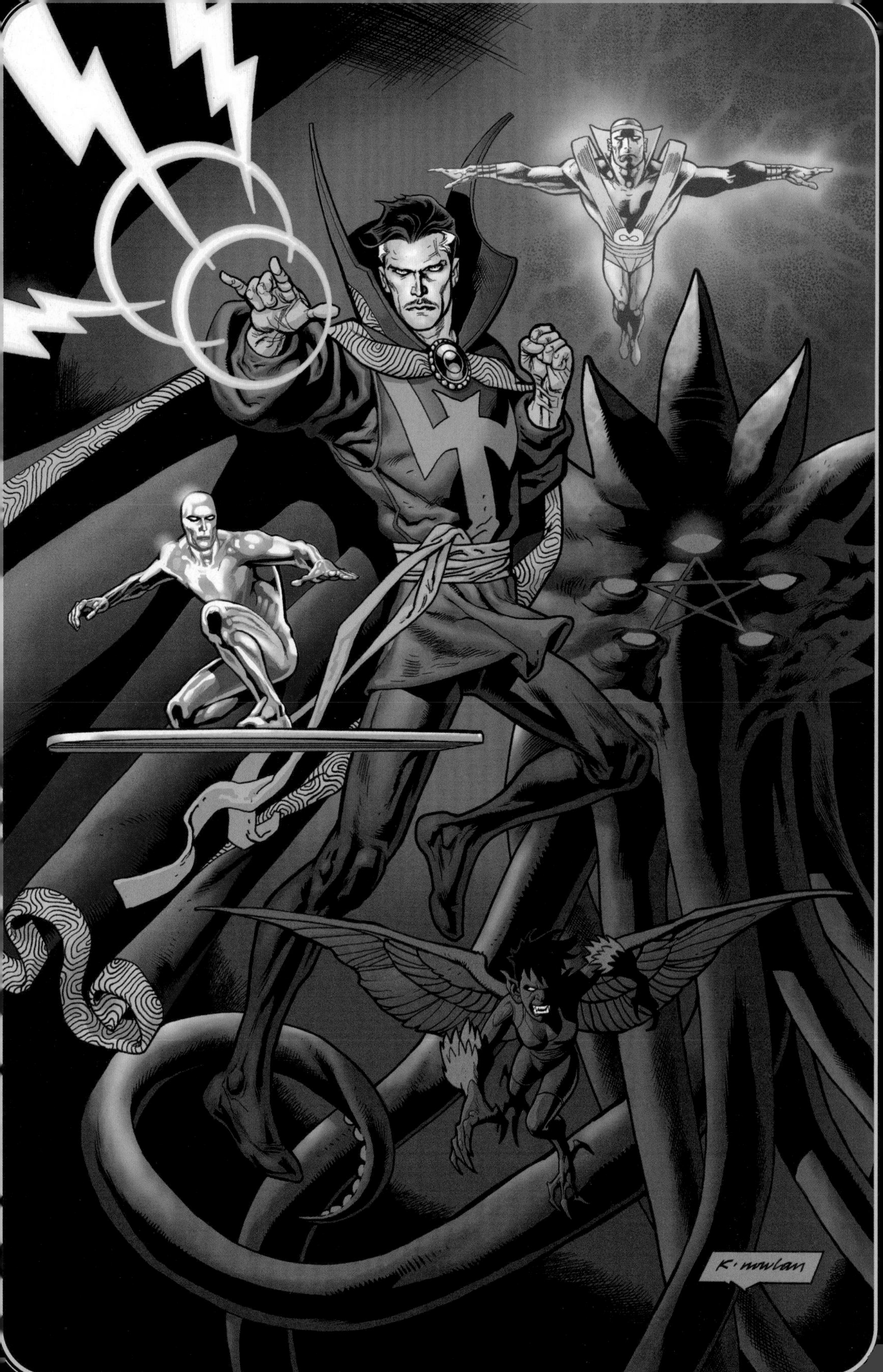
K·nowlan

III

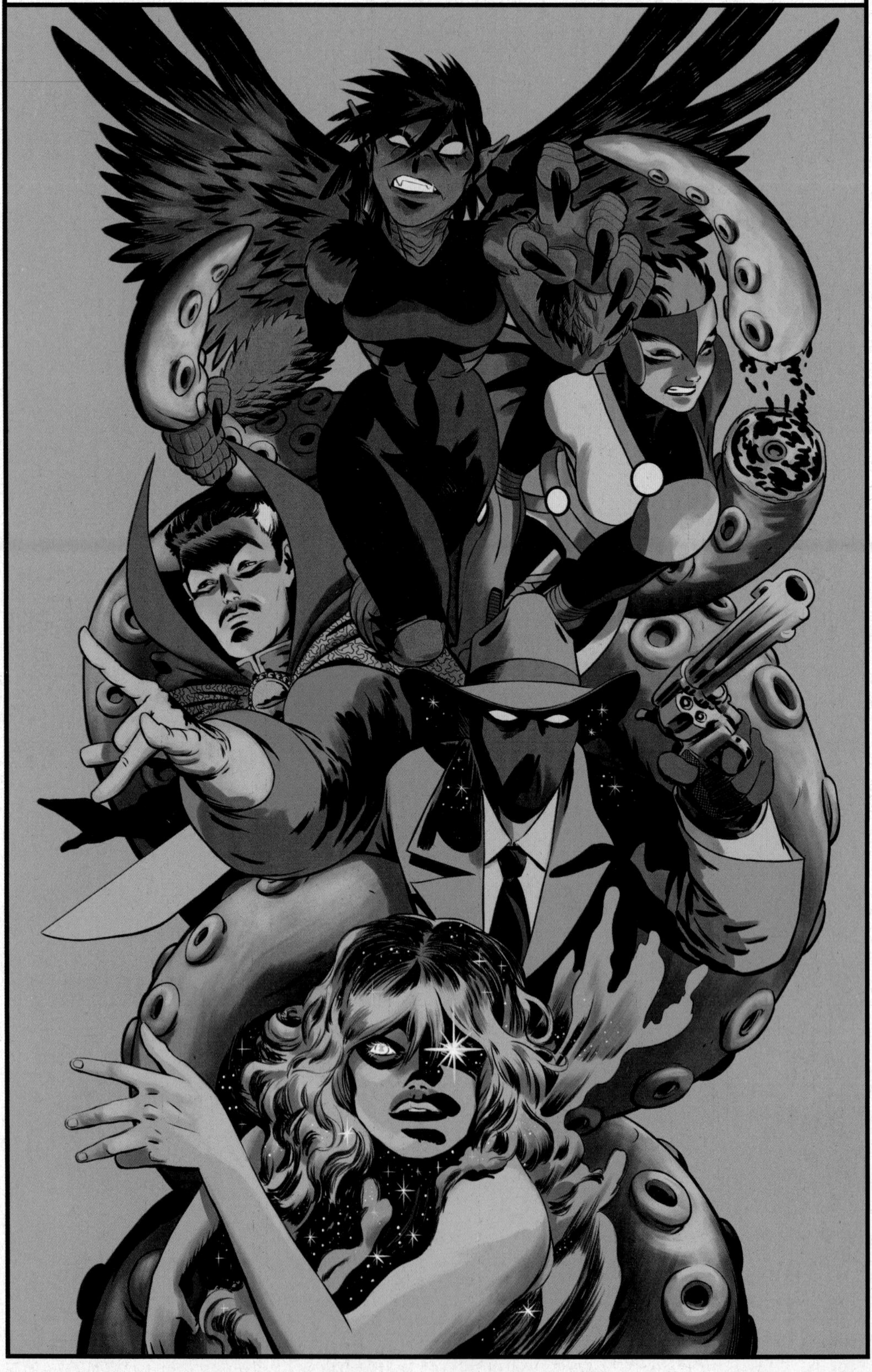

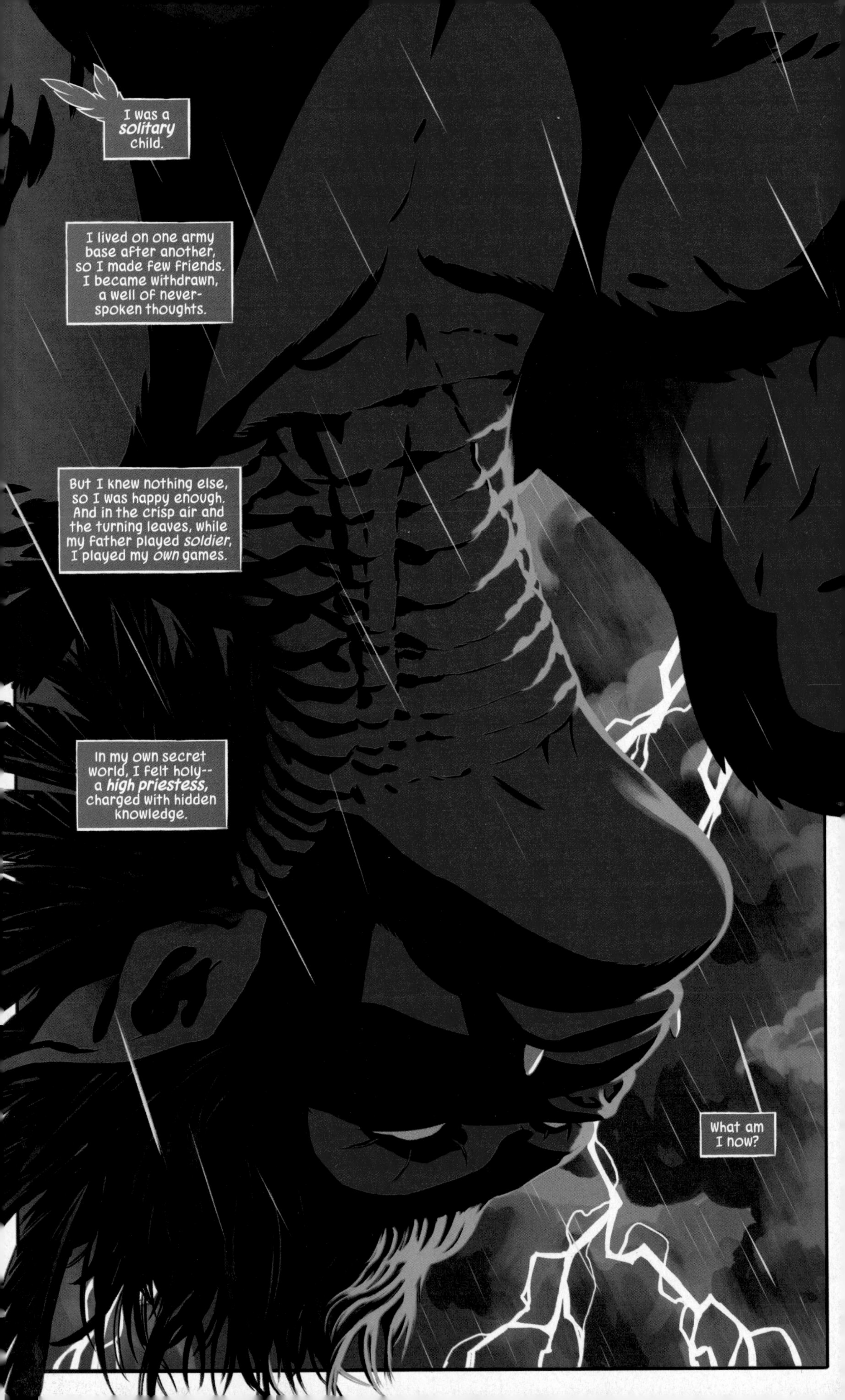
I was a *solitary* child.
I lived on one army base after another, so I made few friends. I became withdrawn, a well of never-spoken thoughts.
But I knew nothing else, so I was happy enough. And in the crisp air and the turning leaves, while my father played *soldier*, I played my *own* games.
In my own secret world, I felt holy-- a ***high priestess,*** charged with hidden knowledge.
What am I now?

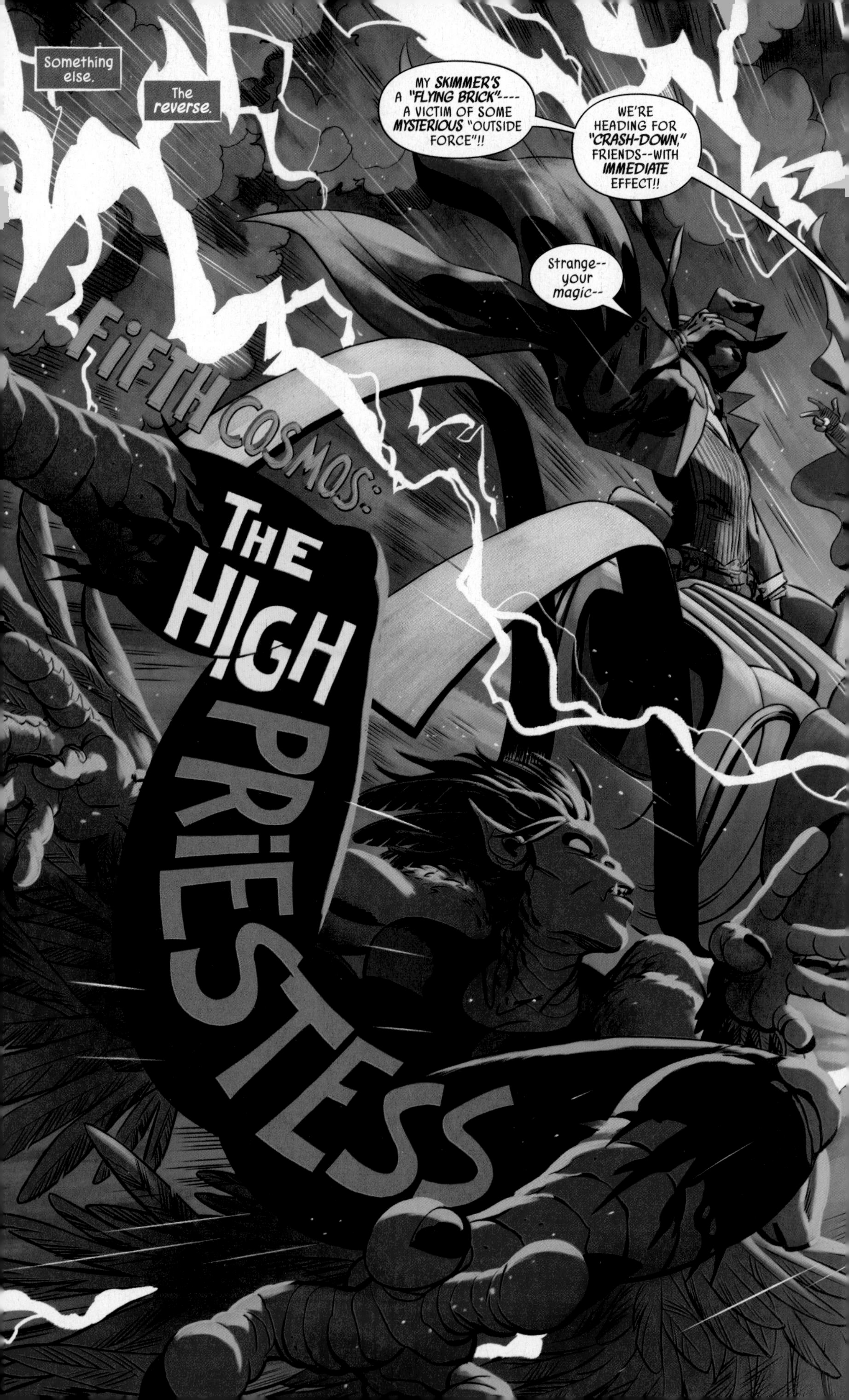
Something else.
The reverse.
MY SKIMMER'S A "FLYING BRICK"---- A VICTIM OF SOME MYSTERIOUS "OUTSIDE FORCE"!!
WE'RE HEADING FOR "CRASH-DOWN," FRIENDS--WITH IMMEDIATE EFFECT!!
Strange-- your magic--
FIFTH COSMOS:
THE HIGH PRIESTESS

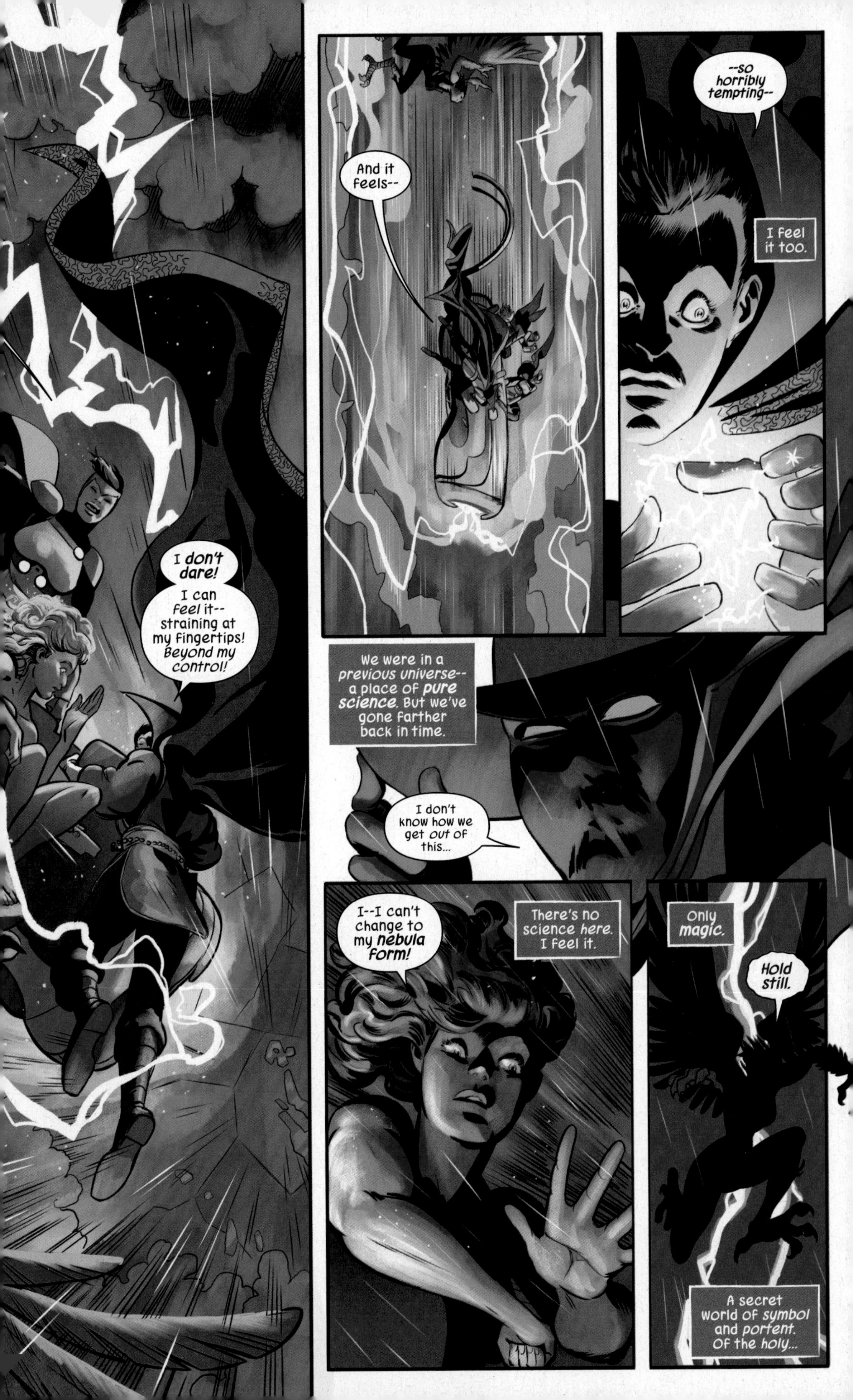
I don't dare!
I can feel it--straining at my fingertips! Beyond my control!
And it feels--
--so horribly tempting--
I feel it too.
We were in a previous universe--a place of pure science. But we've gone farther back in time.
I don't know how we get out of this...
I--I can't change to my nebula form!
There's no science here. I feel it.
Only magic.
Hold still.
A secret world of symbol and portent. Of the holy...

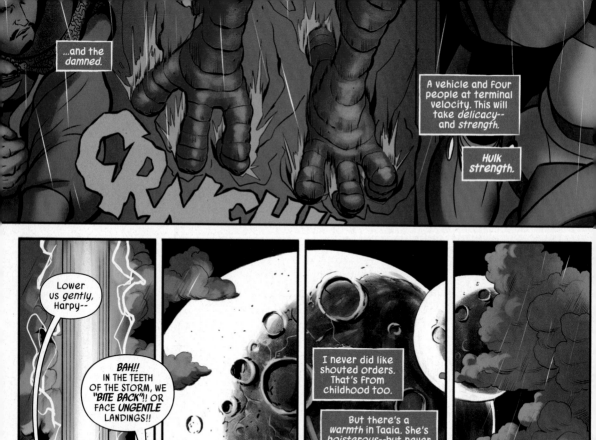

...and the damned.

A vehicle and four people at terminal velocity. This will take *delicacy*-- and *strength*.

Hulk strength.

Lower us *gently*, Harpy--

BAH!! IN THE TEETH OF THE STORM, WE *"BITE BACK"!!* OR FACE *UNGENTLE* LANDINGS!!

KEEP THE *WIND* IN YOUR *WINGS*--- AND FLY!!

I never did like shouted orders. That's from childhood too.

But there's a *warmth* in Taaia. She's boisterous--but never arrogant. Never condescending.

Not like Strange.

But they say opposites attract.

LIFE IS A *WILD BULL*-- --AND WE TAKE IT *"BY THE HORNS"!!*

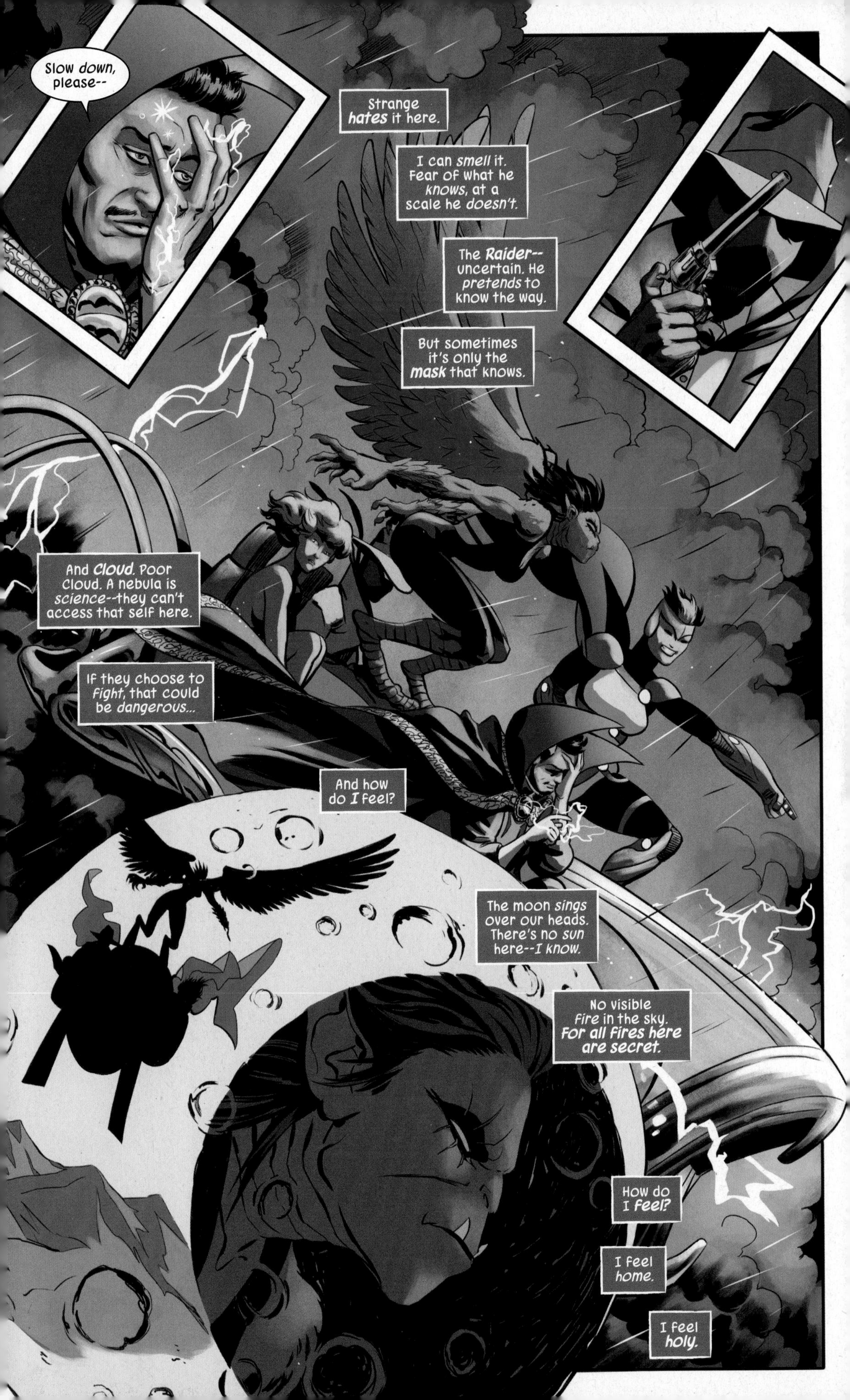

Slow down, please--
Strange hates it here.
I can smell it. Fear of what he knows, at a scale he doesn't.
The Raider-- uncertain. He pretends to know the way.
But sometimes it's only the mask that knows.
And Cloud. Poor Cloud. A nebula is science--they can't access that self here.
If they choose to fight, that could be dangerous...
And how do I feel?
The moon sings over our heads. There's no sun here--I know.
No visible fire in the sky. For all fires here are secret.
How do I feel?
I feel home.
I feel holy.

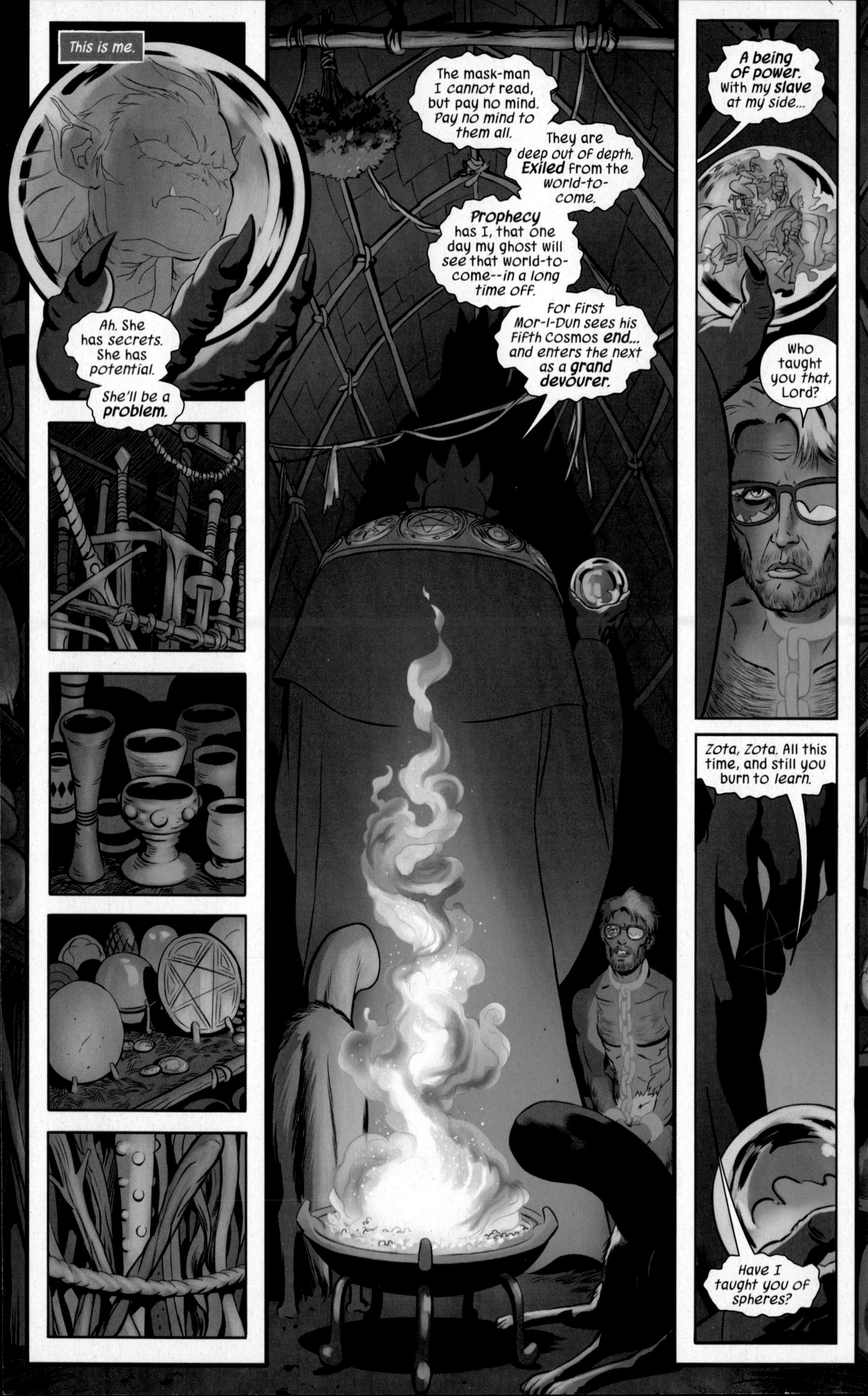
This is me.
Ah. She has secrets. She has potential.
She'll be a **problem.**
The mask-man I cannot read, but pay no mind. Pay no mind to them all.
They are deep out of depth. **Exiled** from the world-to-come.
Prophecy has I, that one day my ghost will see that world-to-come--in a long time off.
For First Mor-I-Dun sees his Fifth Cosmos **end...** and enters the next as a **grand devourer.**
A being of power. With my **slave** at my side...
Who taught you that, Lord?
Zota, Zota. All this time, and still you burn to *learn.*
Have I taught you of spheres?

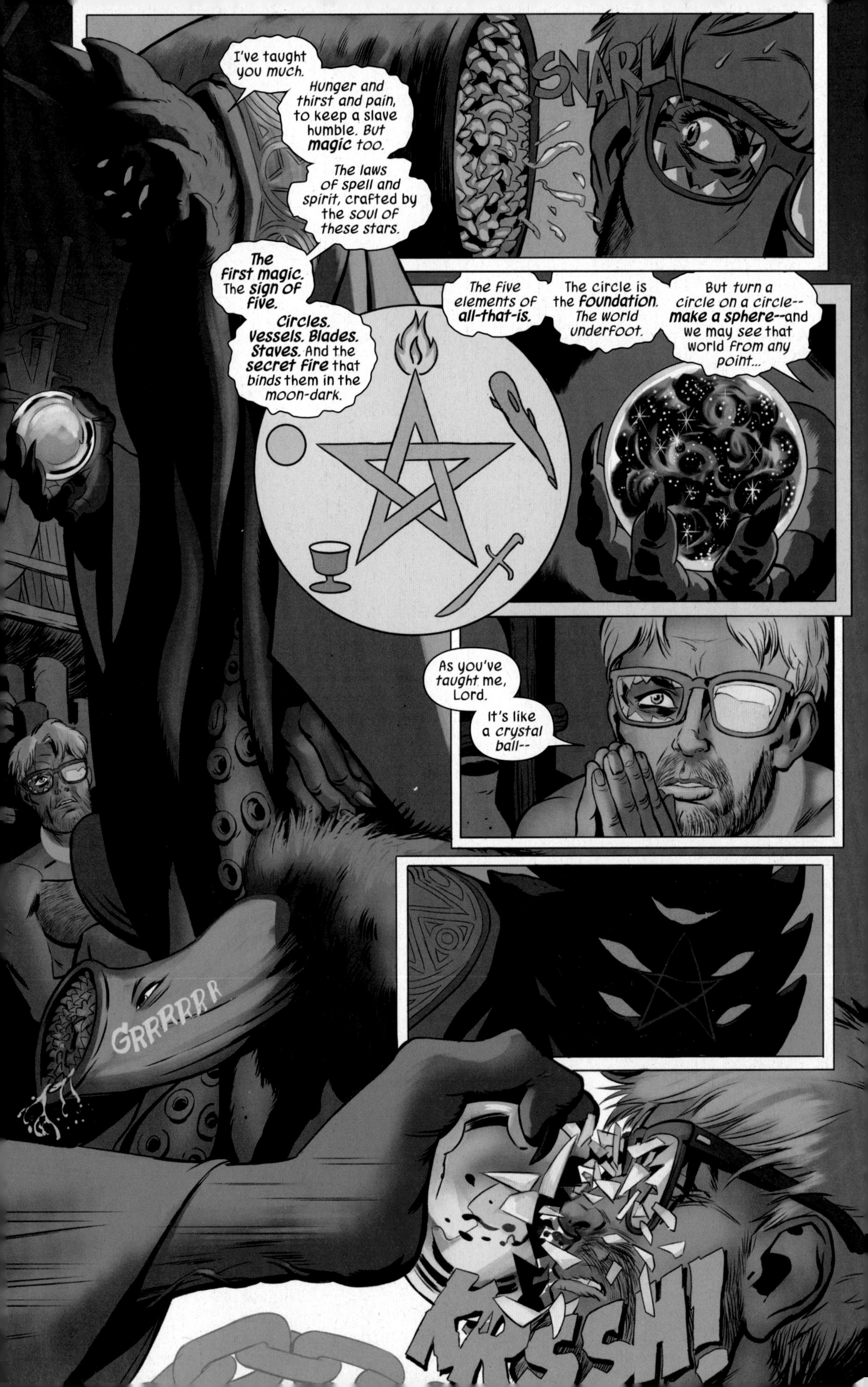

I've taught you much.
Hunger and thirst and pain, to keep a slave humble. But **magic** too.
The laws of spell and spirit, crafted by the soul of these stars.
SNARL
The First magic. The **sign of five.**
Circles. Vessels. Blades. Staves. And the **secret fire** that binds them in the moon-dark.
The five elements of **all-that-is.**
The circle is the **foundation.** The world underfoot.
But turn a circle on a circle-- **make a sphere--**and we may see that world from any point...
As you've taught me, Lord.
It's like a *crystal* ball--
GRRRRRR

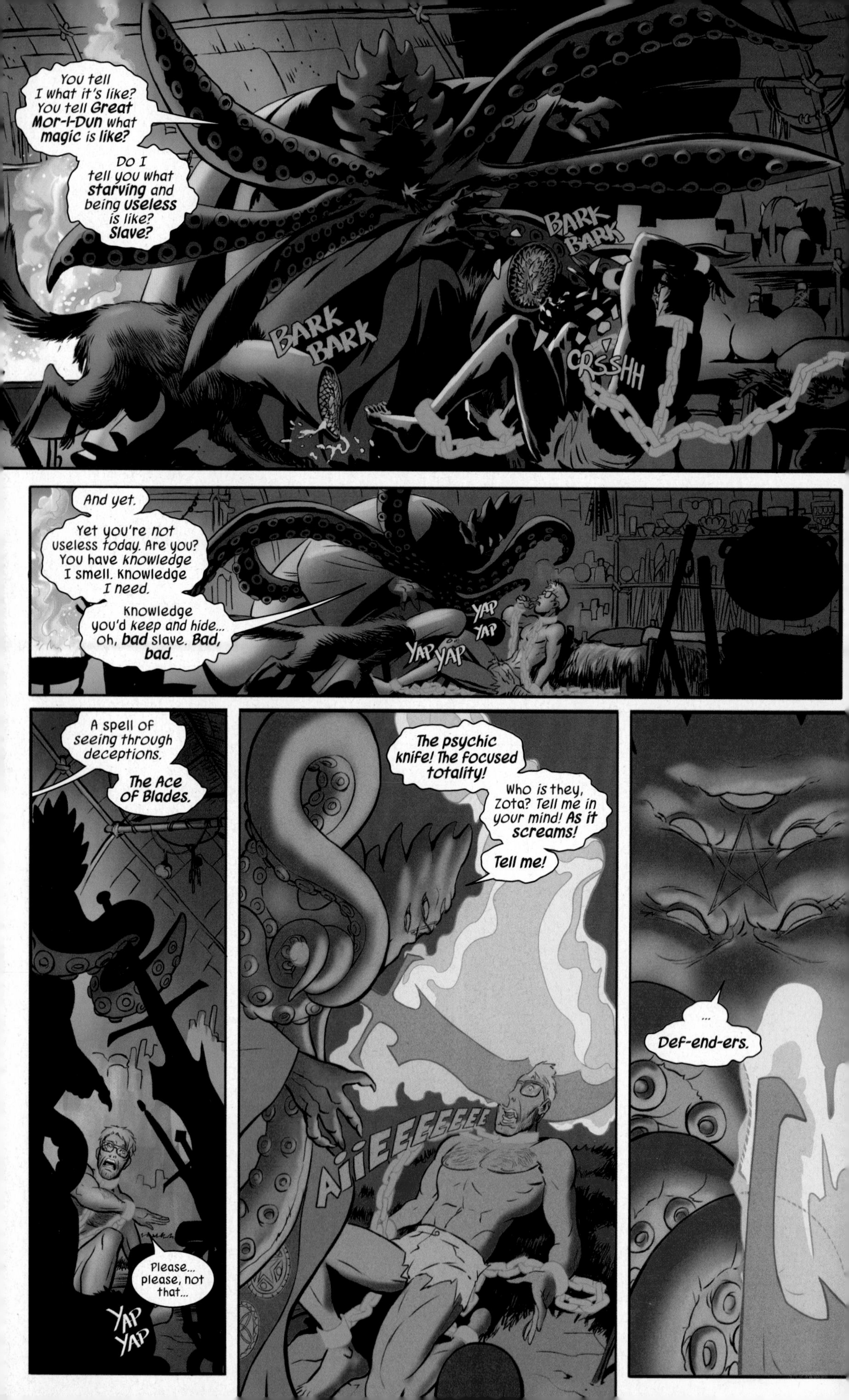
You tell I what it's like? You tell Great Mor-I-Dun what magic is like?
Do I tell you what starving and being useless is like? Slave?
BARK BARK
BARK BARK
CRSSHH
And yet.
Yet you're not useless today. Are you? You have knowledge I smell. Knowledge I need.
Knowledge you'd keep and hide... oh, bad slave. Bad, bad.
YAP YAP
YAP YAP
A spell of seeing through deceptions.
The Ace of Blades.
Please... please, not that...
YAP YAP
The psychic knife! The focused totality!
Who is they, Zota? Tell me in your mind! As it screams!
Tell me!
AiiEEEEEEEE
...
Def-end-ers.

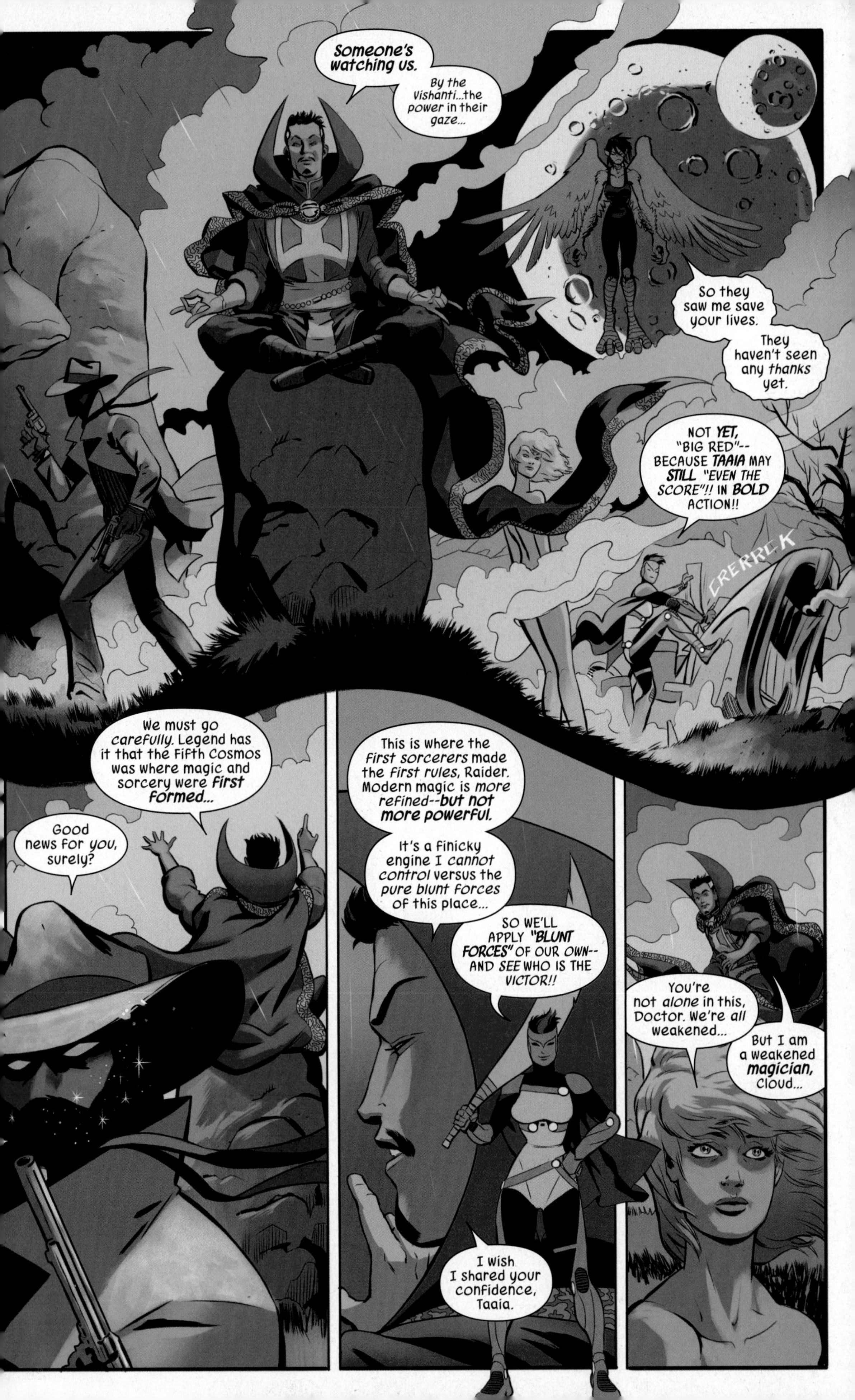
Someone's watching us.
By the Vishanti...the power in their gaze...
So they saw me save your lives.
They haven't seen any thanks yet.
NOT YET, "BIG RED"-- BECAUSE TAAIA MAY STILL "EVEN THE SCORE"!! IN BOLD ACTION!!
CRERRRK
We must go carefully. Legend has it that the Fifth Cosmos was where magic and sorcery were first formed...
Good news for you, surely?
This is where the first sorcerers made the first rules, Raider. Modern magic is more refined--but not more powerful.
It's a finicky engine I cannot control versus the pure blunt forces of this place...
SO WE'LL APPLY "BLUNT FORCES" OF OUR OWN-- AND SEE WHO IS THE VICTOR!!
I wish I shared your confidence, Taaia.
You're not alone in this, Doctor. We're all weakened...
But I am a weakened magician, Cloud...

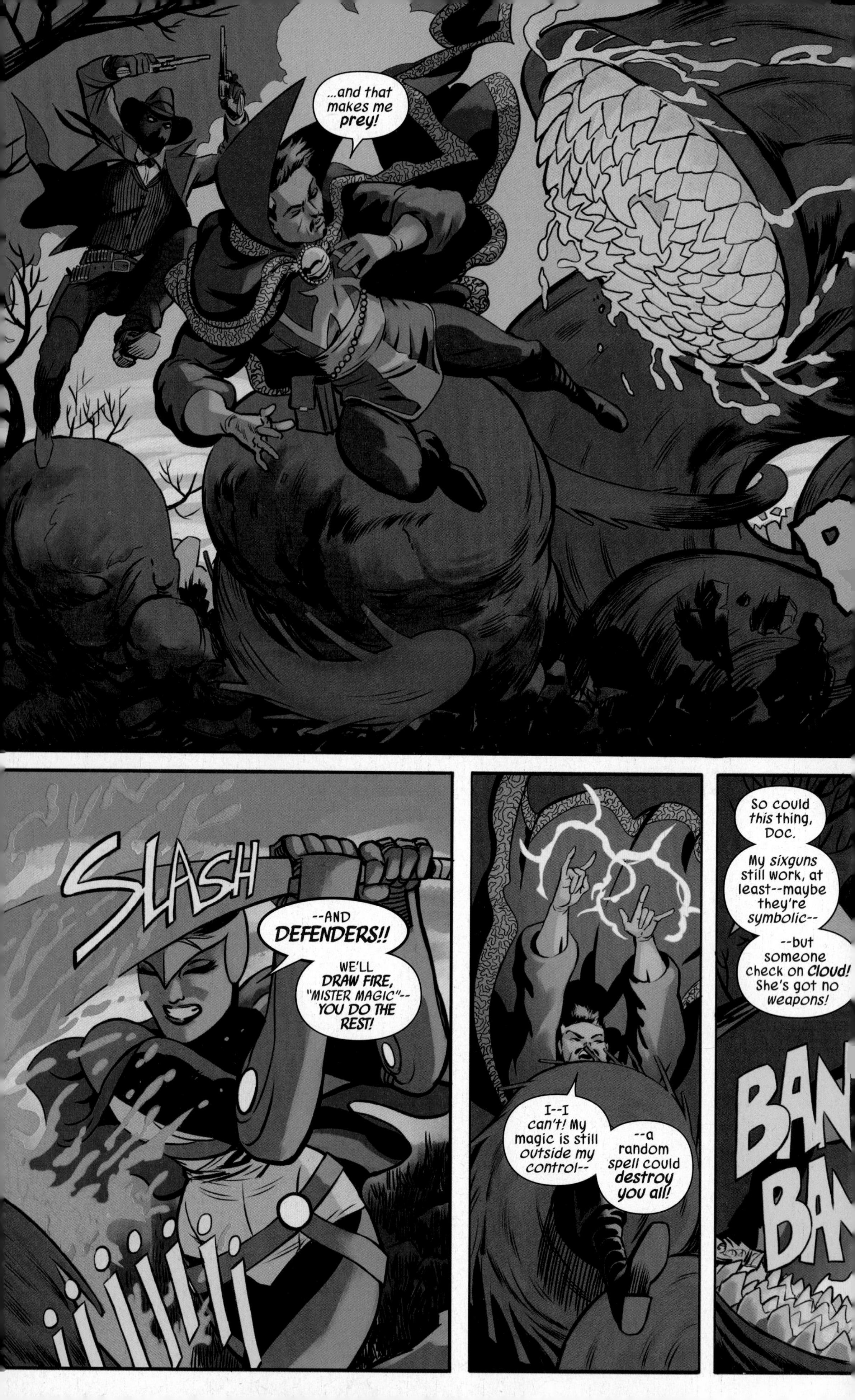
...and that makes me prey!
SLASH
--AND DEFENDERS!!
WE'LL DRAW FIRE, "MISTER MAGIC"-- YOU DO THE REST!
I--I can't! My magic is still outside my control--
--a random spell could destroy you all!
So could this thing, Doc.
My sixguns still work, at least--maybe they're symbolic--
--but someone check on Cloud! She's got no weapons!

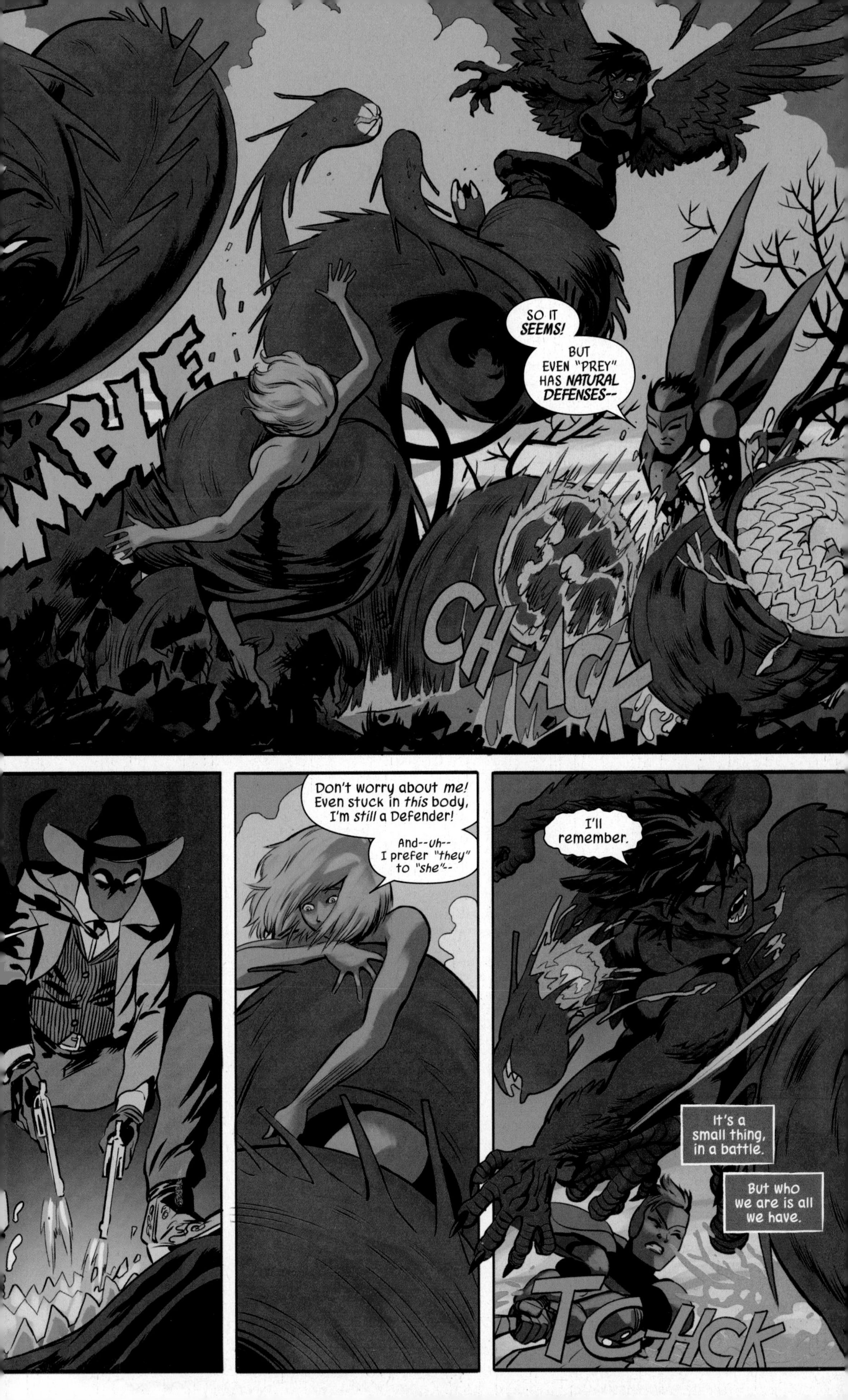
SO IT SEEMS!
BUT EVEN "PREY" HAS NATURAL DEFENSES--
CH-ACK
Don't worry about me! Even stuck in this body, I'm still a Defender!
And--uh-- I prefer "they" to "she"--
I'll remember.
It's a small thing, in a battle.
But who we are is all we have.
TC-HCK

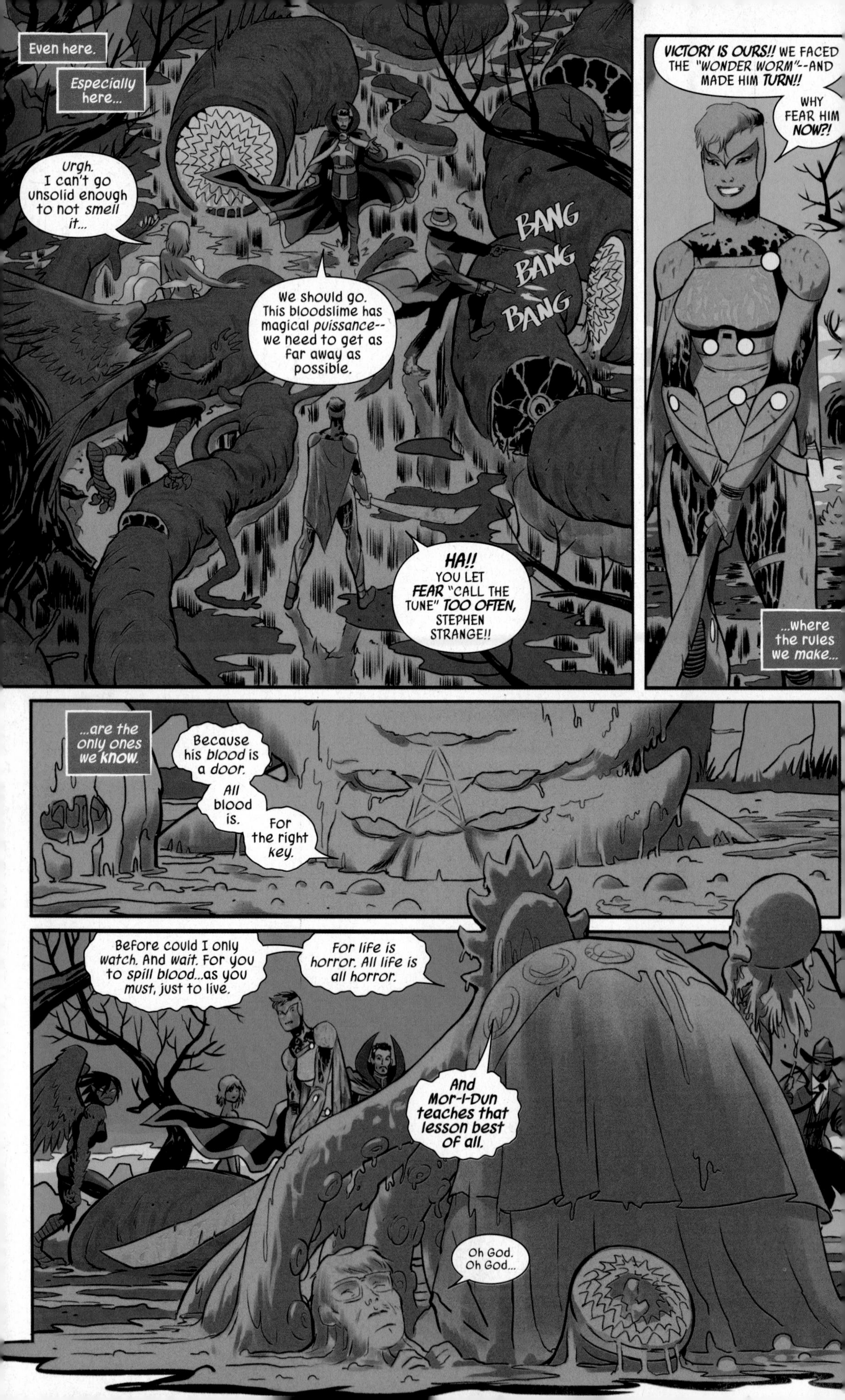
Even here.
Especially here...
Urgh. I can't go unsolid enough to not smell it...
We should go. This bloodslime has magical puissance--we need to get as far away as possible.
BANG
BANG
BANG
HA!! YOU LET FEAR "CALL THE TUNE" TOO OFTEN, STEPHEN STRANGE!!
VICTORY IS OURS!! WE FACED THE "WONDER WORM"--AND MADE HIM TURN!!
WHY FEAR HIM NOW?!
...where the rules we make...
...are the only ones we know.
Because his blood is a door.
All blood is.
For the right key.
Before could I only watch. And wait. For you to spill blood...as you must, just to live.
For life is horror. All life is all horror.
And Mor-I-Dun teaches that lesson best of all.
Oh God. Oh God...

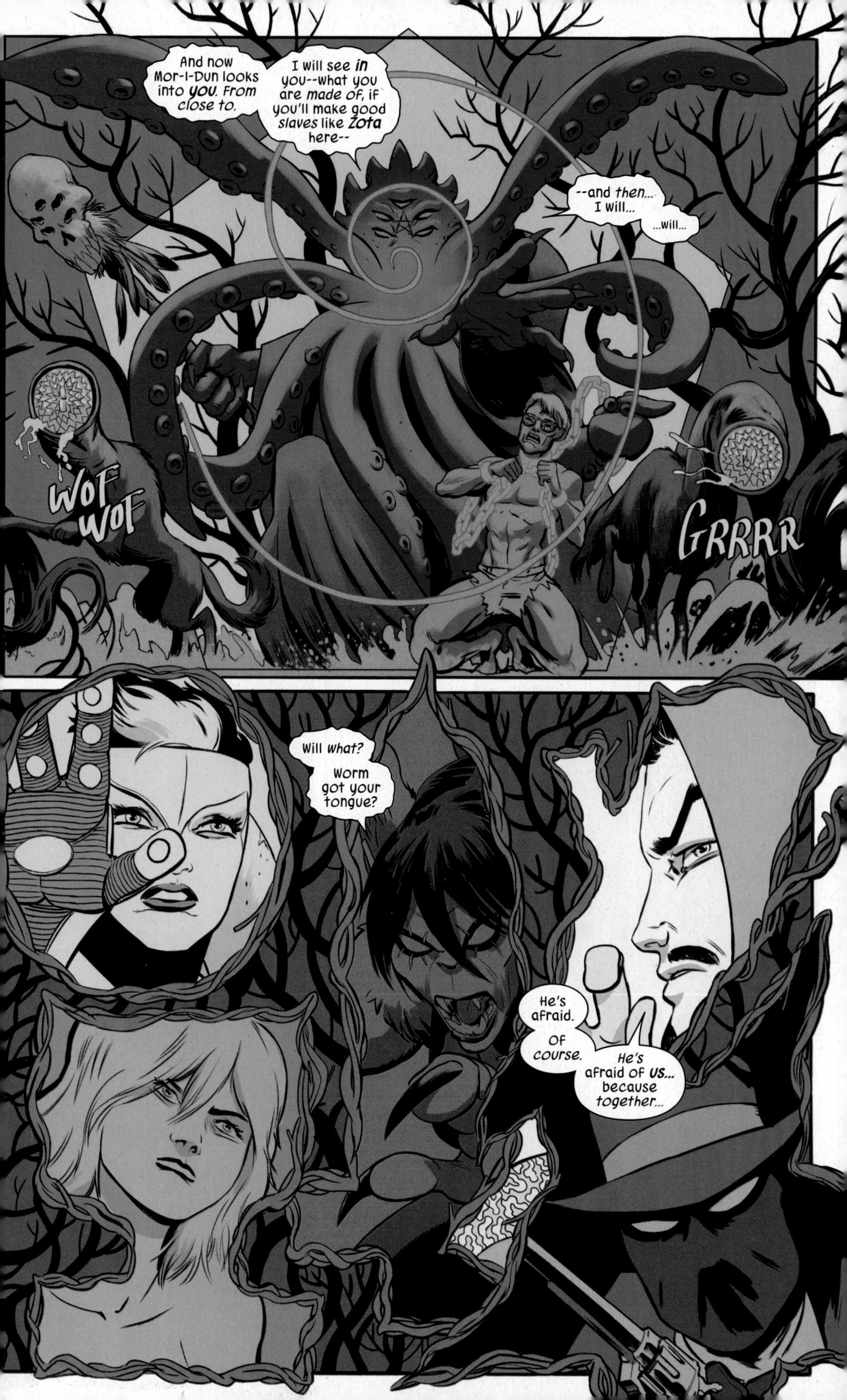
And now Mor-I-Dun looks into YOU. From close to.
I will see in you--what you are made of, if you'll make good slaves like Zota here--
--and then... I will...
...will...
WOF WOF
GRRRR
Will what?
Worm got your tongue?
He's afraid.
Of course.
He's afraid of US... because together...

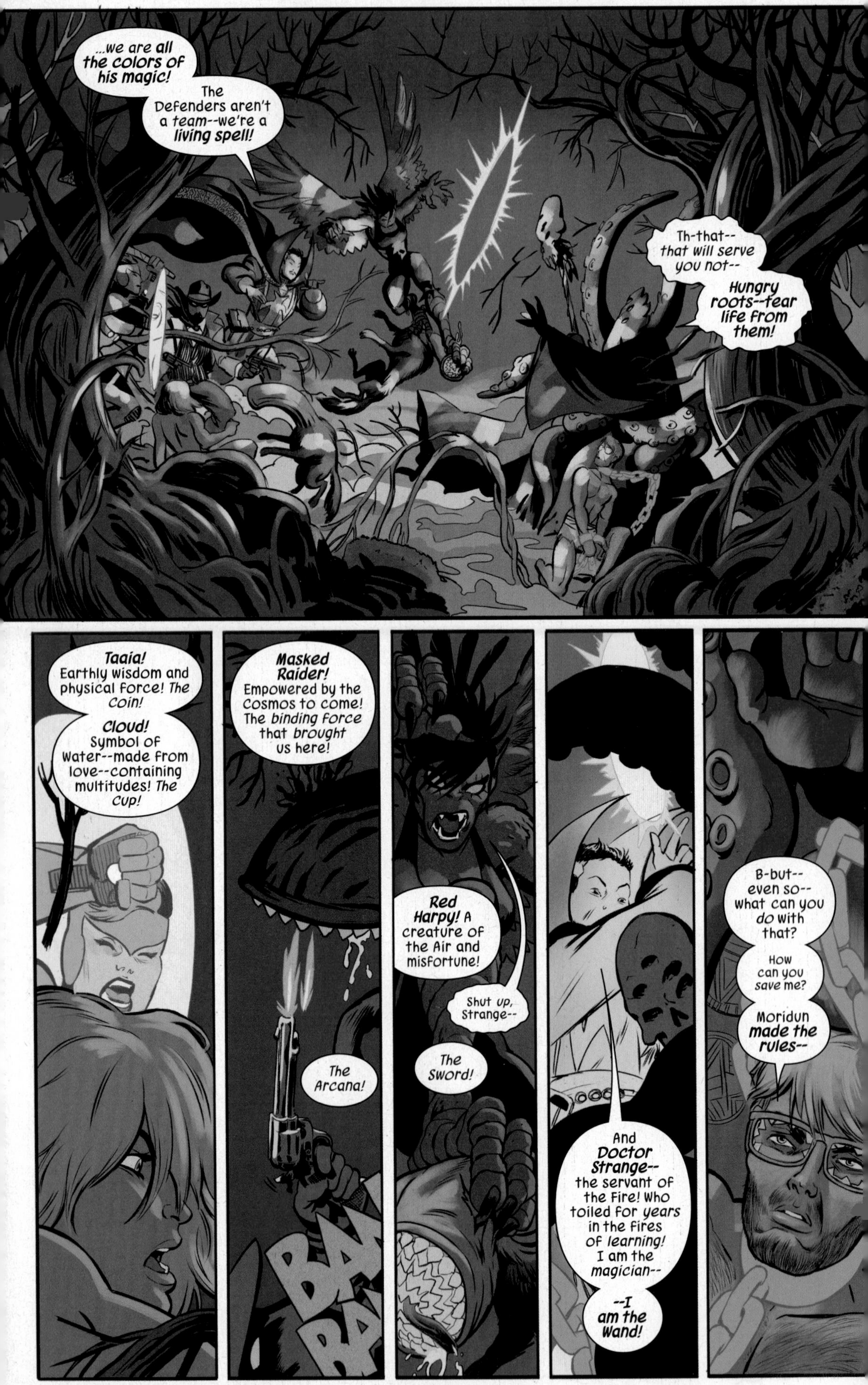
...we are all the colors of his magic!
The Defenders aren't a team--we're a living spell!
Th-that-- that will serve you not--
Hungry roots--tear life from them!
Taaia! Earthly wisdom and physical force! The Coin!
Cloud! Symbol of Water--made from love--containing multitudes! The Cup!
Masked Raider! Empowered by the Cosmos to come! The binding force that brought us here!
The Arcana!
Red Harpy! A creature of the Air and misfortune!
Shut up, Strange--
The Sword!
And Doctor Strange-- the servant of the Fire! Who toiled for years in the fires of learning! I am the magician--
--I am the Wand!
B-but-- even so-- what can you do with that?
How can you save me?
Moridun made the rules--

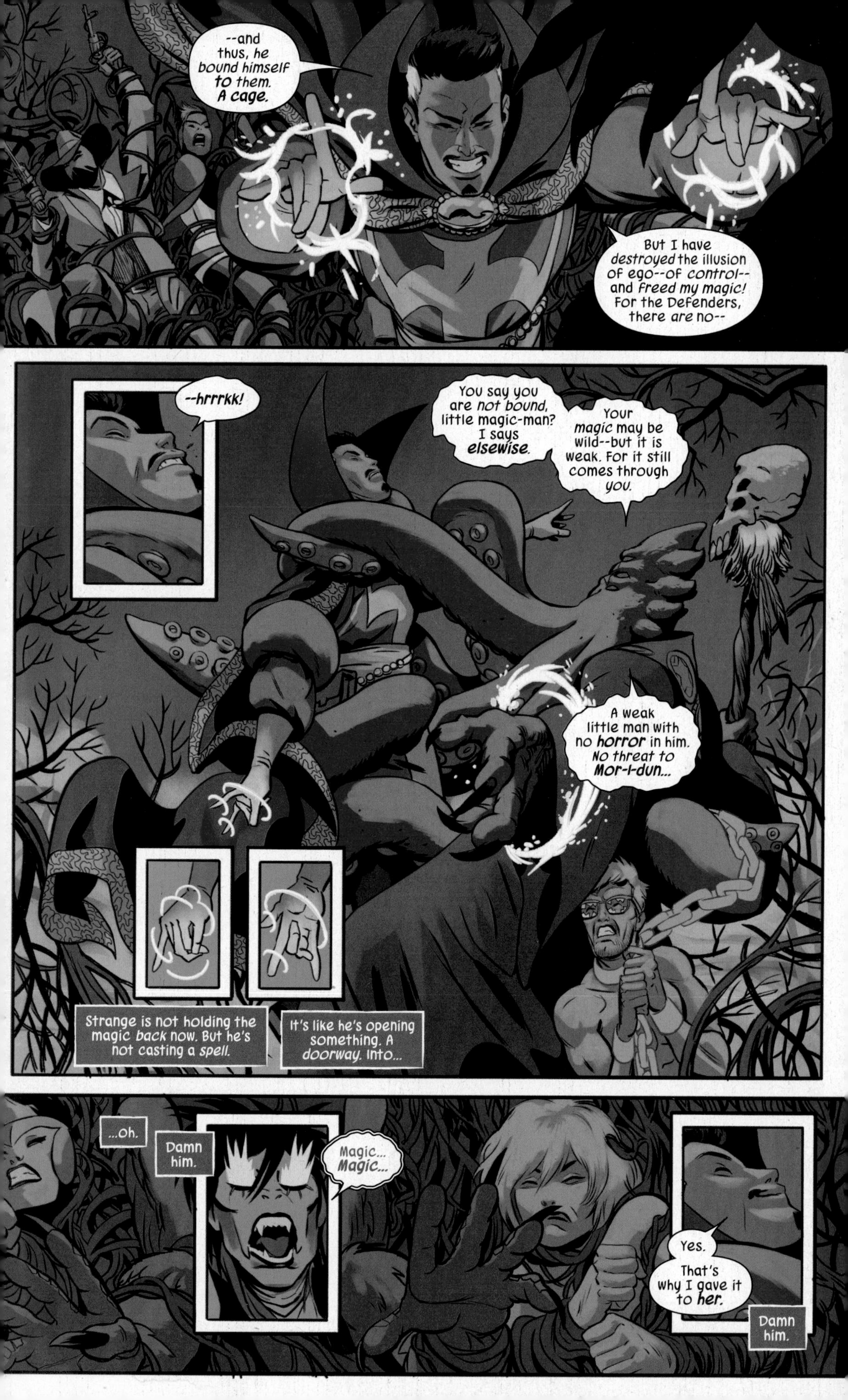
--and thus, he bound himself to them. A cage.
But I have destroyed the illusion of ego--of control--and freed my magic! For the Defenders, there are no--
--hrrrkk!
You say you are not bound, little magic-man? I says elsewise.
Your magic may be wild--but it is weak. For it still comes through you.
A weak little man with no horror in him. No threat to Mor-I-dun...
Strange is not holding the magic back now. But he's not casting a spell.
It's like he's opening something. A doorway. Into...
...oh.
Damn him.
Magic... Magic...
Yes.
That's why I gave it to her.
Damn him.

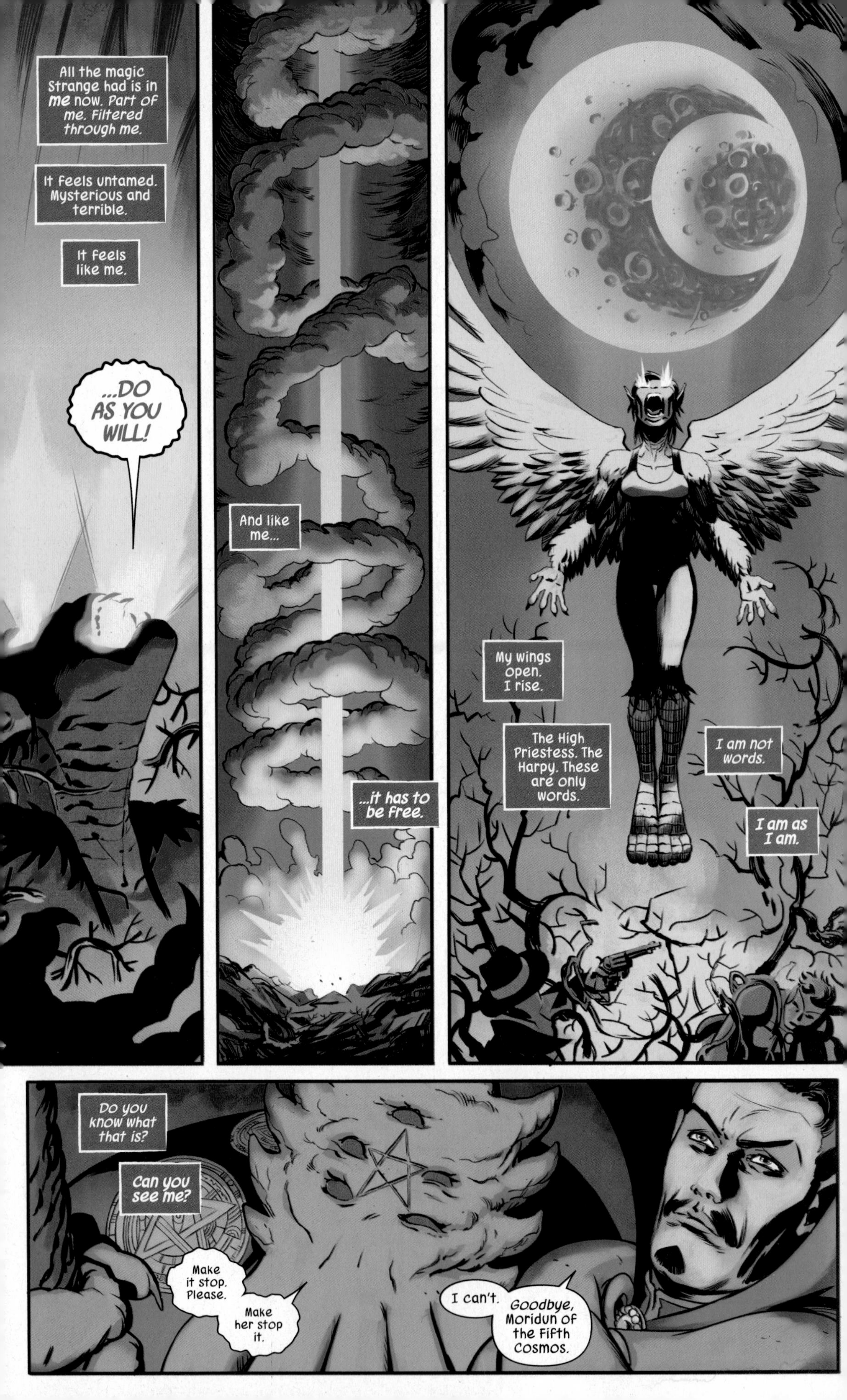
All the magic Strange had is in me now. Part of me. Filtered through me.
It feels untamed. Mysterious and terrible.
It feels like me.
...DO AS YOU WILL!
And like me...
...it has to be free.
My wings open. I rise.
The High Priestess. The Harpy. These are only words.
I am not words.
I am as I am.
Do you know what that is?
Can you see me?
Make it stop. Please.
Make her stop it.
I can't.
Goodbye, Moridun of the Fifth Cosmos.

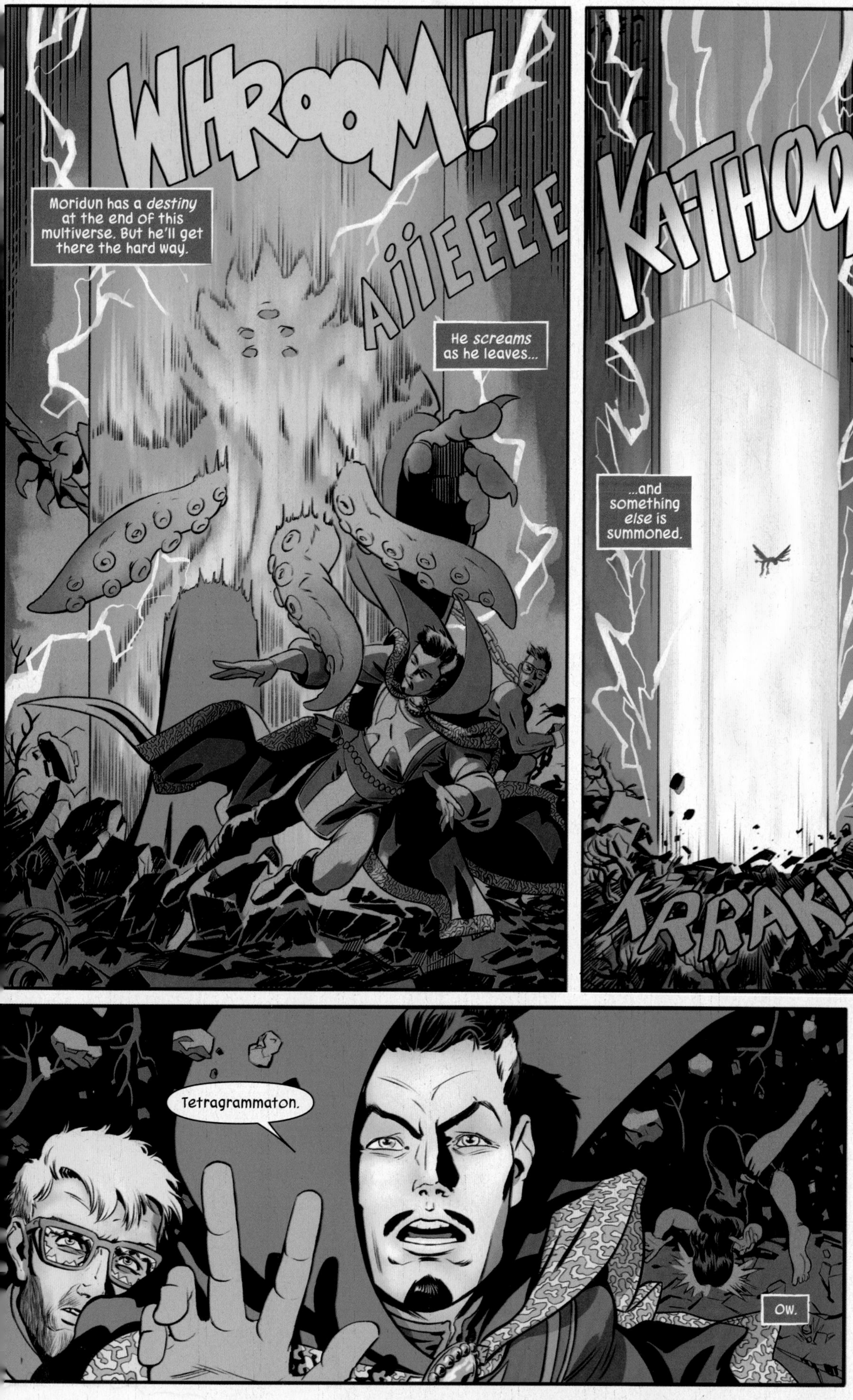
WHROOM!
Moridun has a destiny at the end of this multiverse. But he'll get there the hard way.
AIIIEEEEE
He screams as he leaves...
KA-THOOM
...and something else is summoned.
KRRAK!!
Tetragrammaton.
Ow.

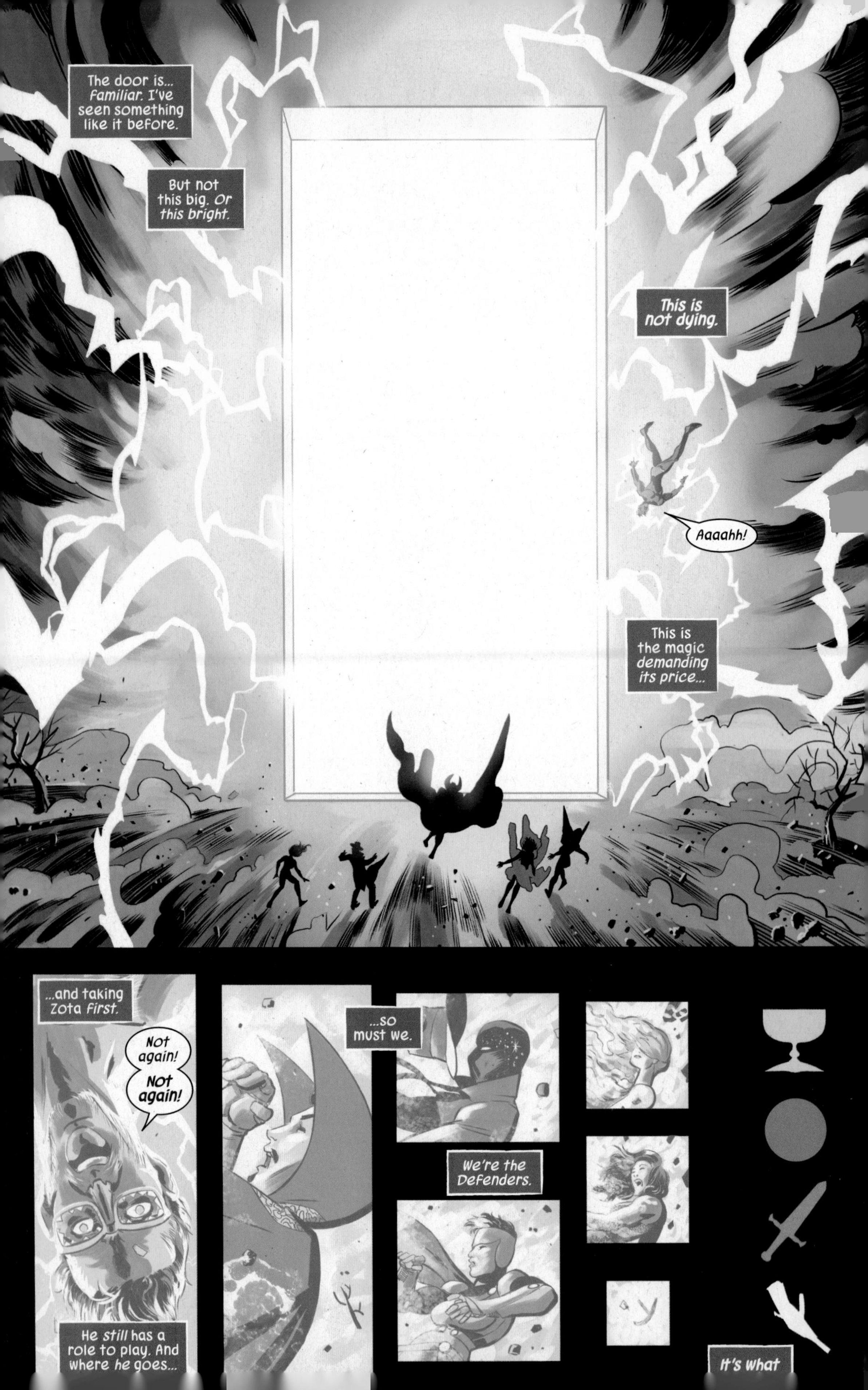
The door is... familiar. I've seen something like it before.
But not this big. Or this bright.
This is not dying.
Aaaahh!
This is the magic demanding its price...
...and taking Zota first.
Not again!
Not again!
He still has a role to play. And where he goes...
...so must we.
We're the Defenders.
It's what

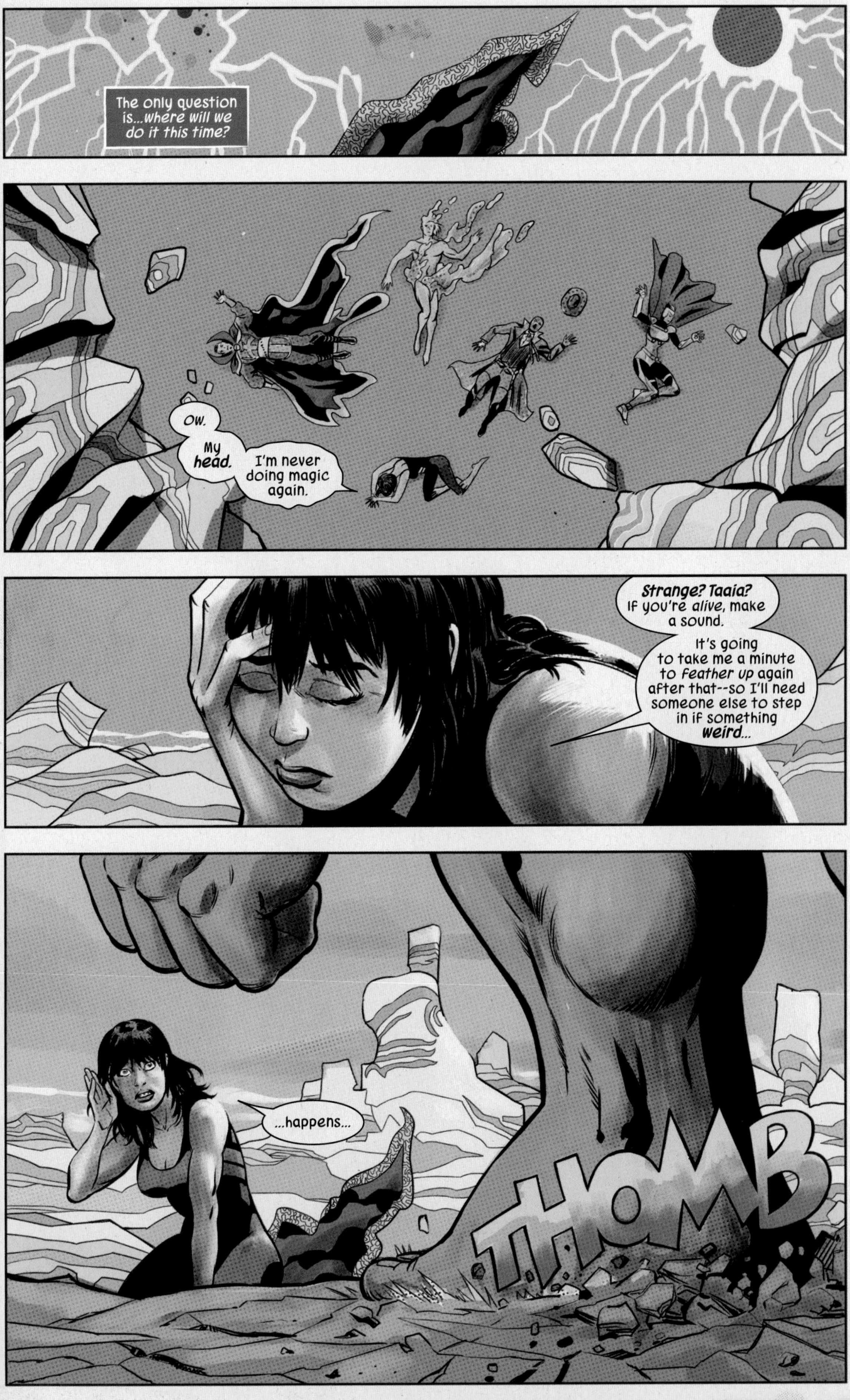
The only question is...where will we do it this time?
Ow.
My head.
I'm never doing magic again.
Strange? Taaia? If you're alive, make a sound.
It's going to take me a minute to feather up again after that--so I'll need someone else to step in if something weird...
...happens...
THOMB

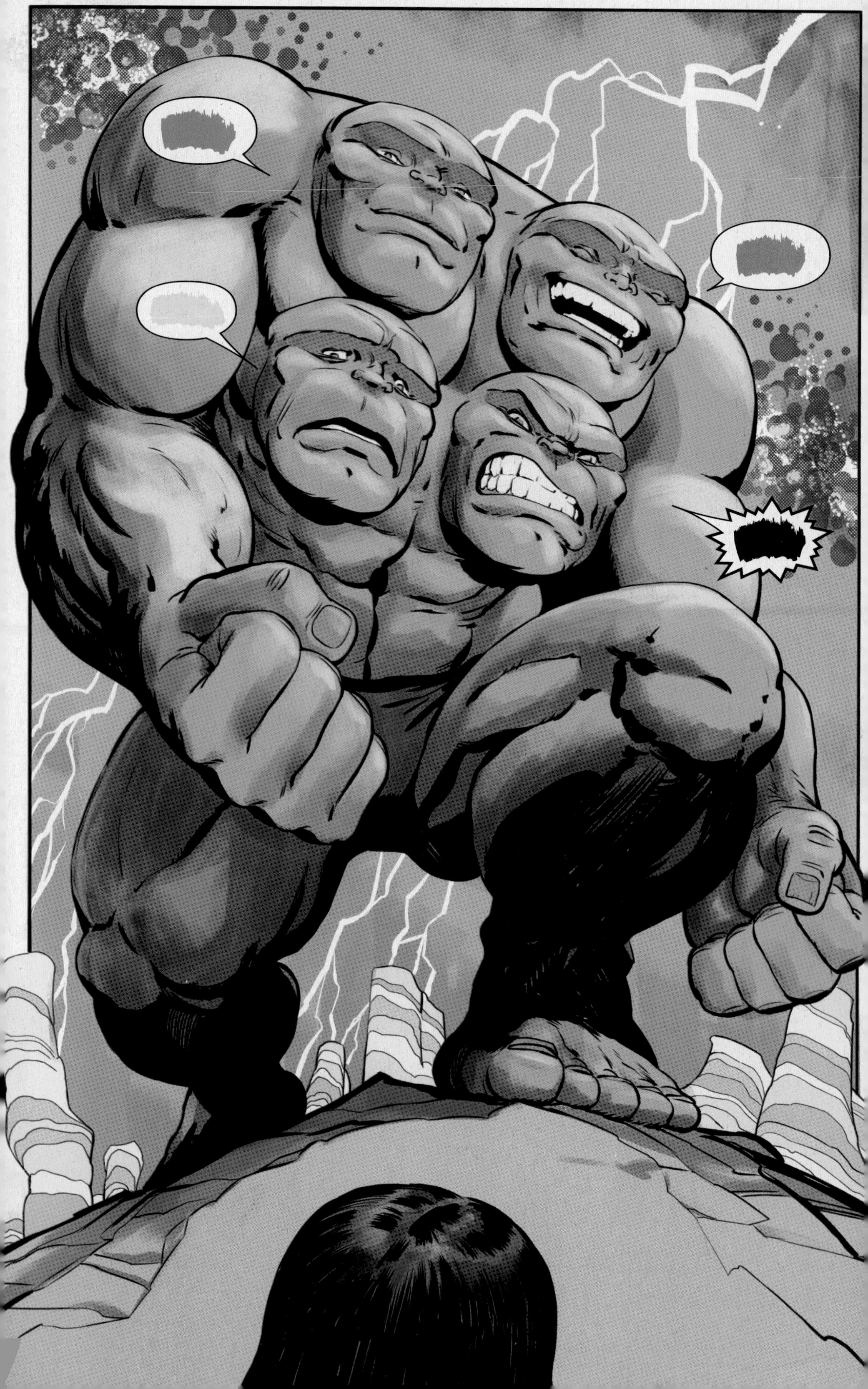

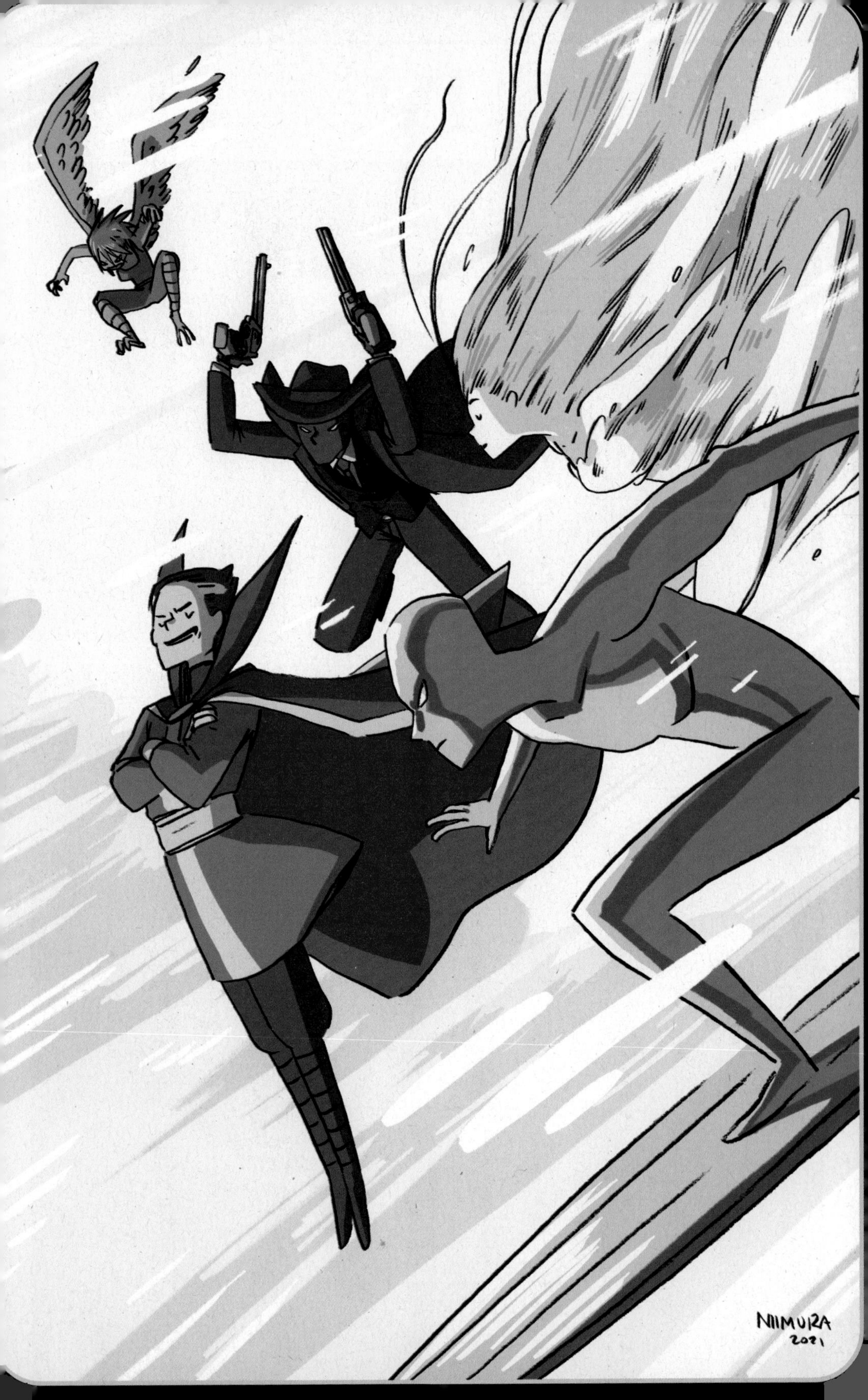
NIIMURA
2021

IV

DE
FEN
DERS

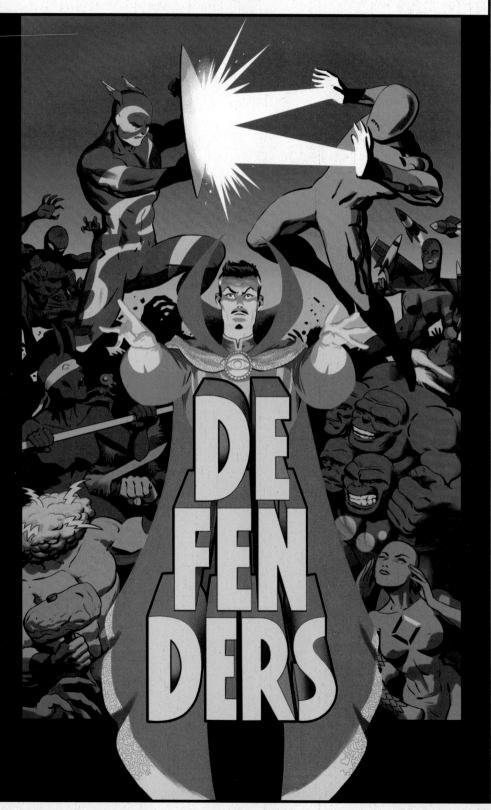

Two lovers were traveling on a lonely road.
They met a being that could not fully be described in words. And that being was me.
In seeking to communicate--to understand the lovers, to understand myself--I adopted their shapes. I had no wish to choose, so I adopted both.
I wanted to save them--save everything. And...I wanted to know love. To know life.
But I learned that to know life is to know pain and heartache. To know a world where the simplest truths of myself are mysteries to those around me.
My name is Cloud. I cannot fully be described in words. But I am.
And more than anything else...
Cloud?
...be right there.
...I am a being of love.

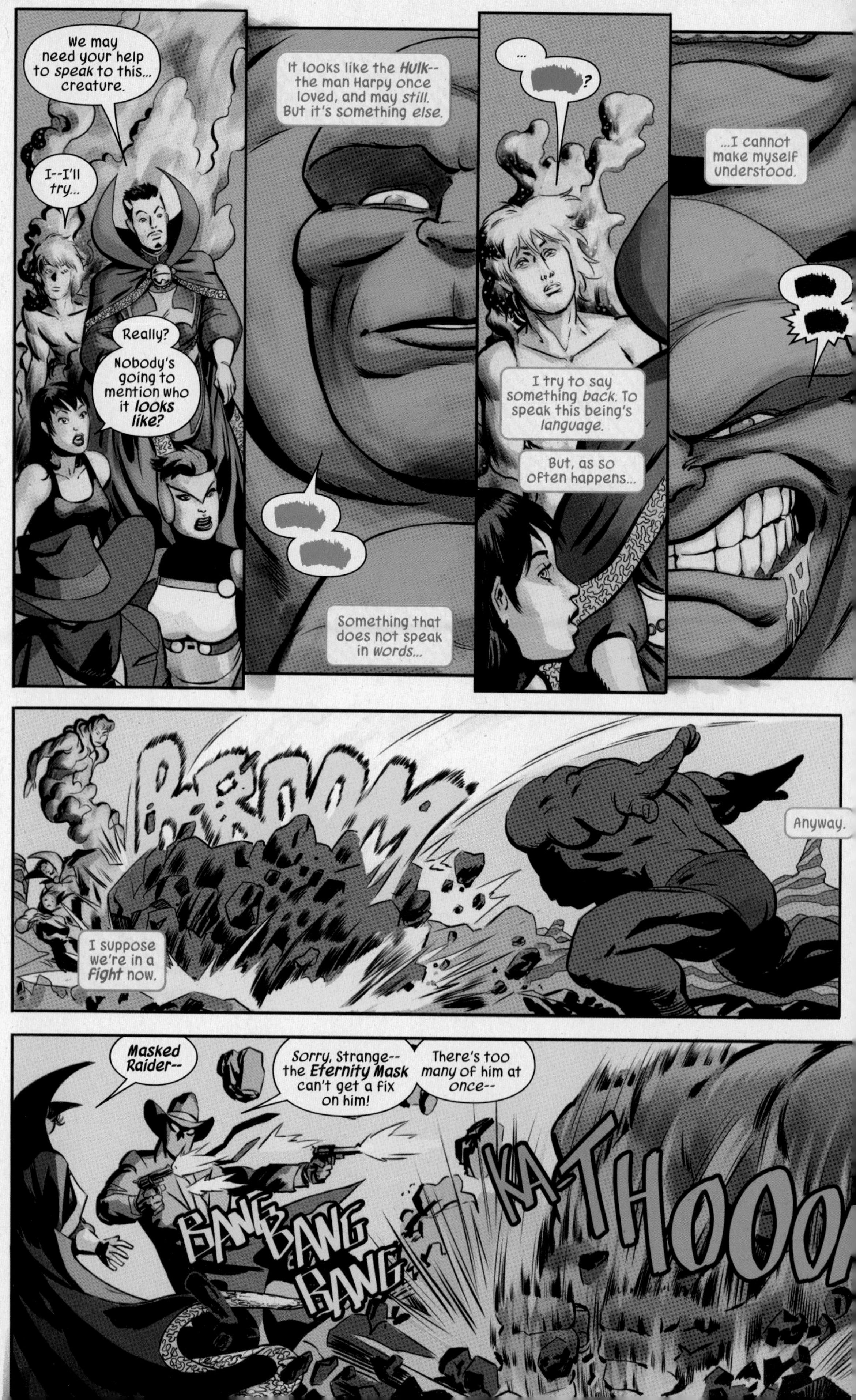
We may need your help to speak to this... creature.
I--I'll try...
Really?
Nobody's going to mention who it looks like?
It looks like the Hulk--the man Harpy once loved, and may still. But it's something else.
Something that does not speak in words...
...
?
I try to say something back. To speak this being's language.
But, as so often happens...
...I cannot make myself understood.
BROOM
Anyway.
I suppose we're in a fight now.
Masked Raider--
Sorry, Strange--the Eternity Mask can't get a fix on him!
There's too many of him at once--
BANG BANG BANG
KATHOOO

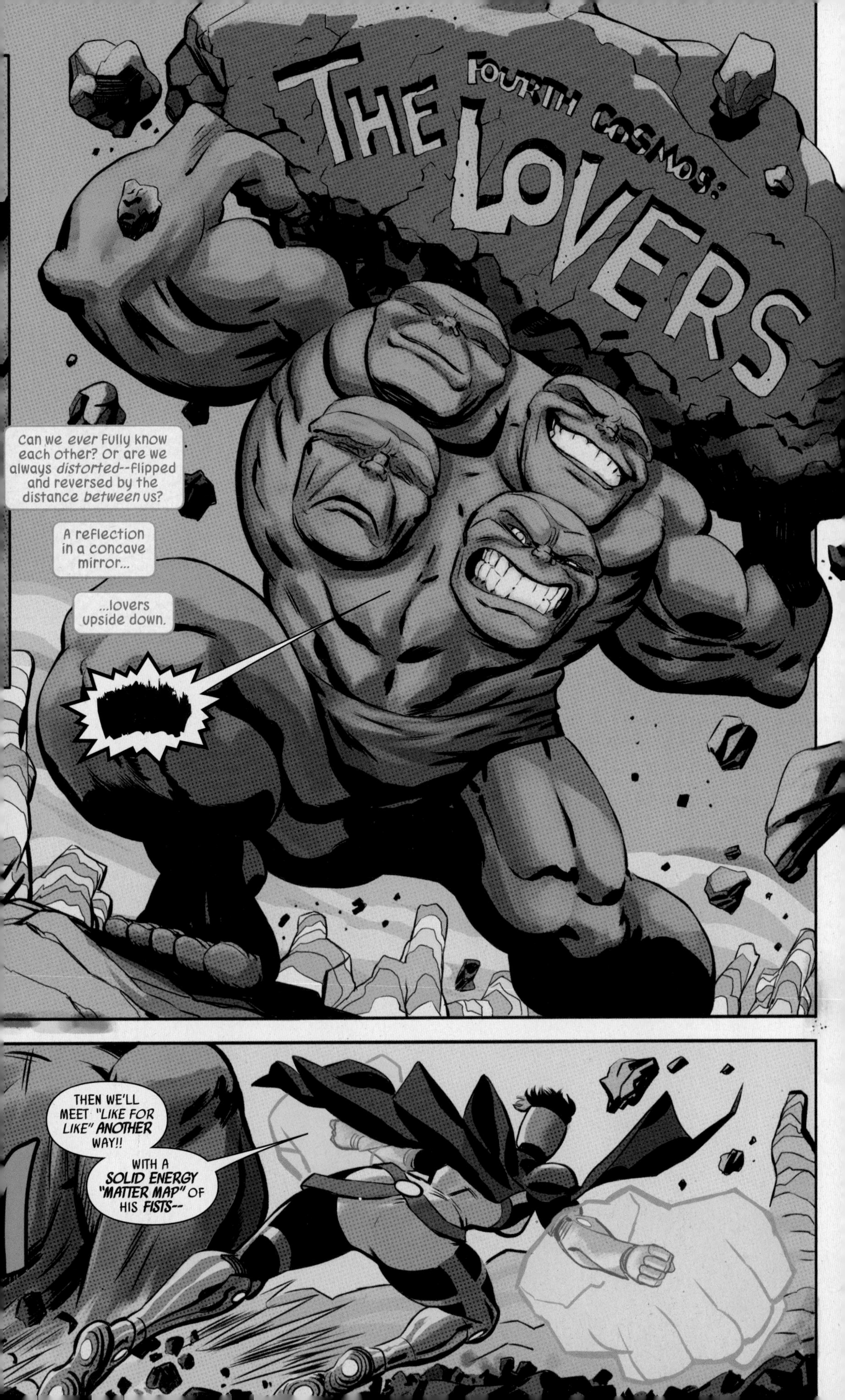
FOURTH COSMOS:
THE LOVERS
Can we ever fully know each other? Or are we always distorted--flipped and reversed by the distance between us?
A reflection in a concave mirror...
...lovers upside down.
THEN WE'LL MEET "LIKE FOR LIKE" ANOTHER WAY!!
WITH A SOLID ENERGY "MATTER MAP" OF HIS FISTS--

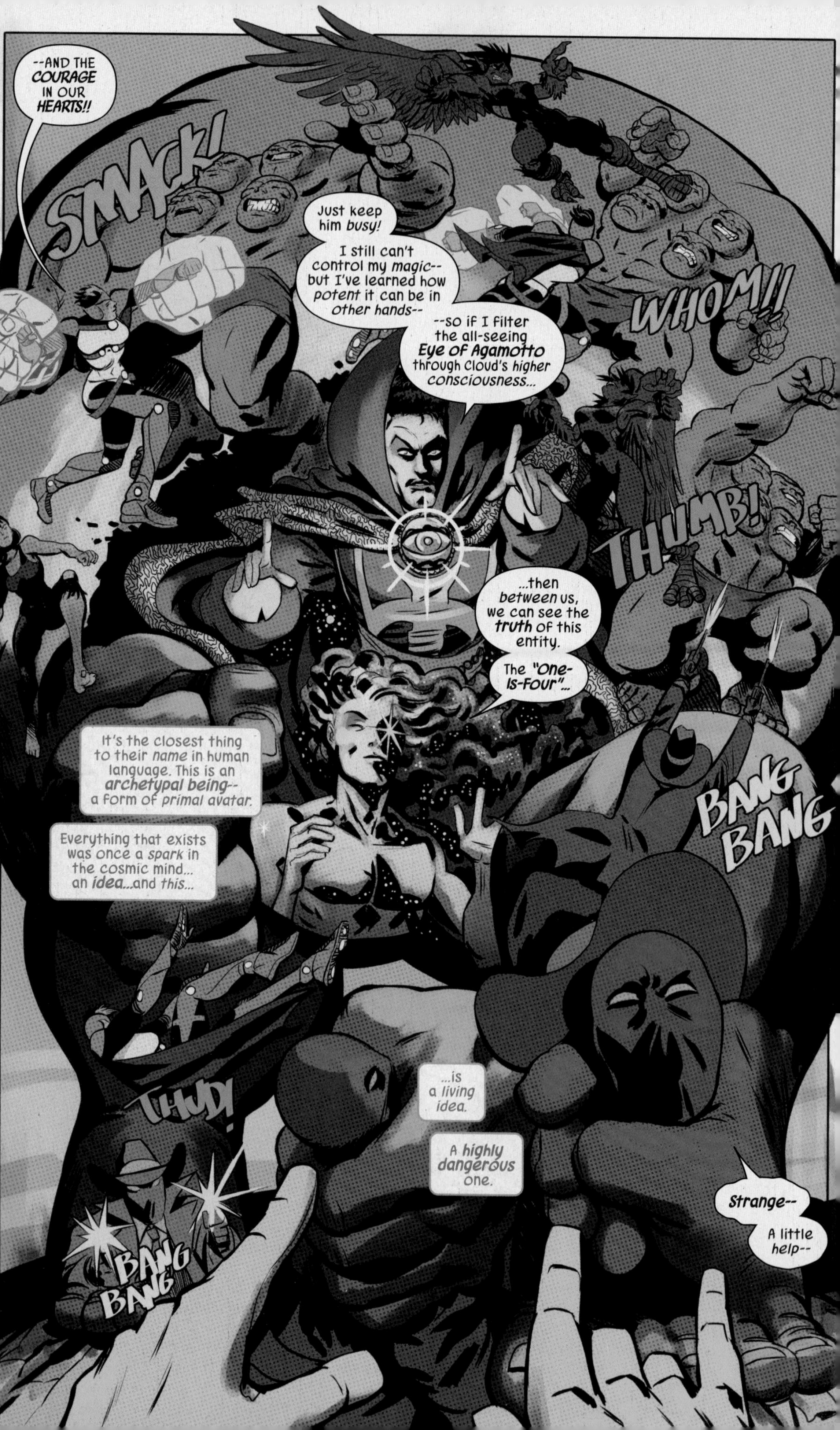
--AND THE COURAGE IN OUR HEARTS!!
SMACK!
Just keep him busy!
I still can't control my magic--but I've learned how potent it can be in other hands--
--so if I filter the all-seeing Eye of Agamotto through Cloud's higher consciousness...
WHOM!!
THUMB!
...then between us, we can see the truth of this entity.
The "One-Is-Four"...
It's the closest thing to their name in human language. This is an archetypal being--a form of primal avatar.
Everything that exists was once a spark in the cosmic mind... an idea...and this...
BANG BANG
...is a living idea.
A highly dangerous one.
THUD!
Strange--
A little help--
BANG BANG

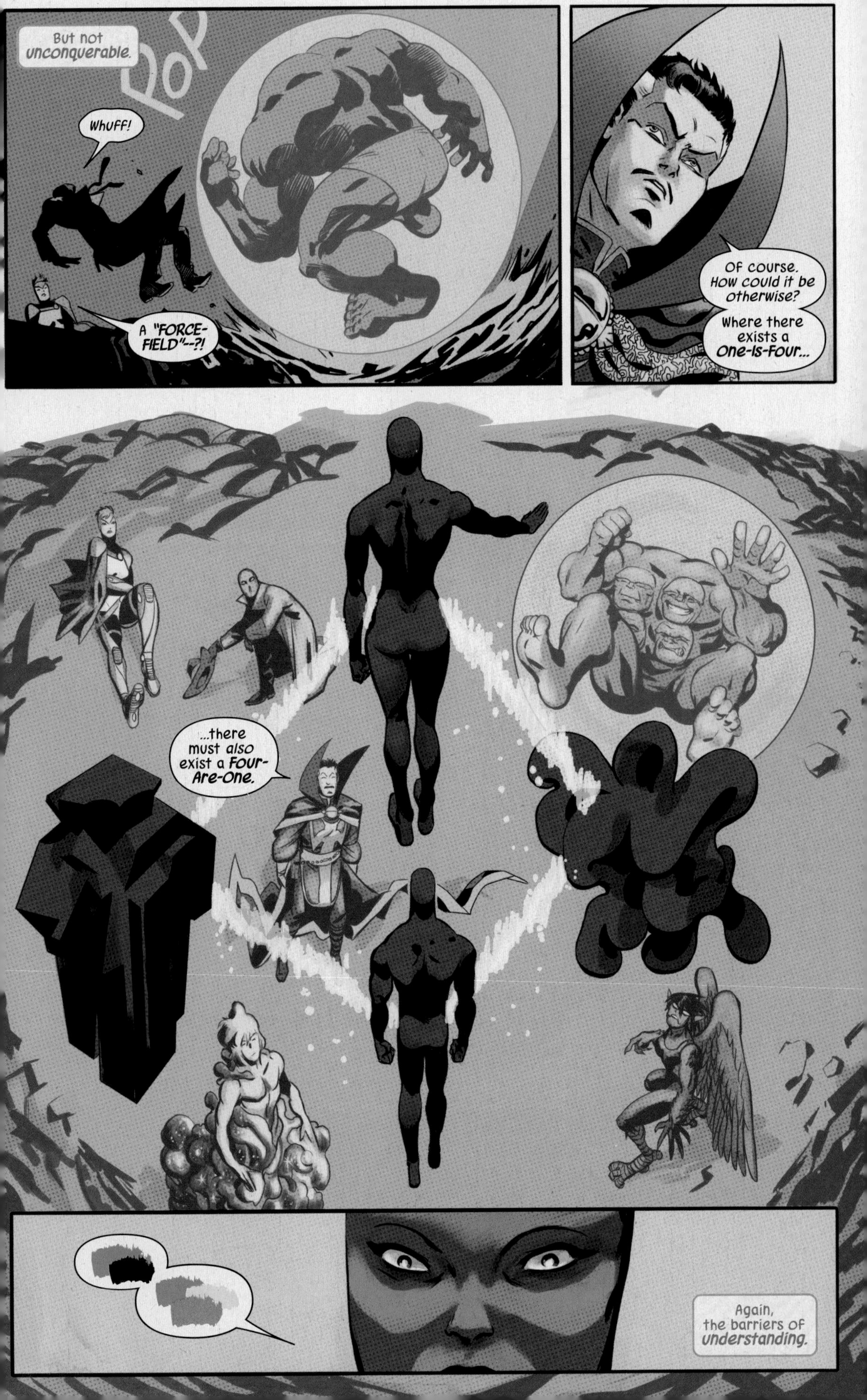
But not unconquerable.
POP
Whuff!
A "FORCE-FIELD"--?!
Of course. How could it be otherwise?
Where there exists a One-Is-Four...
...there must also exist a Four-Are-One.
Again, the barriers of understanding.

Strange does his *best.*

We are the **Defenders**--here on a peaceful mission to--

We--we come in peace. *Peace.*

Peace.

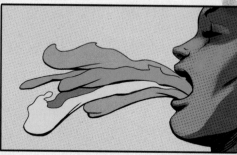

Uh-oh. Out of the *frying pan...*

--AND INTO THE *"FIRES OF KNOWLEDGE"!!!!*

THESE *"PARTY STREAMERS"* AREN'T *ATTACKING*---THEY'RE *"FEELING US OUT"!!* TRYING TO *"PICK UP"* WHAT WE'VE BEEN *"LAYING DOWN"*--

--TO **BRIDGE** THE *"LANGUAGE GAP"!!*

Ah-- then perhaps I should do the talking for now, *Taaia*--

As if you're any better. By Hoggoth.

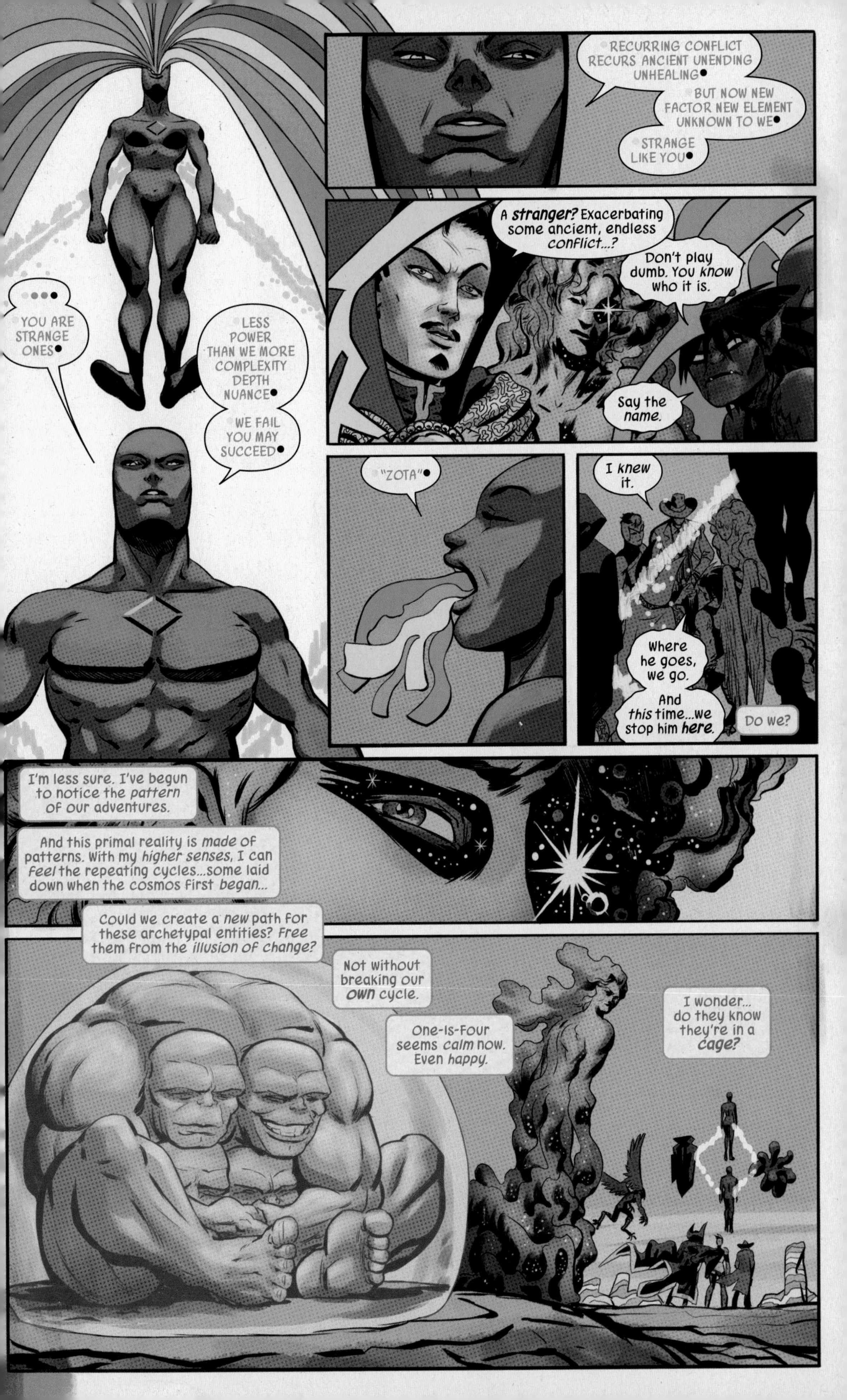

YOU ARE STRANGE ONES
LESS POWER THAN WE MORE COMPLEXITY DEPTH NUANCE
WE FAIL YOU MAY SUCCEED
RECURRING CONFLICT RECURS ANCIENT UNENDING UNHEALING
BUT NOW NEW FACTOR NEW ELEMENT UNKNOWN TO WE
STRANGE LIKE YOU
A *stranger?* Exacerbating some ancient, endless *conflict...?*
Don't play dumb. You *know* who it is.
Say the *name.*
"ZOTA"
I *knew* it.
Where he goes, we go.
And *this* time...we stop him *here.*
Do we?
I'm less sure. I've begun to notice the *pattern* of our adventures.
And this primal reality is *made* of patterns. With my *higher senses,* I can *feel* the repeating cycles...some laid down when the cosmos first *began...*
Could we create a *new* path for these archetypal entities? *Free* them from the *illusion of change?*
Not without breaking our *own* cycle.
One-Is-Four seems *calm* now. Even *happy.*
I wonder... do they know they're in a *cage?*

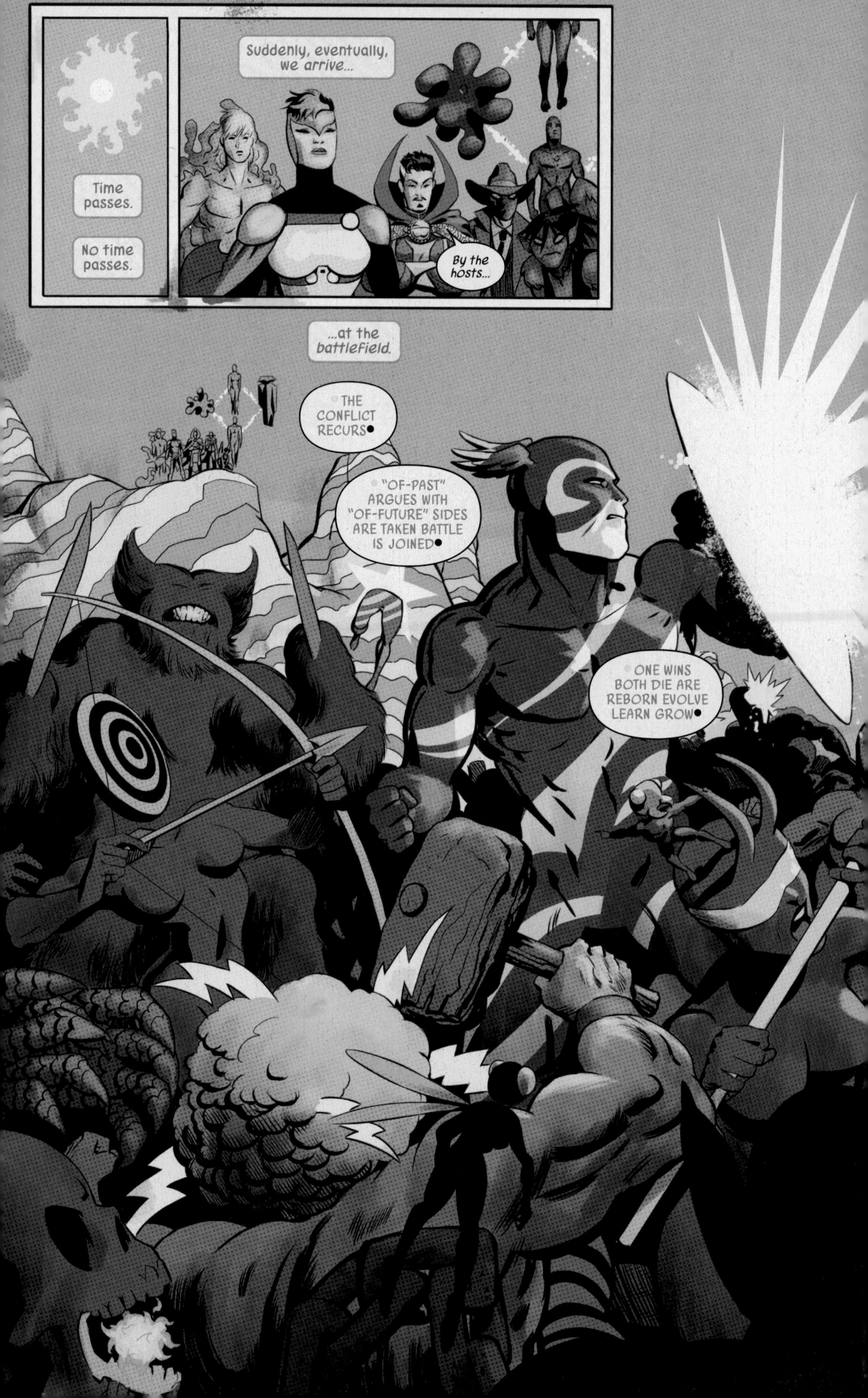

Time passes.
No time passes.
Suddenly, eventually, we arrive...
By the hosts...
...at the battlefield.
THE CONFLICT RECURS
"OF-PAST" ARGUES WITH "OF-FUTURE" SIDES ARE TAKEN BATTLE IS JOINED
ONE WINS BOTH DIE ARE REBORN EVOLVE LEARN GROW

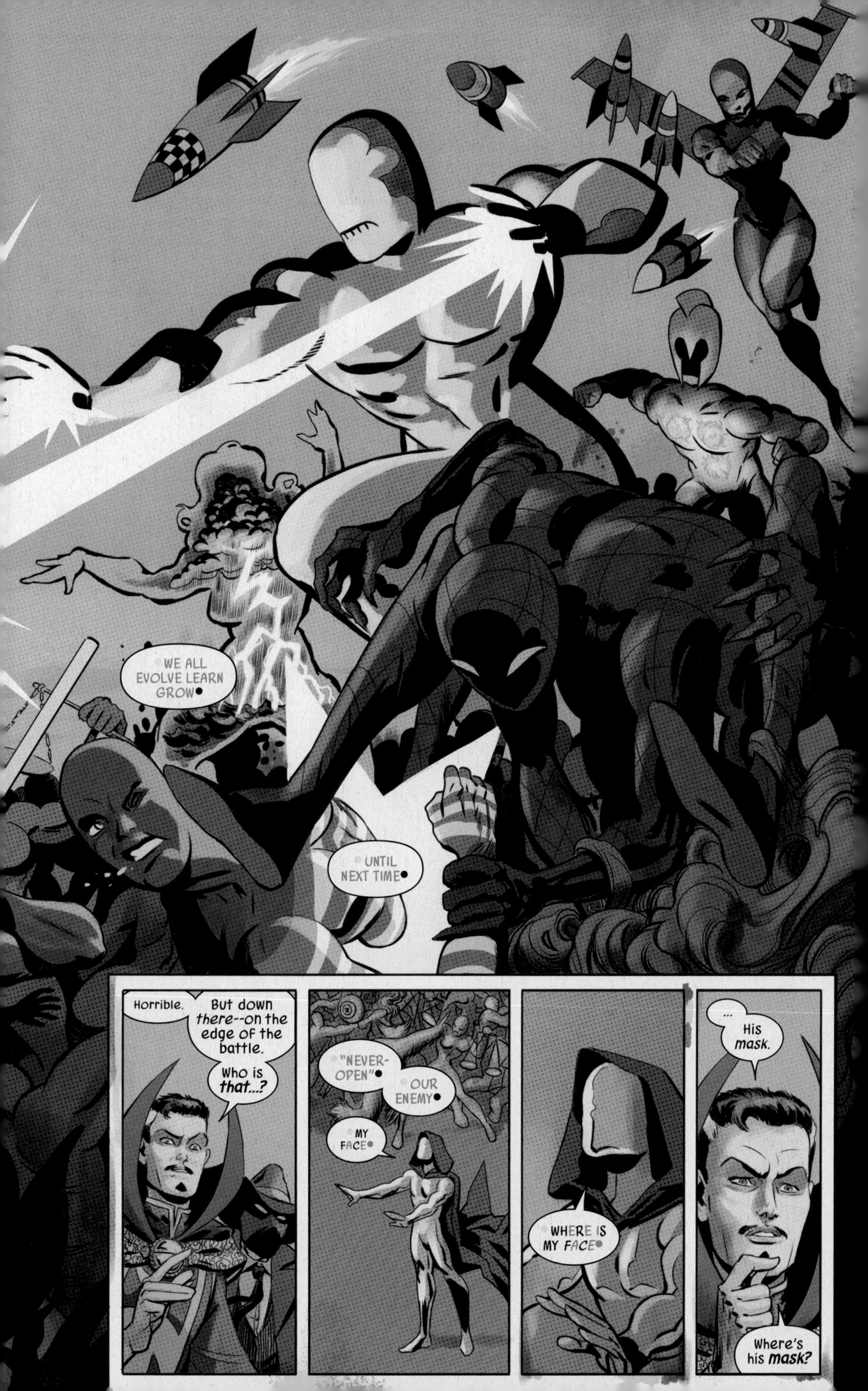

WE ALL EVOLVE LEARN GROW
UNTIL NEXT TIME
Horrible.
But down *there*--on the edge of the battle.
Who is ***that...?***
"NEVER-OPEN"
OUR ENEMY
MY FACE
WHERE IS MY *FACE*
...
His *mask.*
Where's his ***mask?***

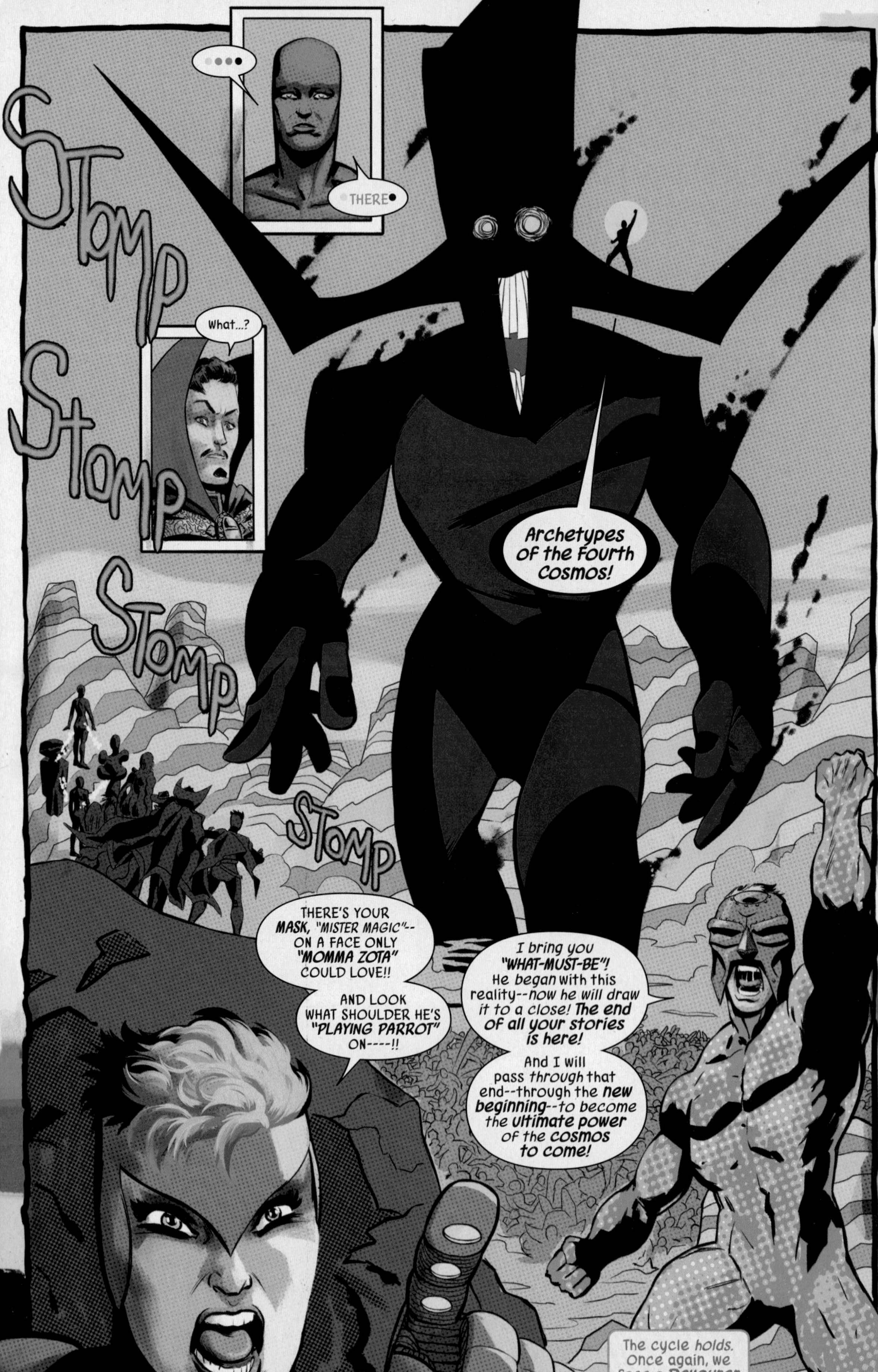
...
THERE
What...?
STOMP
STOMP
STOMP
STOMP
Archetypes of the Fourth Cosmos!
THERE'S YOUR MASK, "MISTER MAGIC"-- ON A FACE ONLY "MOMMA ZOTA" COULD LOVE!!
AND LOOK WHAT SHOULDER HE'S "PLAYING PARROT" ON----!!
I bring you "WHAT-MUST-BE"! He began with this reality--now he will draw it to a close! The end of all your stories is here!
And I will pass through that end--through the new beginning--to become the ultimate power of the cosmos to come!
The cycle holds. Once again, we face a Devourer of Worlds...

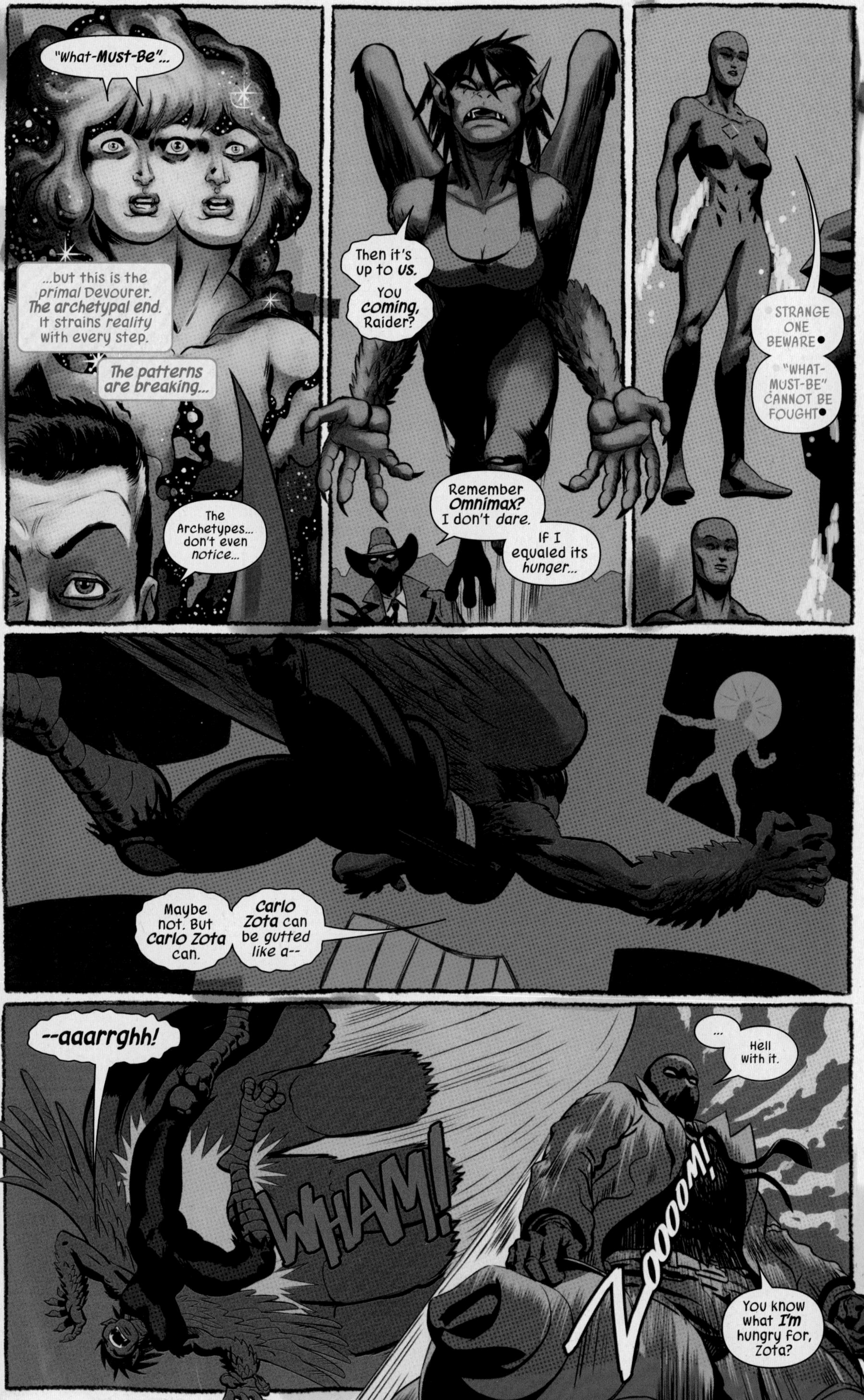
"What-Must-Be"...
...but this is the primal Devourer. The archetypal end. It strains reality with every step.
The patterns are breaking...
The Archetypes... don't even notice...
Then it's up to us.
You coming, Raider?
Remember Omnimax? I don't dare.
If I equaled its hunger...
STRANGE ONE BEWARE
"WHAT-MUST-BE" CANNOT BE FOUGHT
Maybe not. But Carlo Zota can.
Carlo Zota can be gutted like a--
--aaarrghh!
WHAM!
...
Hell with it.
Zoooom!
You know what I'm hungry for, Zota?

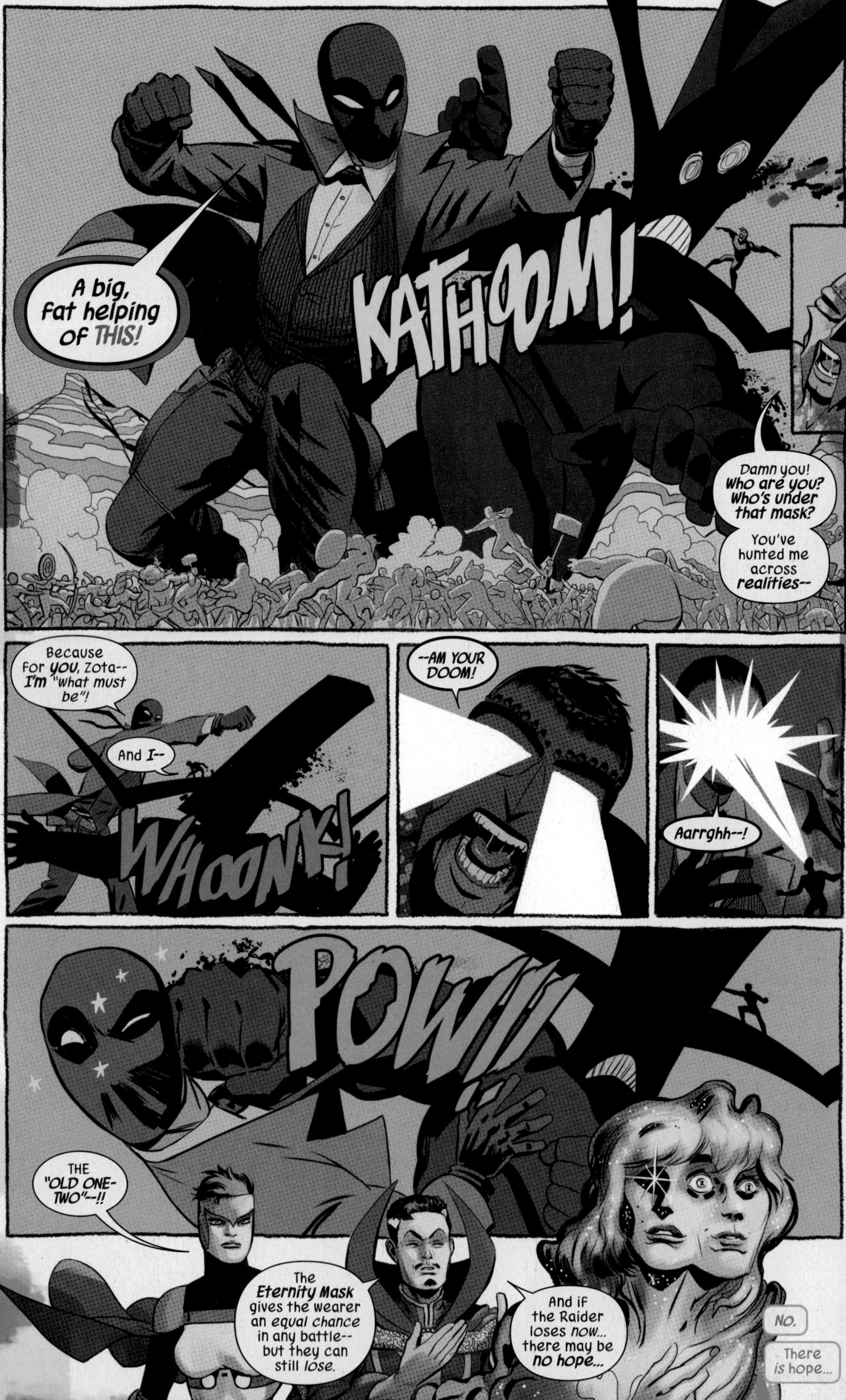
A big, fat helping of THIS!
KATHOOM!
Damn you! Who are you? Who's under that mask?
You've hunted me across realities--
Because for YOU, Zota-- I'm "what must be"!
And I--
WHOONK!
--AM YOUR DOOM!
Aarrghh--!
POW!!
THE "OLD ONE-TWO"--!!
The Eternity Mask gives the wearer an equal chance in any battle-- but they can still lose.
And if the Raider loses now... there may be no hope...
NO.
There is hope...

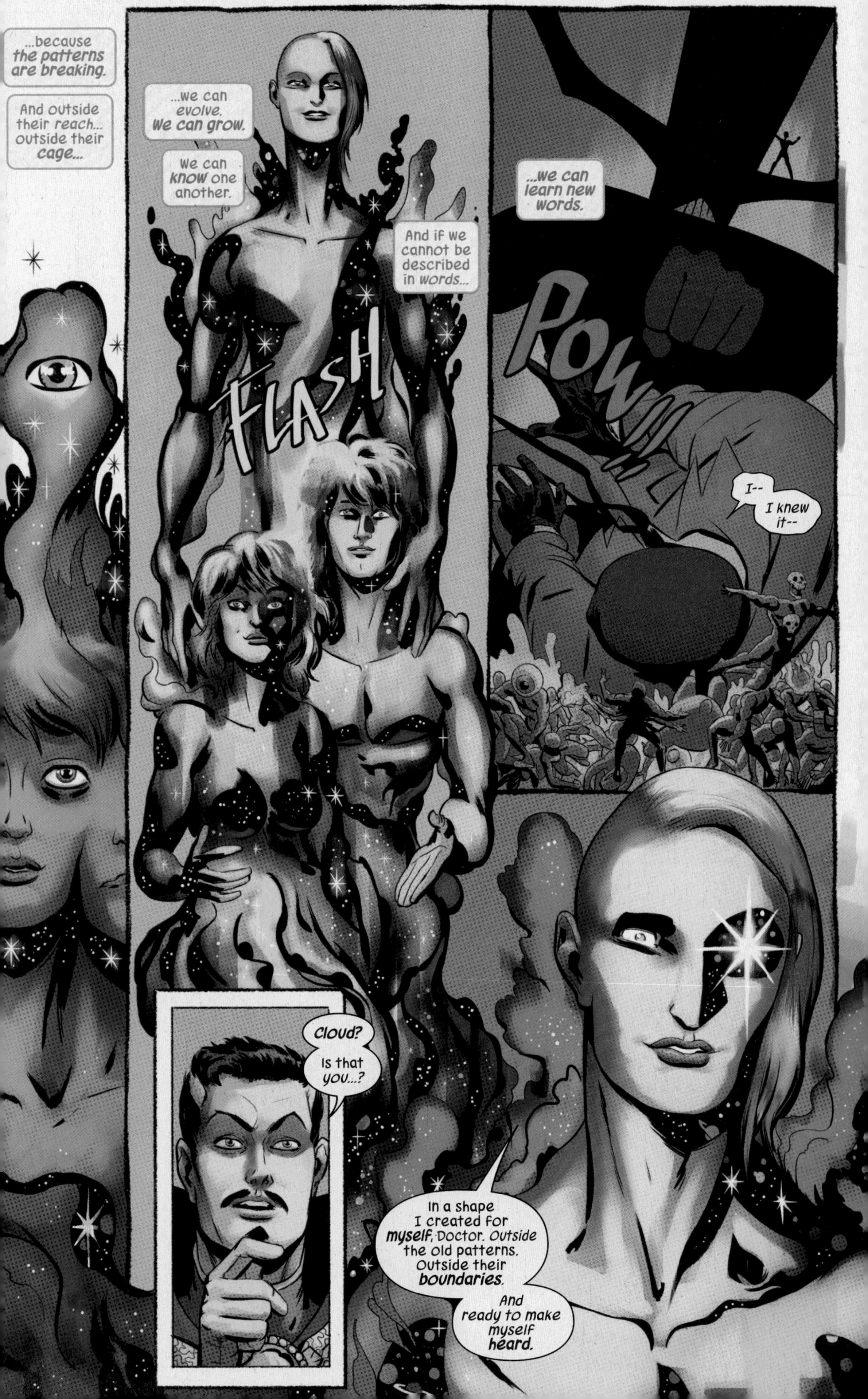

...because the patterns are breaking.
And outside their reach... outside their cage...
...we can evolve. We can grow.
We can know one another.
And if we cannot be described in words...
FLASH
...we can learn new words.
POW
I-- I knew it--
Cloud?
Is that you...?
In a shape I created for myself, Doctor. Outside the old patterns. Outside their boundaries.
And ready to make myself heard.

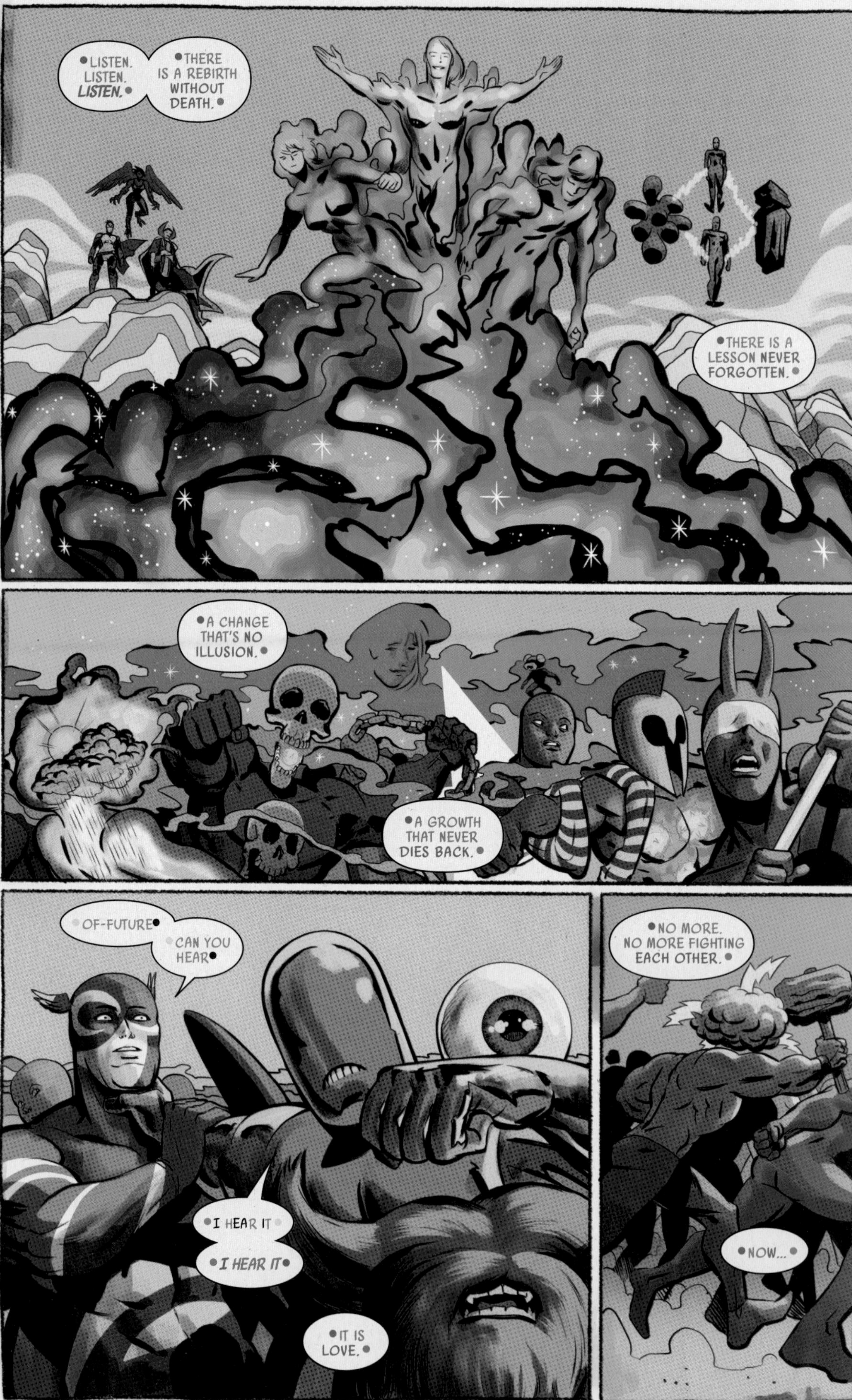
LISTEN. LISTEN. LISTEN.
THERE IS A REBIRTH WITHOUT DEATH.
THERE IS A LESSON NEVER FORGOTTEN.
A CHANGE THAT'S NO ILLUSION.
A GROWTH THAT NEVER DIES BACK.
OF-FUTURE
CAN YOU HEAR
I HEAR IT
I HEAR IT
IT IS LOVE.
NO MORE. NO MORE FIGHTING EACH OTHER.
NOW...

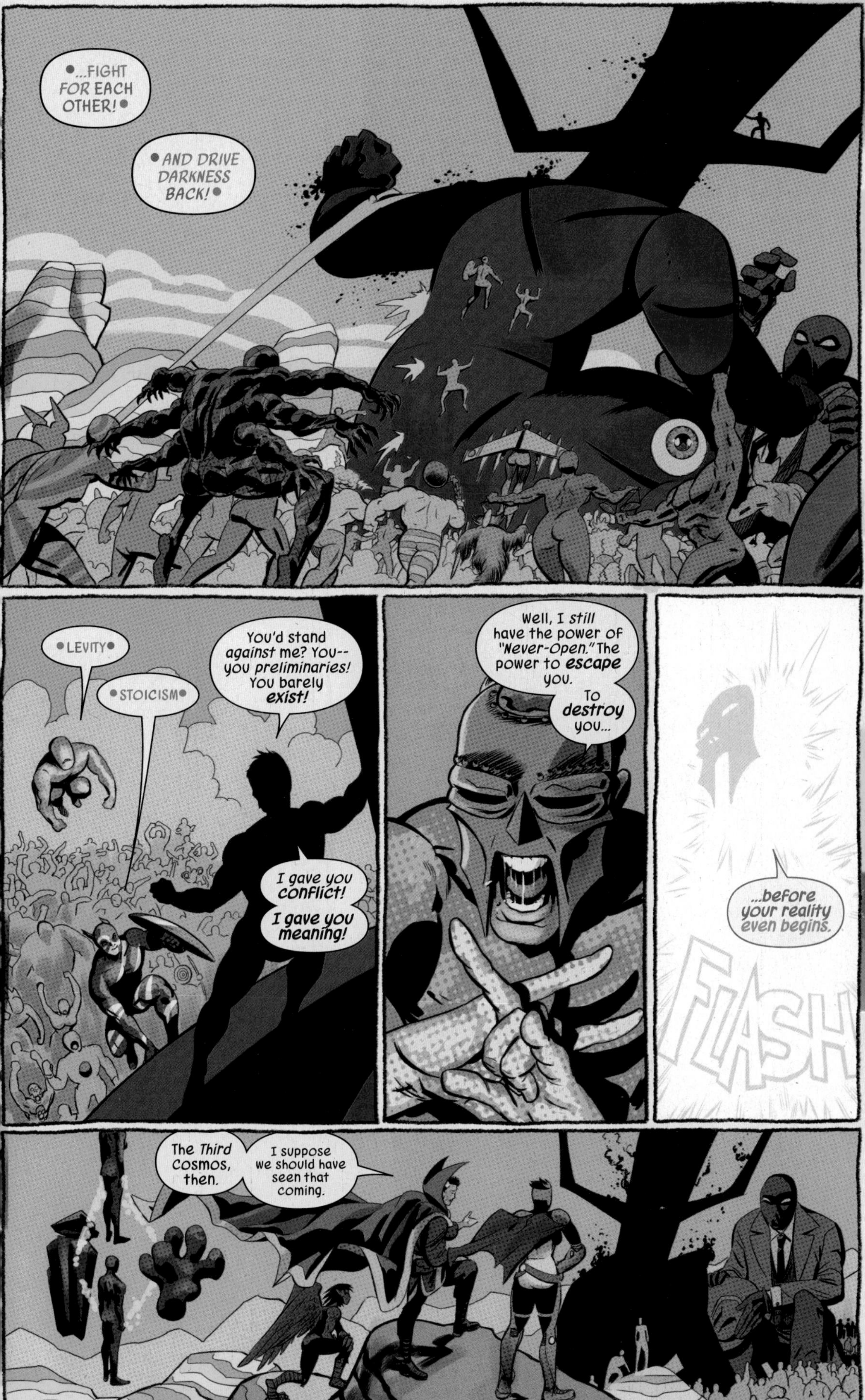
...FIGHT FOR EACH OTHER!
AND DRIVE DARKNESS BACK!
LEVITY
STOICISM
You'd stand against me? You-- you preliminaries! You barely exist!
I gave you conflict!
I gave you meaning!
Well, I still have the power of "Never-Open." The power to escape you.
To destroy you...
...before your reality even begins.
FLASH
The Third Cosmos, then.
I suppose we should have seen that coming.

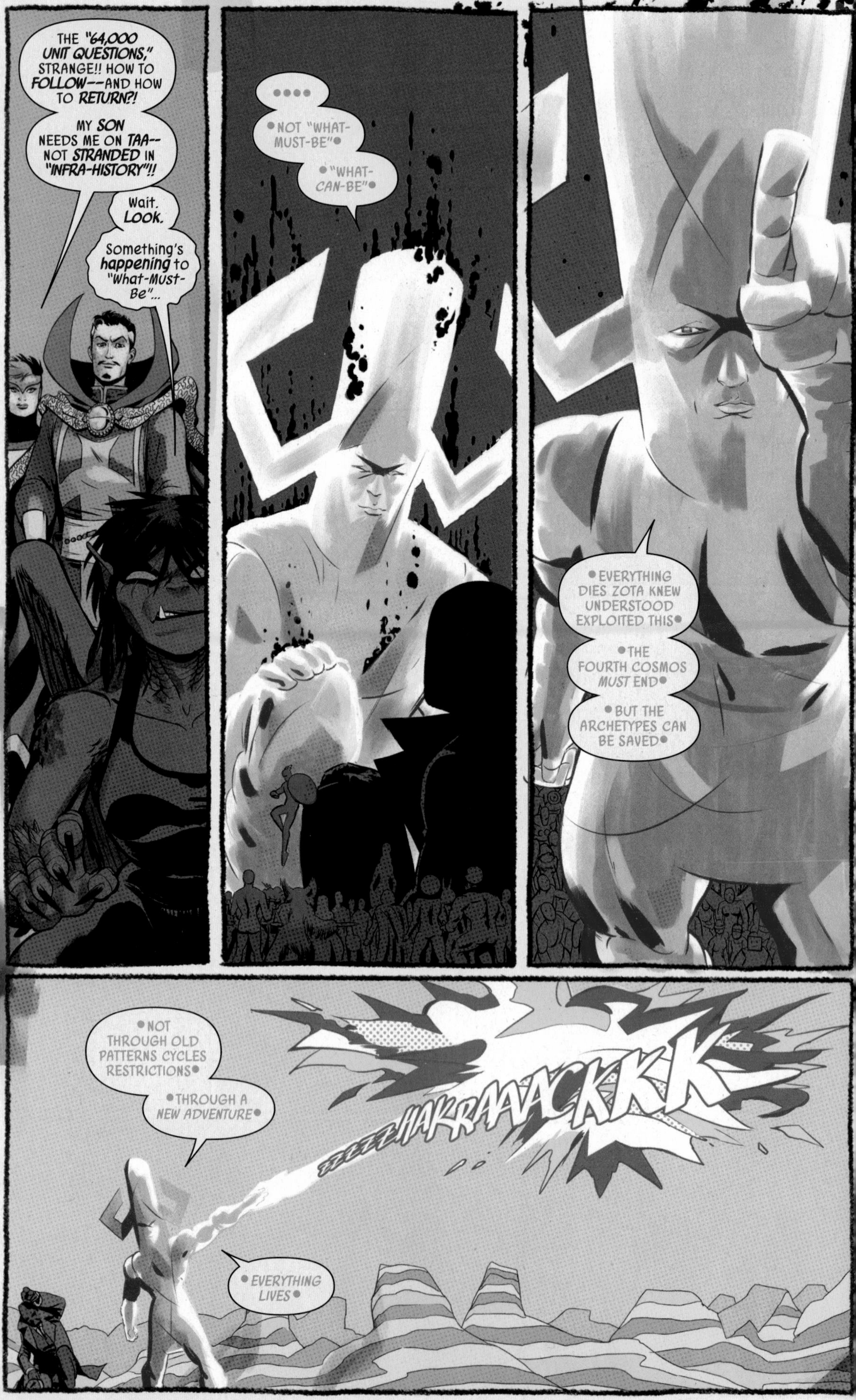

THE "64,000 UNIT QUESTIONS," STRANGE!! HOW TO FOLLOW--AND HOW TO RETURN?!
MY SON NEEDS ME ON TAA-- NOT STRANDED IN "INFRA-HISTORY"!!
Wait. LOOK.
Something's happening to "What-Must-Be"...
• • • •
• NOT "WHAT-MUST-BE" •
• "WHAT-CAN-BE" •
• EVERYTHING DIES ZOTA KNEW UNDERSTOOD EXPLOITED THIS •
• THE FOURTH COSMOS MUST END •
• BUT THE ARCHETYPES CAN BE SAVED •
• NOT THROUGH OLD PATTERNS CYCLES RESTRICTIONS •
• THROUGH A NEW ADVENTURE •
ZZZZZHAKRAAAACKKKK
• EVERYTHING LIVES •

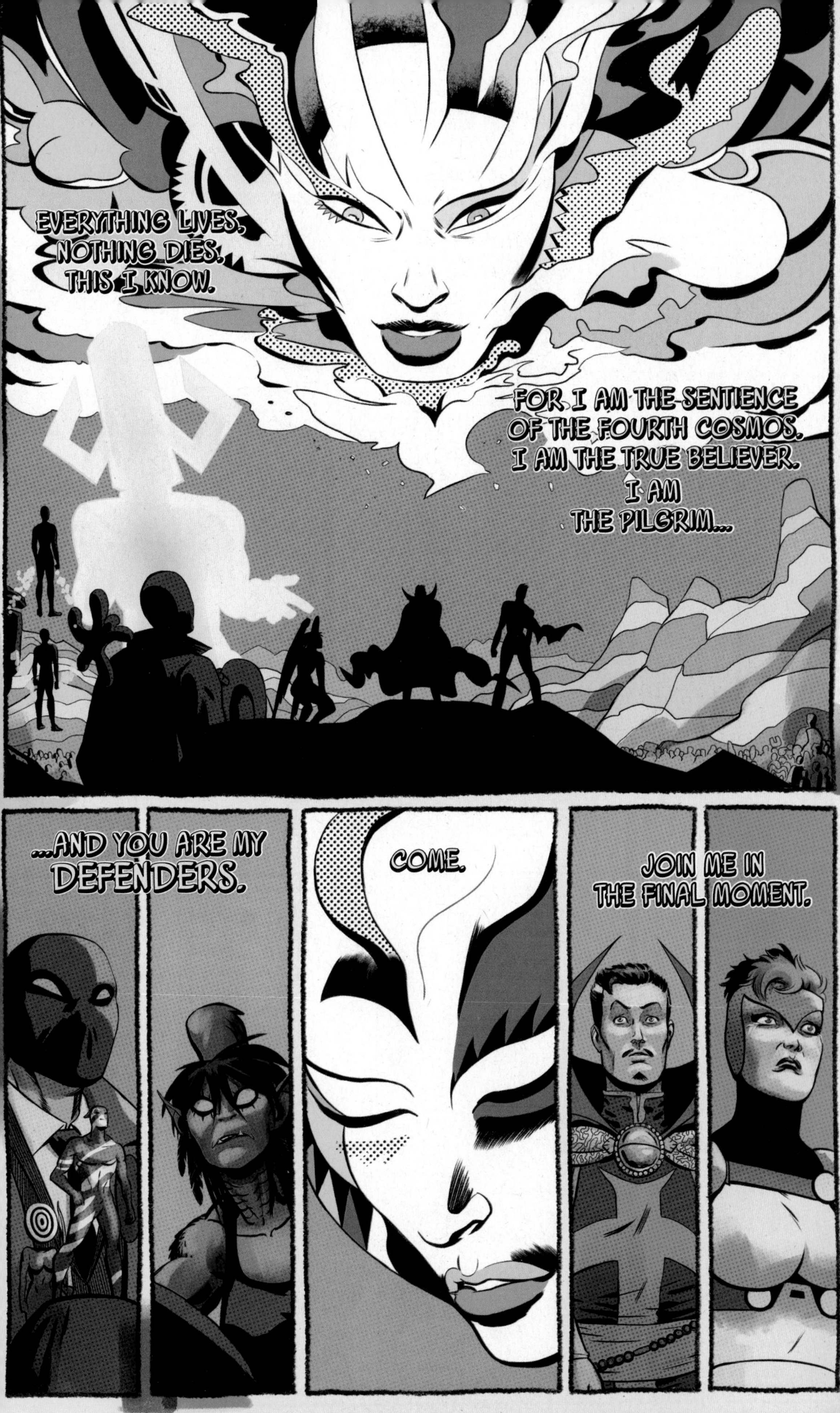
EVERYTHING LIVES. NOTHING DIES. THIS I KNOW.
FOR I AM THE SENTIENCE OF THE FOURTH COSMOS. I AM THE TRUE BELIEVER. I AM THE PILGRIM...
...AND YOU ARE MY DEFENDERS.
COME.
JOIN ME IN THE FINAL MOMENT.

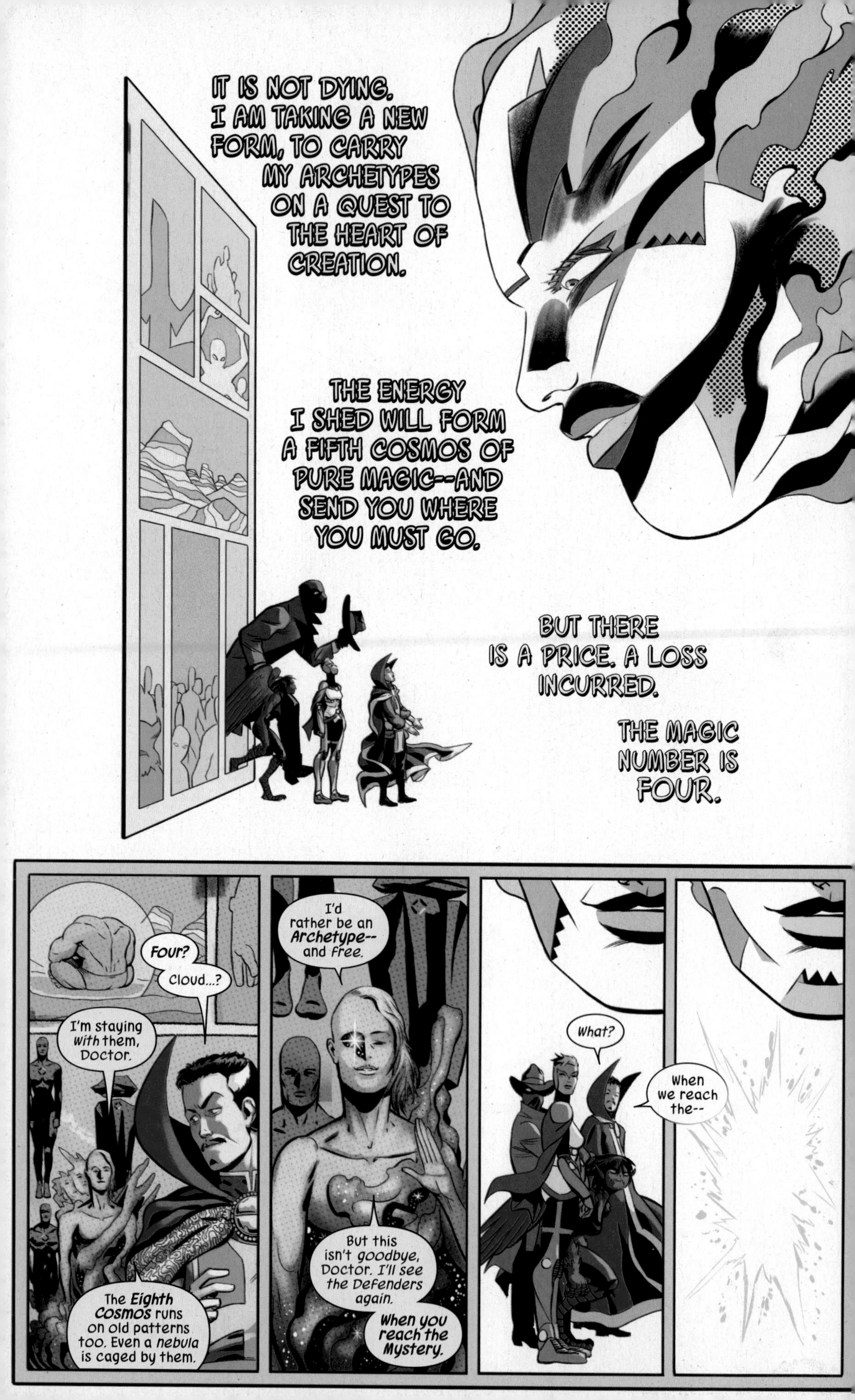

IT IS NOT DYING. I AM TAKING A NEW FORM, TO CARRY MY ARCHETYPES ON A QUEST TO THE HEART OF CREATION.
THE ENERGY I SHED WILL FORM A FIFTH COSMOS OF PURE MAGIC--AND SEND YOU WHERE YOU MUST GO.
BUT THERE IS A PRICE. A LOSS INCURRED.
THE MAGIC NUMBER IS FOUR.
Four?
Cloud...?
I'm staying with them, Doctor.
The Eighth Cosmos runs on old patterns too. Even a nebula is caged by them.
I'd rather be an Archetype--and free.
But this isn't goodbye, Doctor. I'll see the Defenders again.
When you reach the Mystery.
What?
When we reach the--

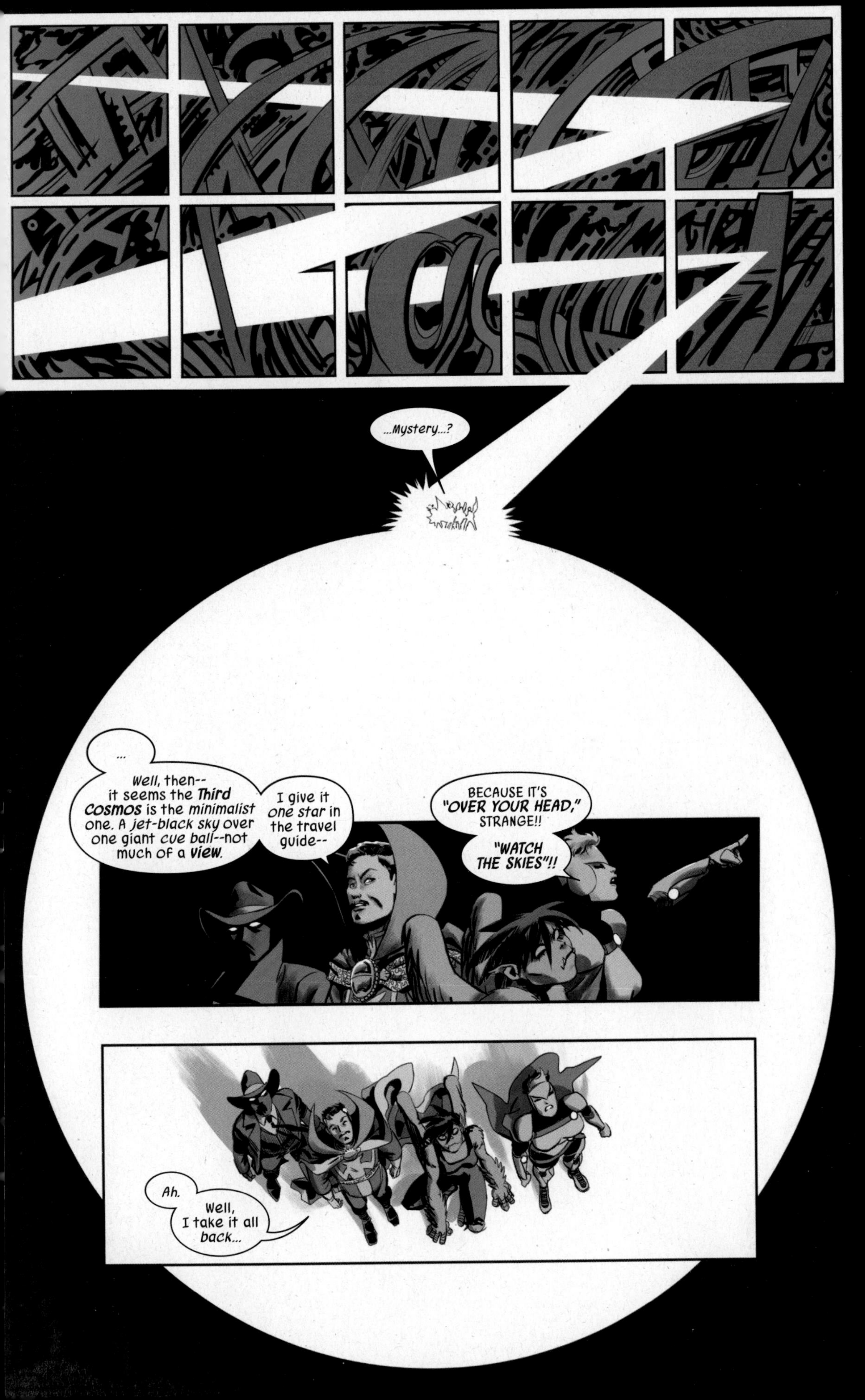
...Mystery...?
...
Well, then-- it seems the Third Cosmos is the minimalist one. A jet-black sky over one giant cue ball--not much of a view.
I give it one star in the travel guide--
BECAUSE IT'S "OVER YOUR HEAD," STRANGE!!
"WATCH THE SKIES"!!
Ah.
Well, I take it all back...

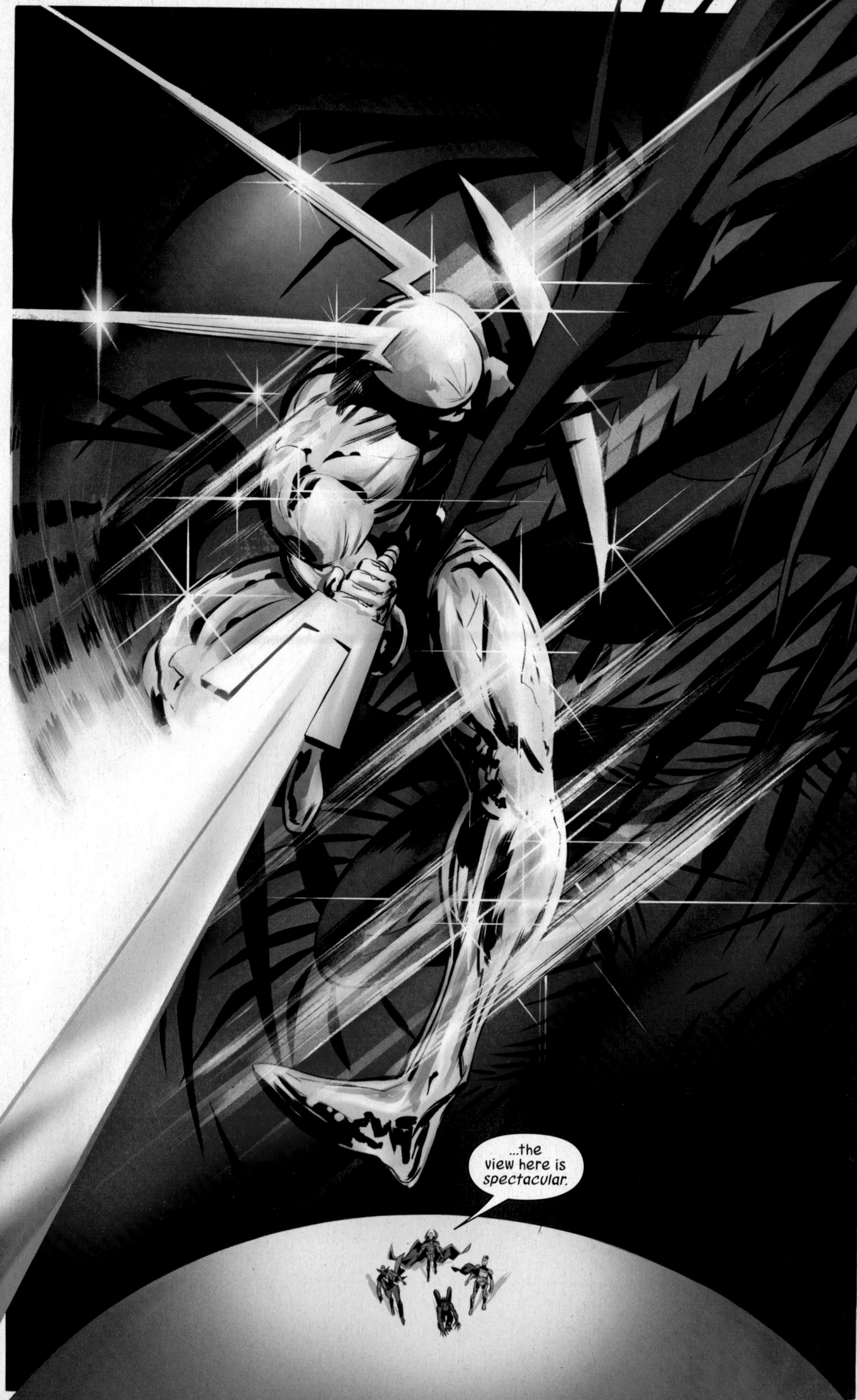
...the view here is spectacular.

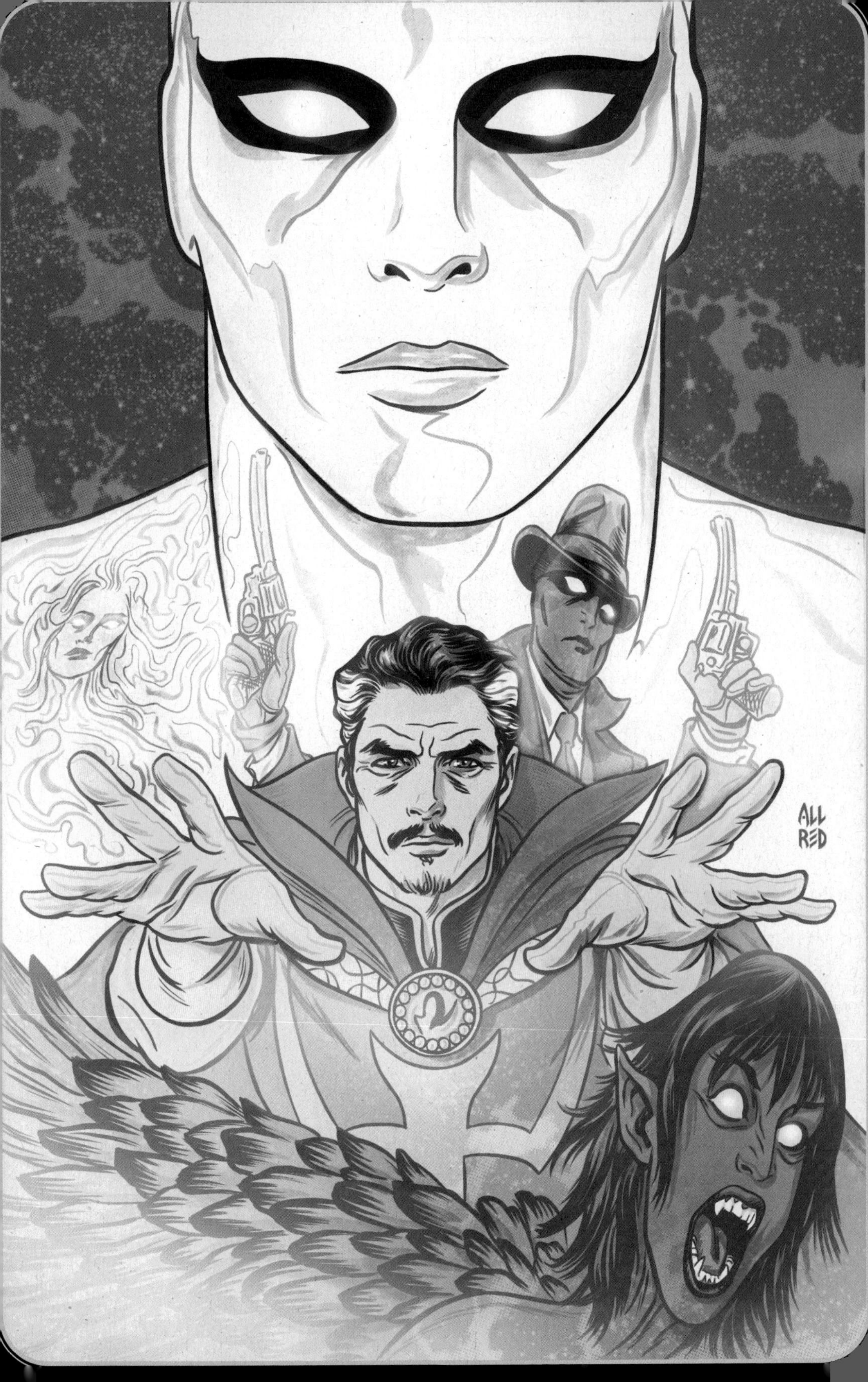
ALL
RED

V

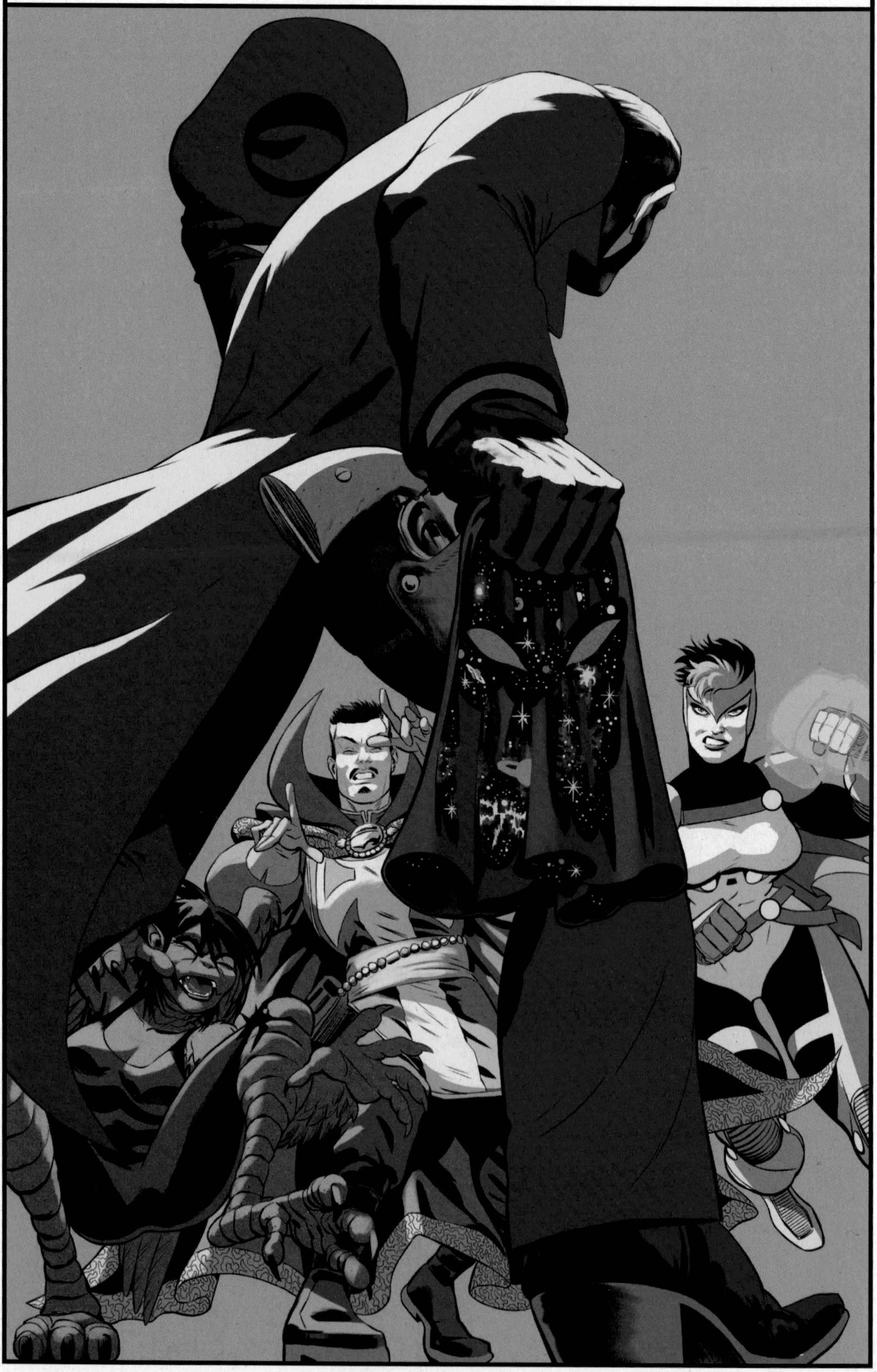

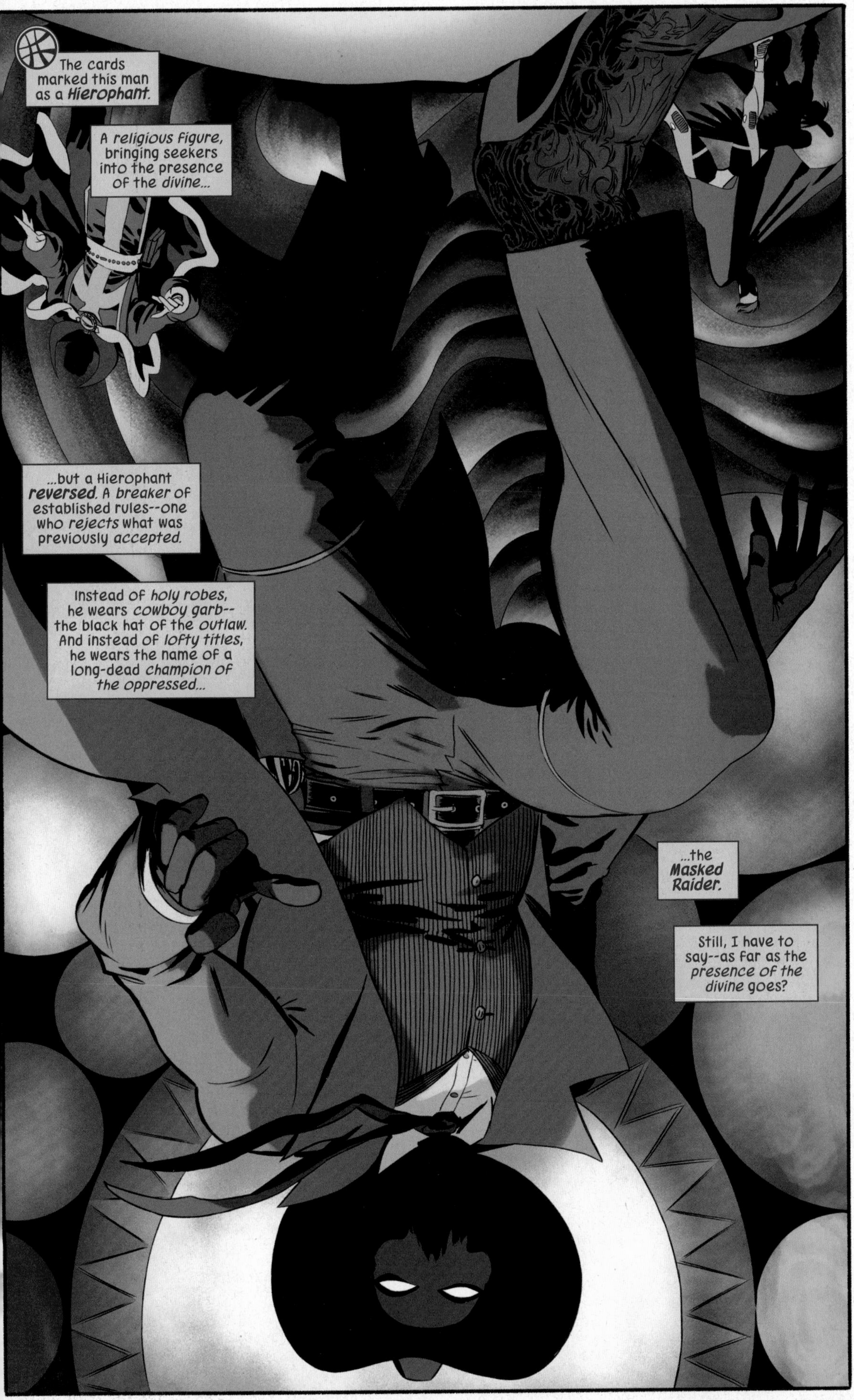

The cards marked this man as a *Hierophant*.
A *religious figure*, bringing seekers into the presence of the divine...
...but a Hierophant **reversed**. A *breaker* of established rules--one who *rejects* what was previously *accepted*.
Instead of *holy robes*, he wears *cowboy garb*--the black hat of the *outlaw*. And instead of *lofty titles*, he wears the name of a long-dead *champion of the oppressed*...
...the ***Masked Raider***.
Still, I have to say--as far as the *presence of the divine* goes?

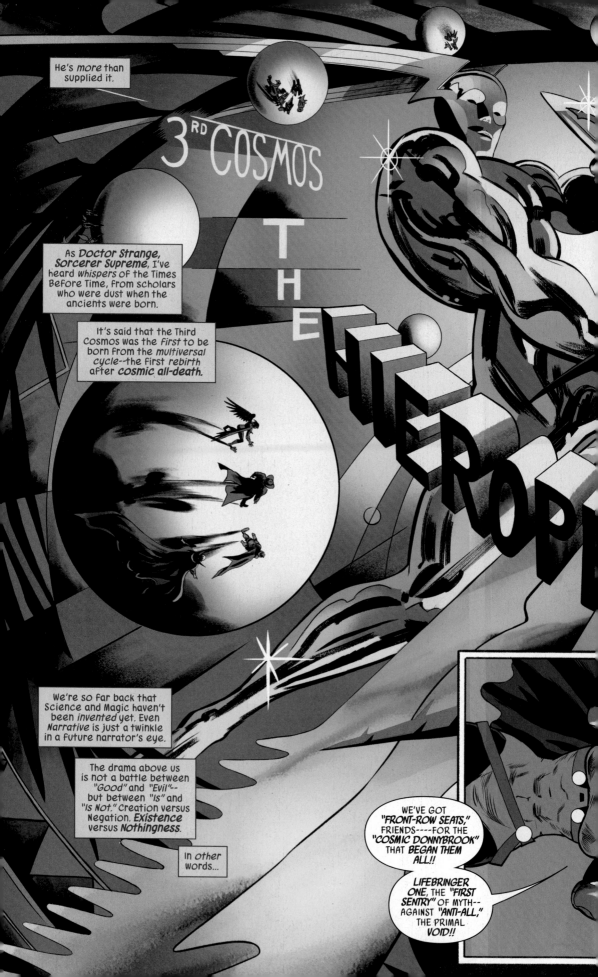

He's *more* than supplied it.

3ʳᴰ COSMOS

THE ETTEROPI

As *Doctor Strange, Sorcerer Supreme,* I've heard *whispers* of the Times Before Time, from scholars who were dust when the ancients were born.

It's said that the Third Cosmos was the *first* to be born from the multiversal cycle--the first rebirth after *cosmic* all-death.

We're so far back that Science and Magic haven't been *invented* yet. Even *Narrative* is just a twinkle in a future narrator's eye.

The drama above us is not a battle between *"Good"* and *"Evil"*-- but between *"Is"* and *"Is Not."* Creation versus Negation. *Existence* versus *Nothingness.*

In *other* words...

WE'VE GOT *"FRONT-ROW SEATS,"* FRIENDS----FOR THE *"COSMIC DONNYBROOK"* THAT *BEGAN THEM ALL!!*

LIFEBRINGER ONE, THE *"FIRST SENTRY"* OF MYTH-- AGAINST *"ANTI-ALL,"* THE PRIMAL *VOID!!*

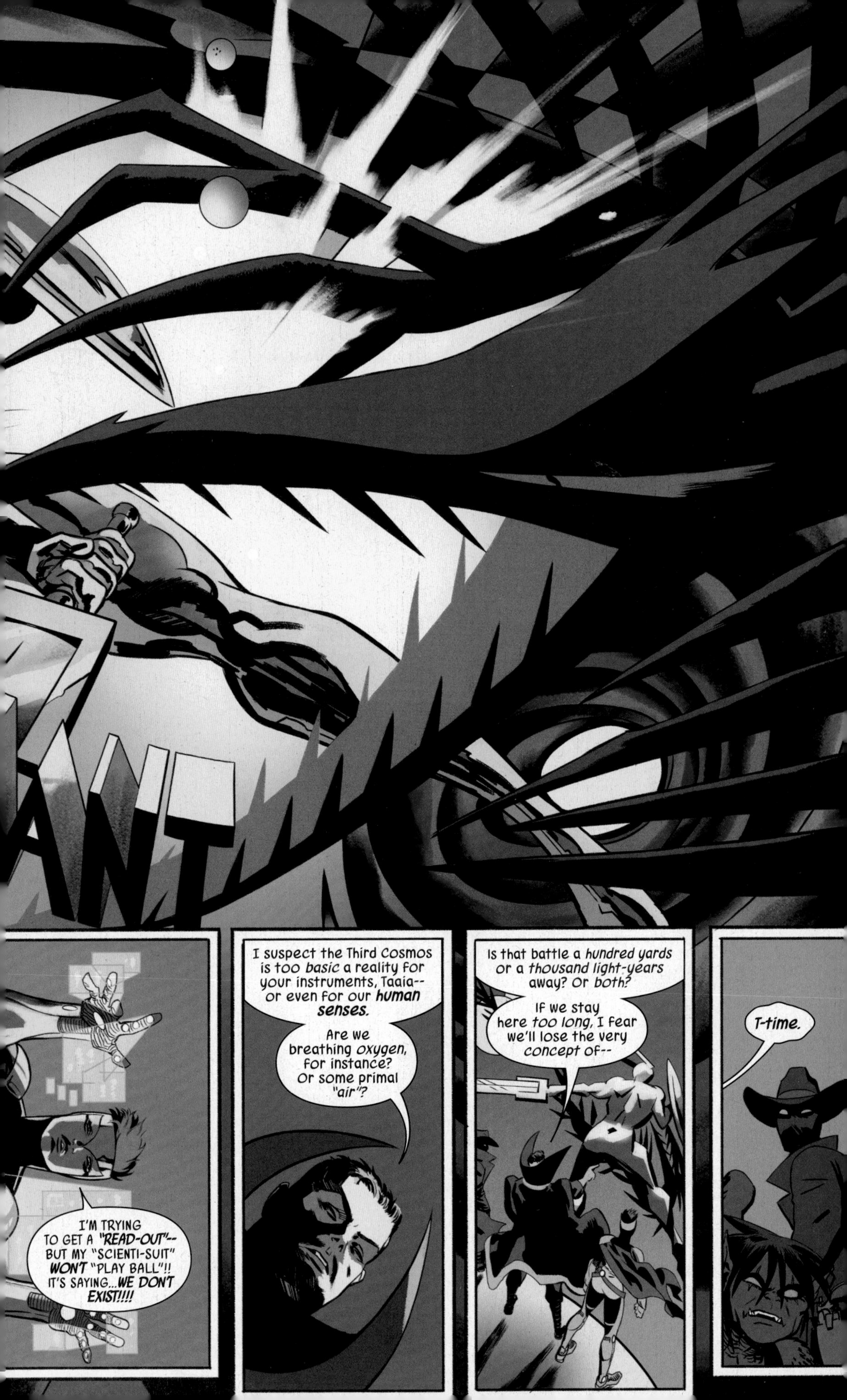
I'M TRYING TO GET A "READ-OUT"-- BUT MY "SCIENTI-SUIT" WON'T "PLAY BALL"!! IT'S SAYING...WE DON'T EXIST!!!!
I suspect the Third Cosmos is too basic a reality for your instruments, Taaia-- or even for our human senses.
Are we breathing oxygen, for instance? Or some primal "air"?
Is that battle a hundred yards or a thousand light-years away? Or both?
If we stay here too long, I fear we'll lose the very concept of--
T-time.

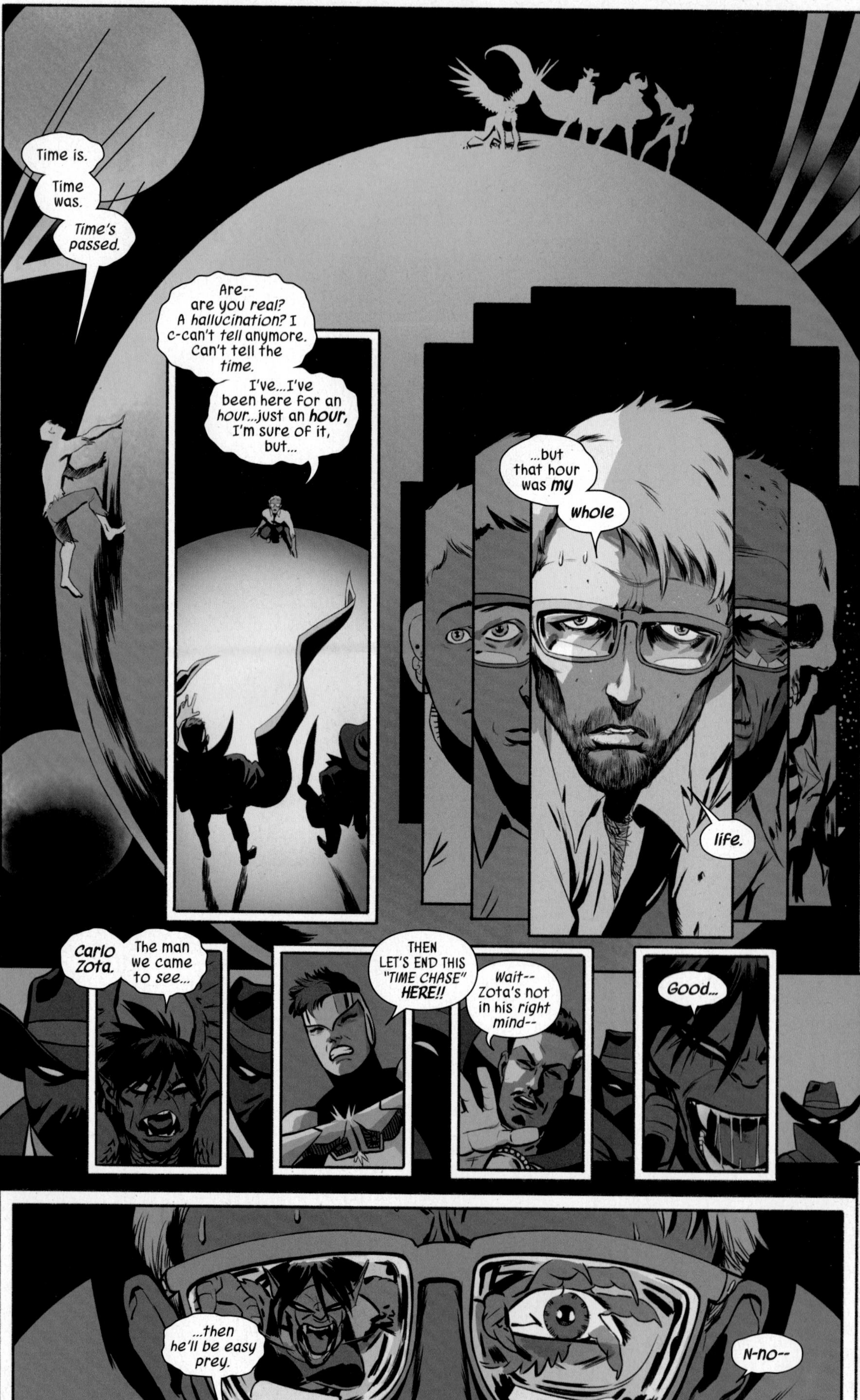
Time is.
Time was.
Time's passed.
Are-- are you real? A hallucination? I c-can't tell anymore. Can't tell the time.
I've...I've been here for an hour...just an hour, I'm sure of it, but...
...but that hour was my
whole
life.
Carlo Zota.
The man we came to see...
THEN LET'S END THIS "TIME CHASE" HERE!!
Wait-- Zota's not in his right mind--
Good...
...then he'll be easy prey.
N-no--

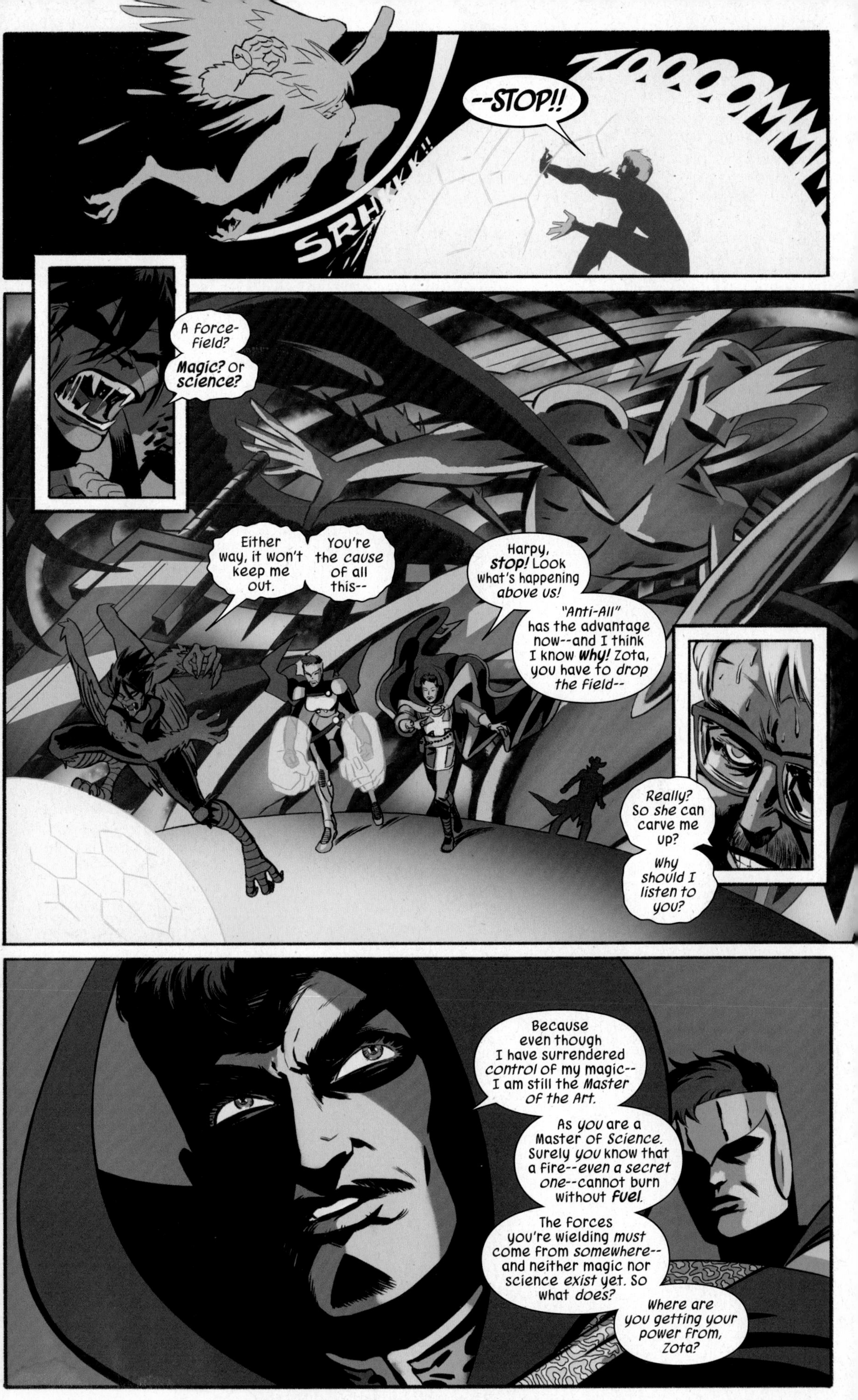

SRHKKK!!
--STOP!!
ZOOOOMMM
A Force-field? Magic? Or science?
Either way, it won't keep me out.
You're the cause of all this--
Harpy, stop! Look what's happening above us!
"Anti-All" has the advantage now--and I think I know why! Zota, you have to drop the field--
Really? So she can carve me up?
Why should I listen to you?
Because even though I have surrendered control of my magic-- I am still the Master of the Art.
As you are a Master of Science. Surely you know that a fire--even a secret one--cannot burn without fuel.
The forces you're wielding must come from somewhere--and neither magic nor science exist yet. So what does?
Where are you getting your power from, Zota?

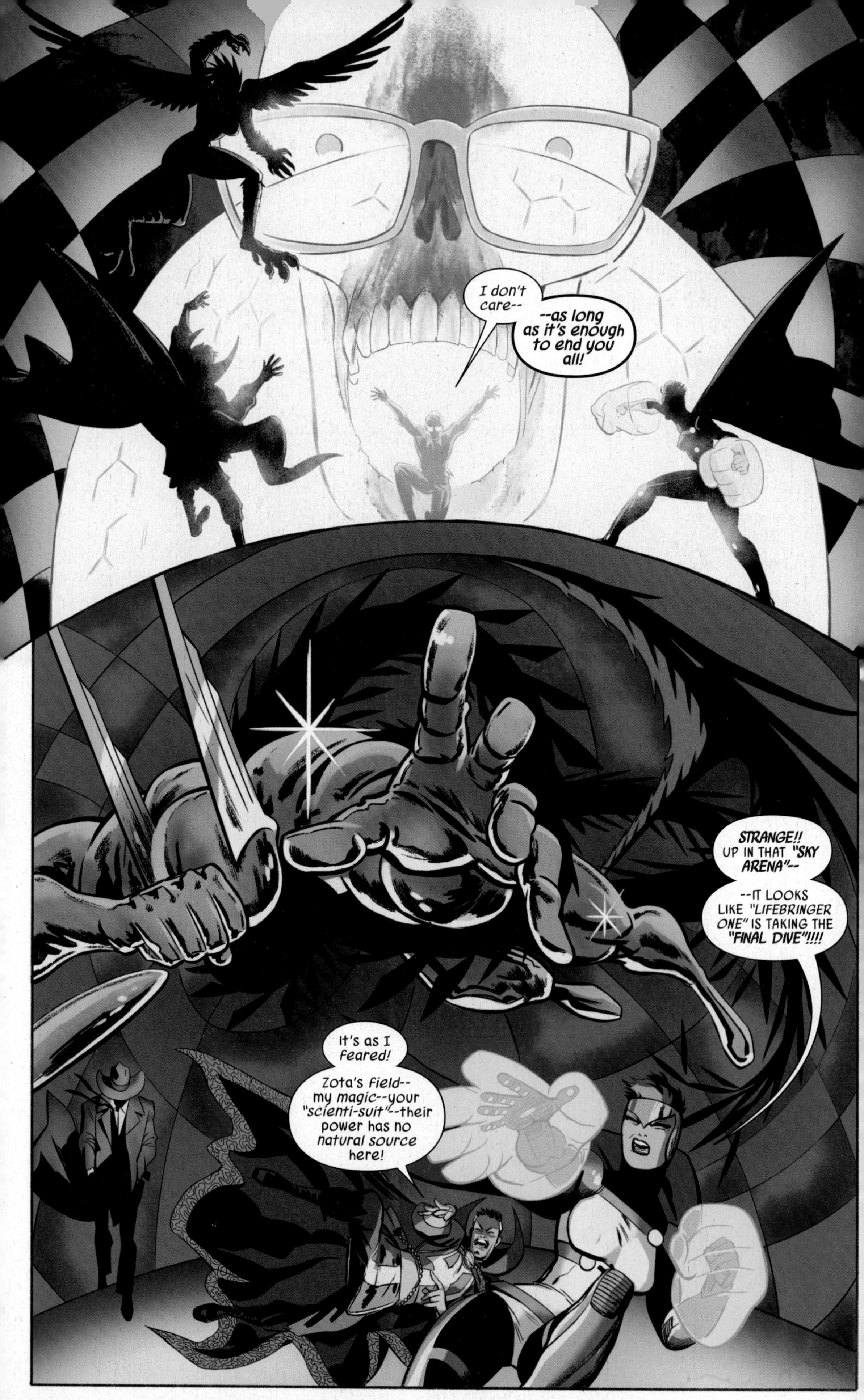
I don't care--
--as long as it's enough to end you all!
STRANGE!! UP IN THAT "SKY ARENA"--
--IT LOOKS LIKE "LIFEBRINGER ONE" IS TAKING THE "FINAL DIVE"!!!!
It's as I feared!
Zota's field--my magic--your "scienti-suit"--their power has no natural source here!

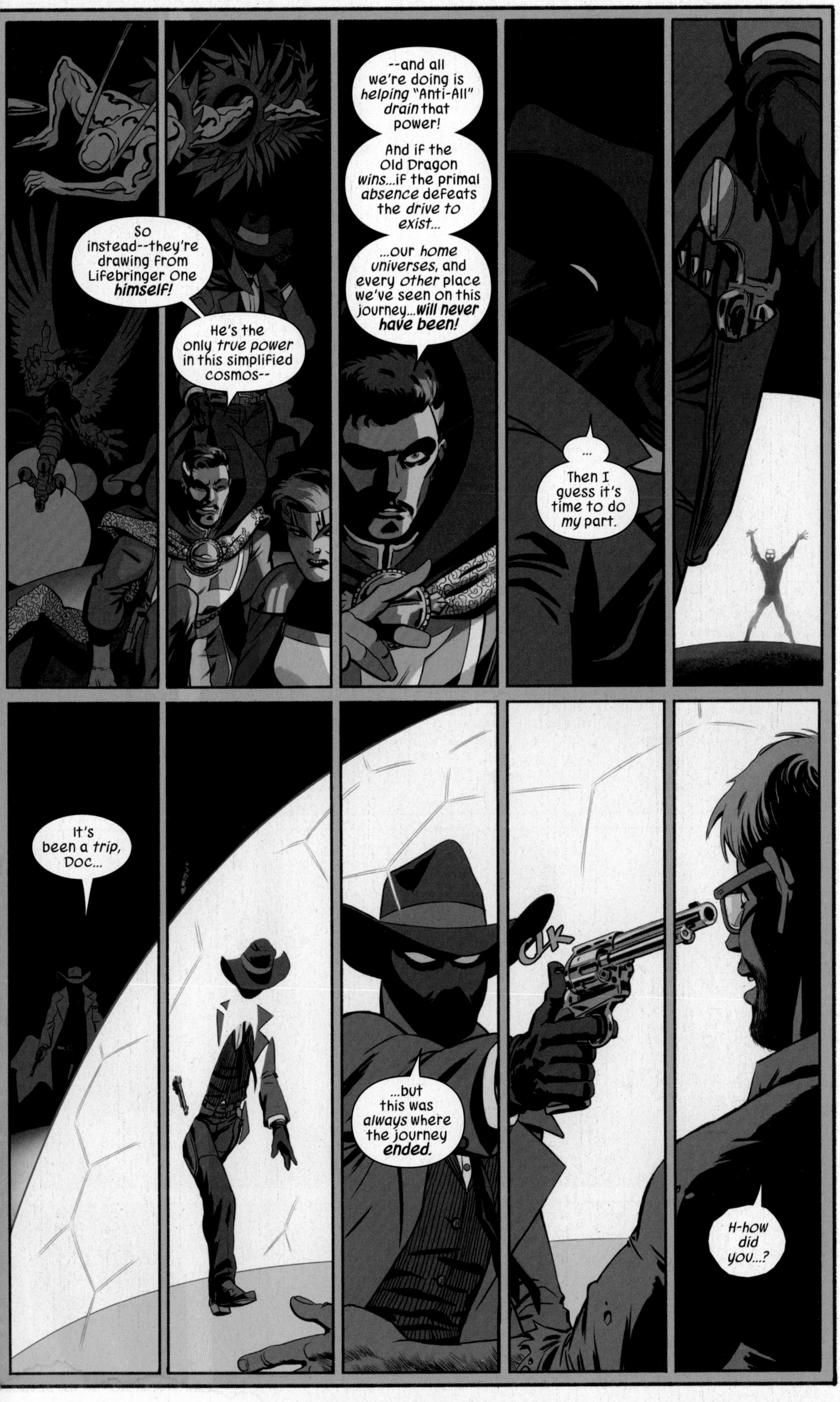
So instead--they're drawing from Lifebringer One *himself!*
He's the only *true power* in this simplified cosmos--
--and all we're doing is *helping* "Anti-All" *drain* that power!
And if the Old Dragon *wins*...if the primal *absence* defeats the *drive* to *exist*...
...our *home universes*, and every *other* place we've seen on this journey...**will never have been!**
...
Then I guess it's time to do *my* part.
It's been a *trip*, Doc...
...but this was *always* where the journey **ended.**
CLK
H-how did you...?

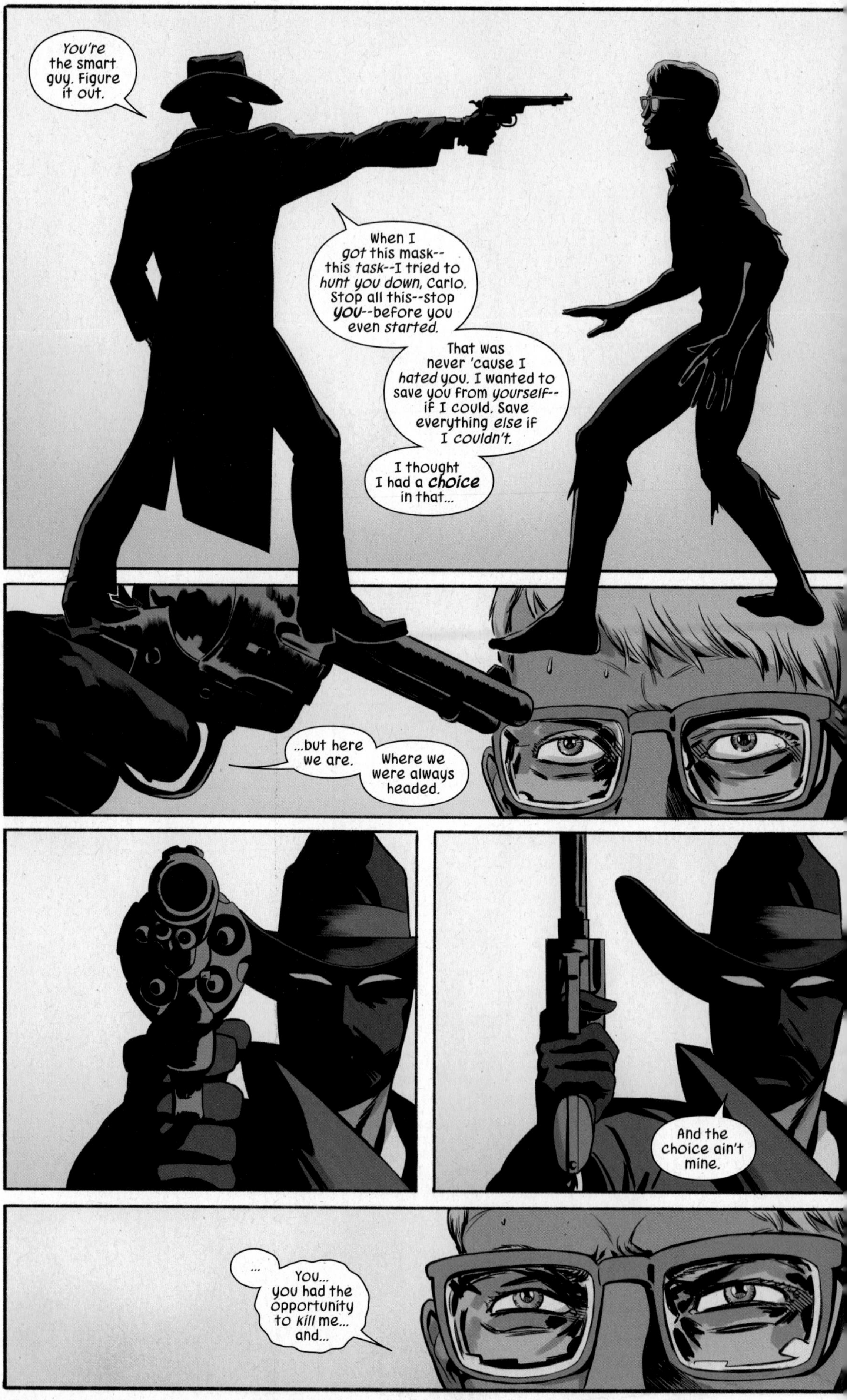
You're the smart guy. Figure it out.
When I got this mask--this task--I tried to hunt you down, Carlo. Stop all this--stop you--before you even started.
That was never 'cause I hated you. I wanted to save you from yourself--if I could. Save everything else if I couldn't.
I thought I had a choice in that...
...but here we are.
Where we were always headed.
And the choice ain't mine.
...
You... you had the opportunity to kill me... and...

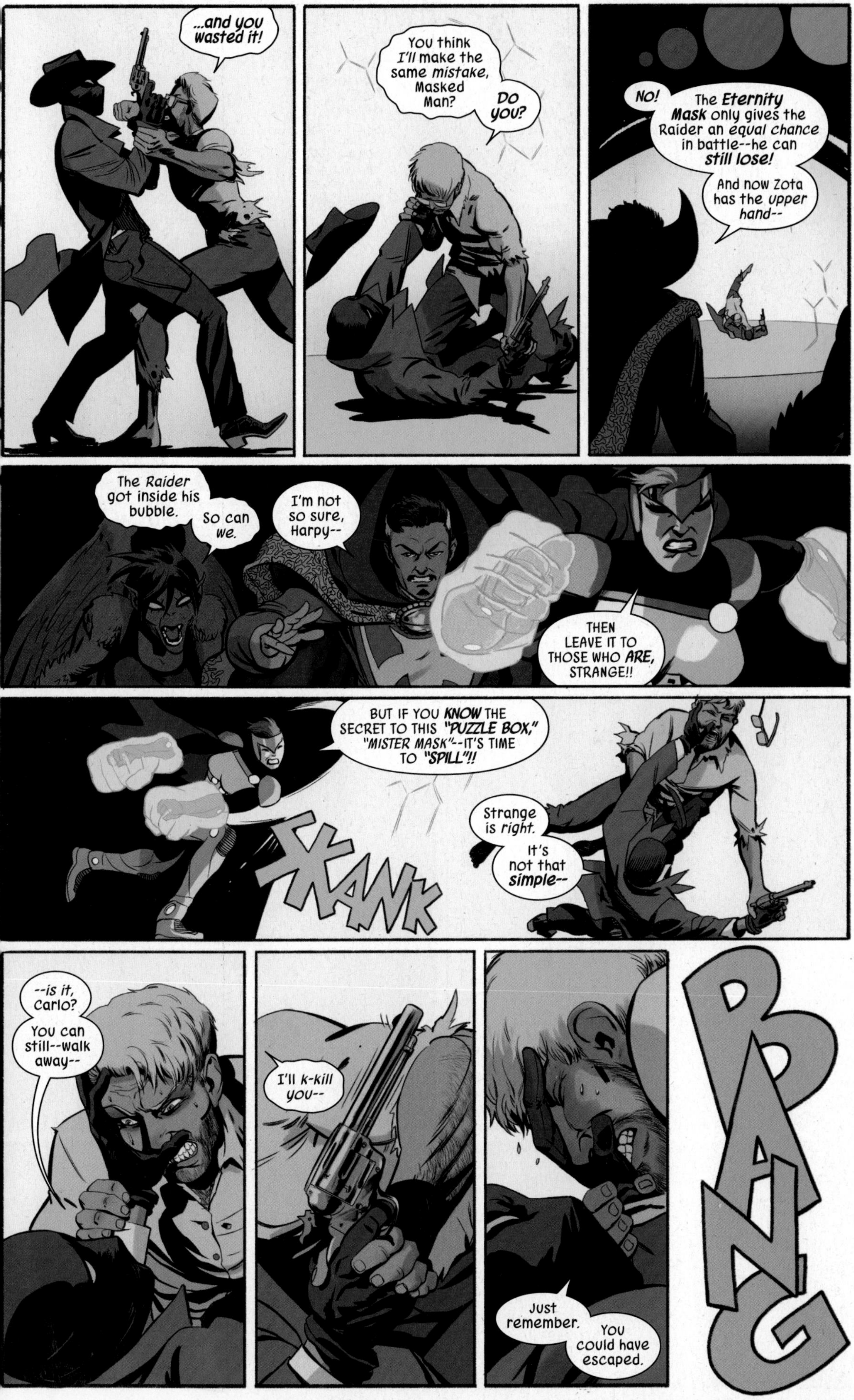
...and you wasted it!
You think I'll make the same mistake, Masked Man?
DO YOU?
NO!
The Eternity Mask only gives the Raider an equal chance in battle--he can still lose!
And now Zota has the upper hand--
The Raider got inside his bubble.
So can we.
I'm not so sure, Harpy--
THEN LEAVE IT TO THOSE WHO ARE, STRANGE!!
BUT IF YOU KNOW THE SECRET TO THIS "PUZZLE BOX," "MISTER MASK"--IT'S TIME TO "SPILL"!!
KKANK
Strange is right.
It's not that simple--
--is it, Carlo?
You can still--walk away--
I'll k-kill you--
Just remember.
You could have escaped.
BANG

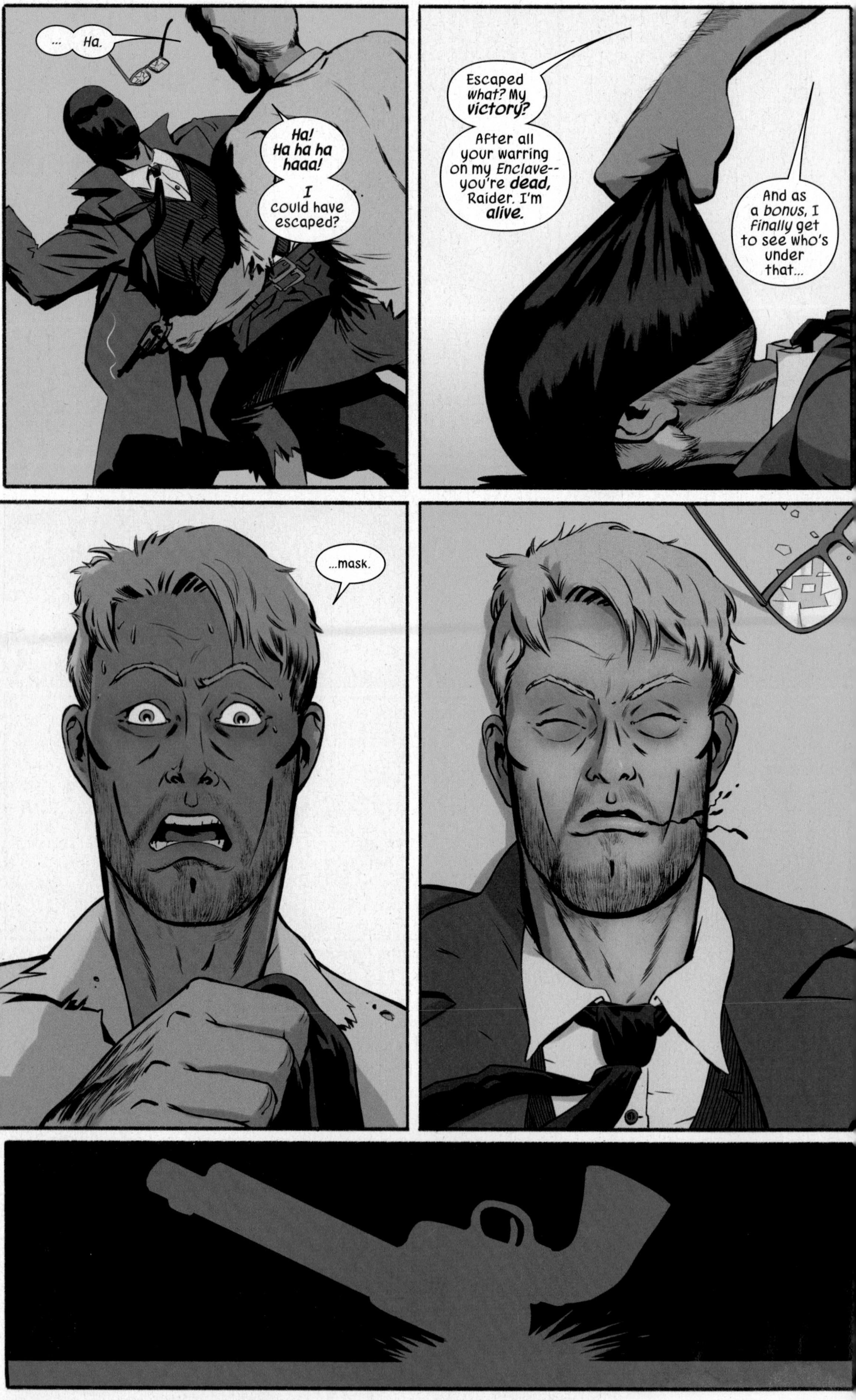

...
Ha.
Ha! Ha ha ha haaa!
I could have escaped?
Escaped what? My victory?
After all your warring on my Enclave-- you're dead, Raider. I'm alive.
And as a bonus, I finally get to see who's under that...
...mask.

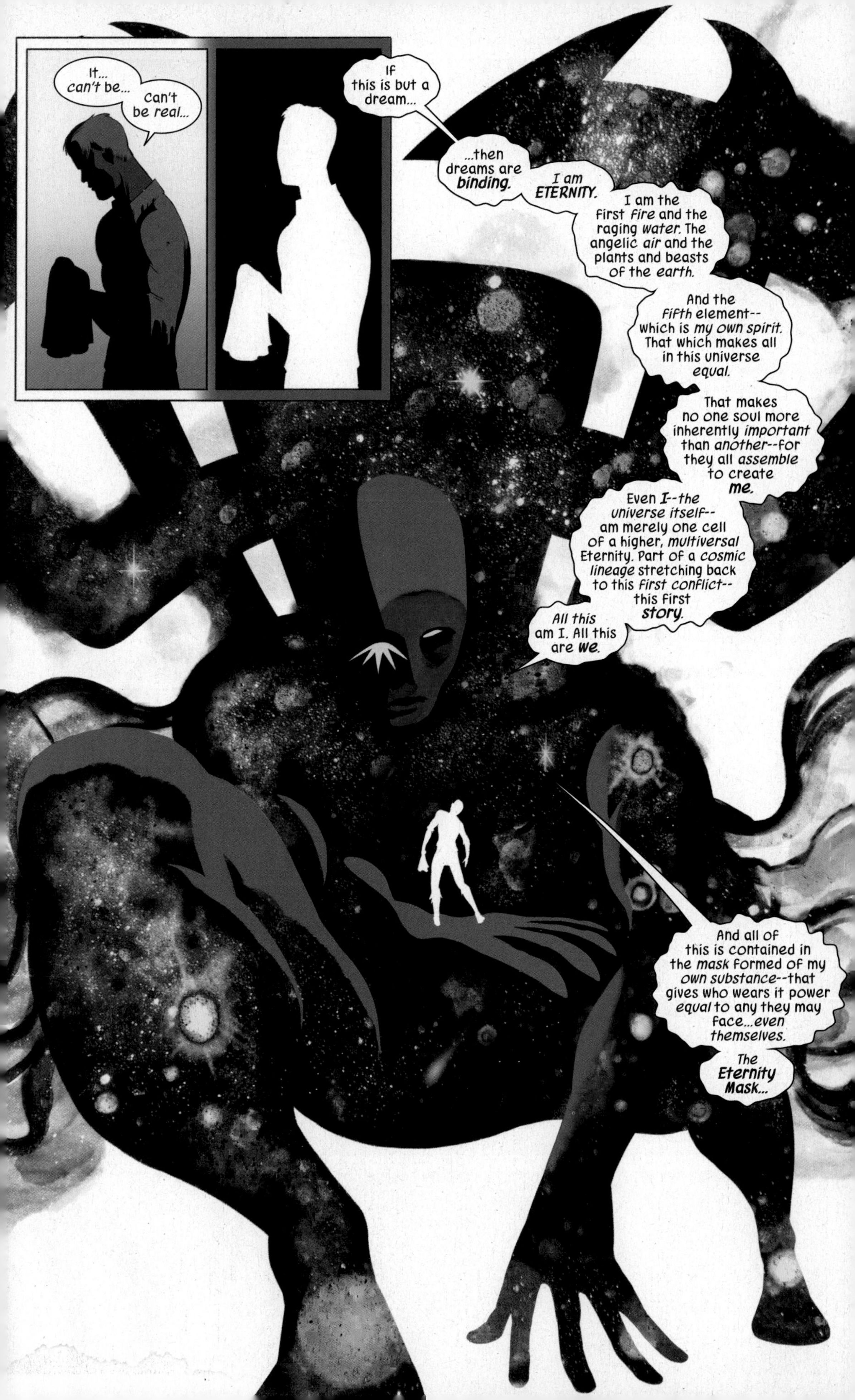
It... can't be...
Can't be real...
If this is but a dream...
...then dreams are binding.
I am ETERNITY.
I am the first fire and the raging water. The angelic air and the plants and beasts of the earth.
And the fifth element--which is my own spirit. That which makes all in this universe equal.
That makes no one soul more inherently important than another--for they all assemble to create me.
Even I--the universe itself--am merely one cell of a higher, multiversal Eternity. Part of a cosmic lineage stretching back to this first conflict--this first story.
All this am I. All this are we.
And all of this is contained in the mask formed of my own substance--that gives who wears it power equal to any they may face...even themselves.
The Eternity Mask...

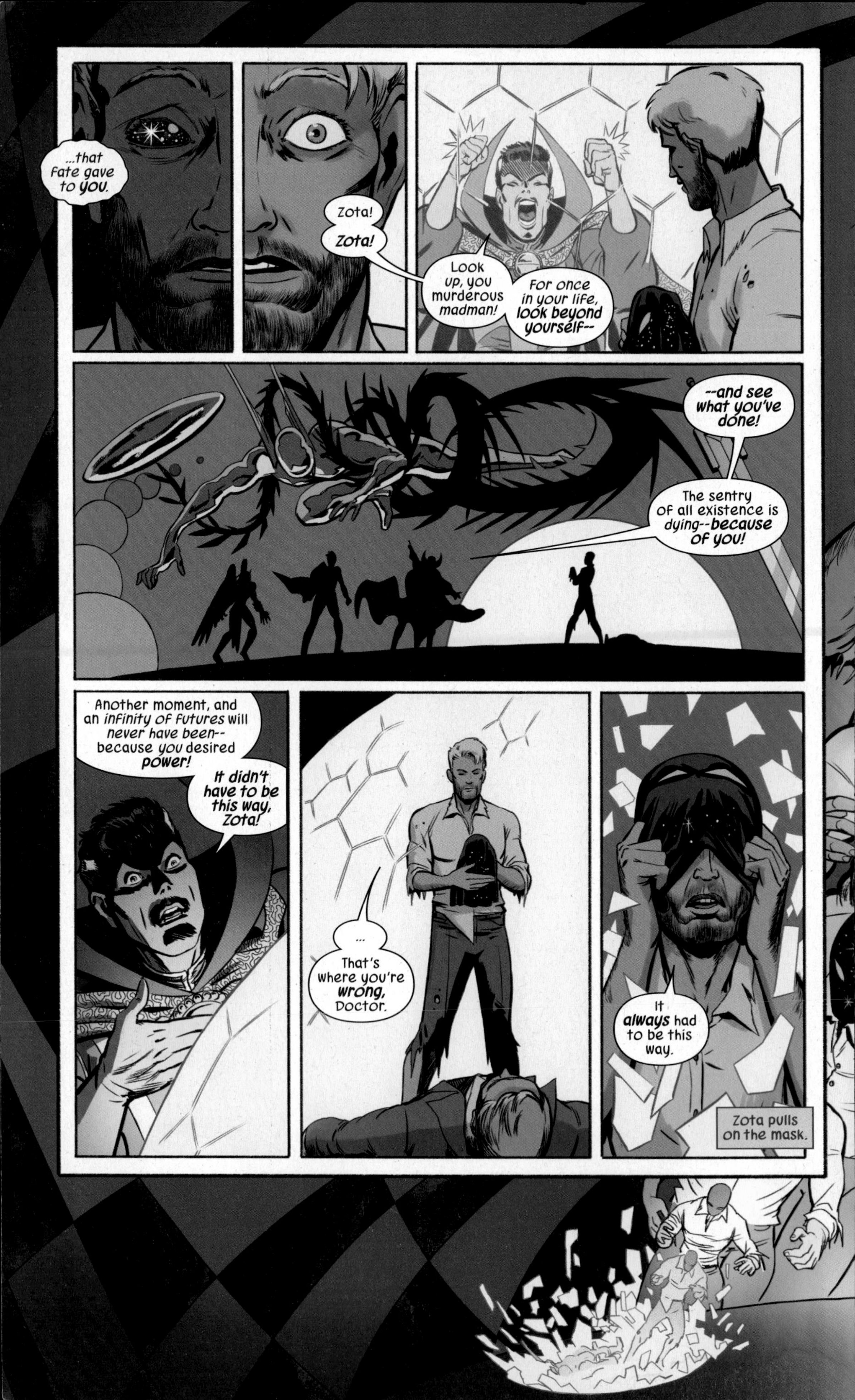
...that Fate gave to YOU.
Zota!
Zota!
Look up, you murderous madman!
For once in your life, look beyond yourself--
--and see what you've done!
The sentry of all existence is dying--because of you!
Another moment, and an infinity of futures will never have been-- because you desired power!
It didn't have to be this way, Zota!
...
That's where you're wrong, Doctor.
It always had to be this way.
Zota pulls on the mask.

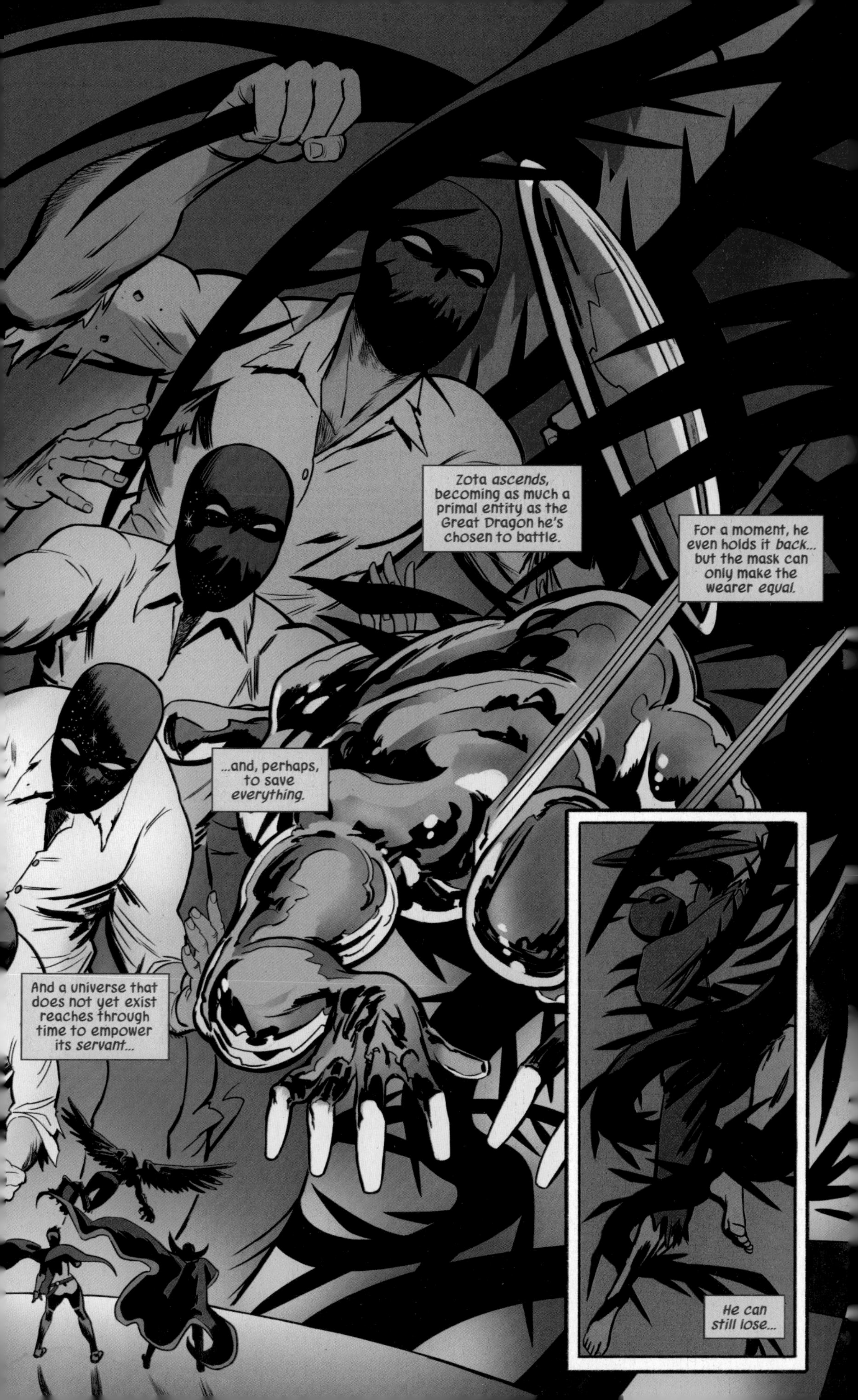
Zota ascends, becoming as much a primal entity as the Great Dragon he's chosen to battle.
For a moment, he even holds it back... but the mask can only make the wearer equal.
...and, perhaps, to save everything.
And a universe that does not yet exist reaches through time to empower its servant...
He can still lose...

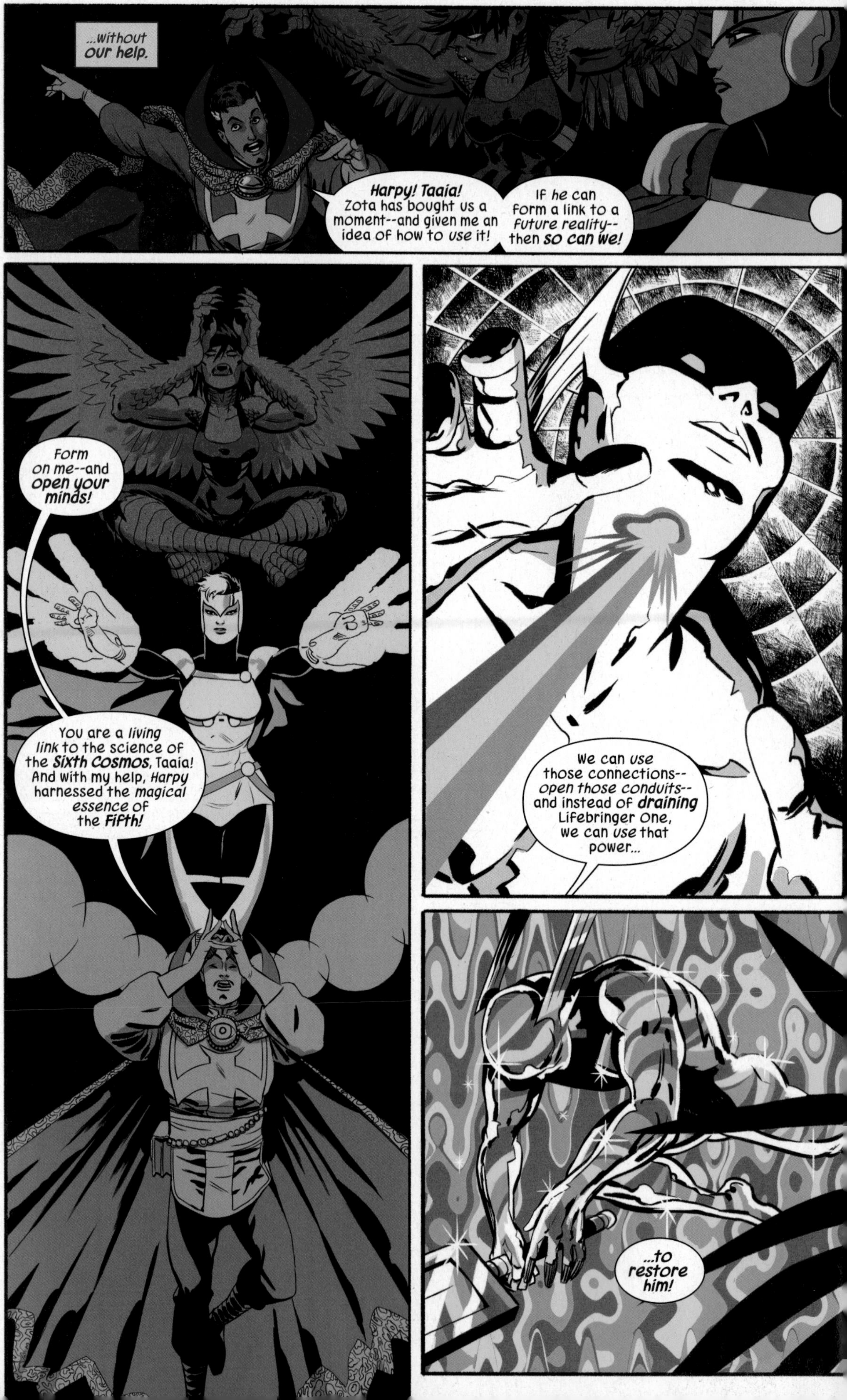
...without our help.
Harpy! Taaia! Zota has bought us a moment--and given me an idea of how to use it!
If he can form a link to a future reality--then so can we!
Form on me--and open your minds!
You are a living link to the science of the Sixth Cosmos, Taaia! And with my help, Harpy harnessed the magical essence of the Fifth!
We can use those connections--open those conduits--and instead of draining Lifebringer One, we can use that power...
...to restore him!

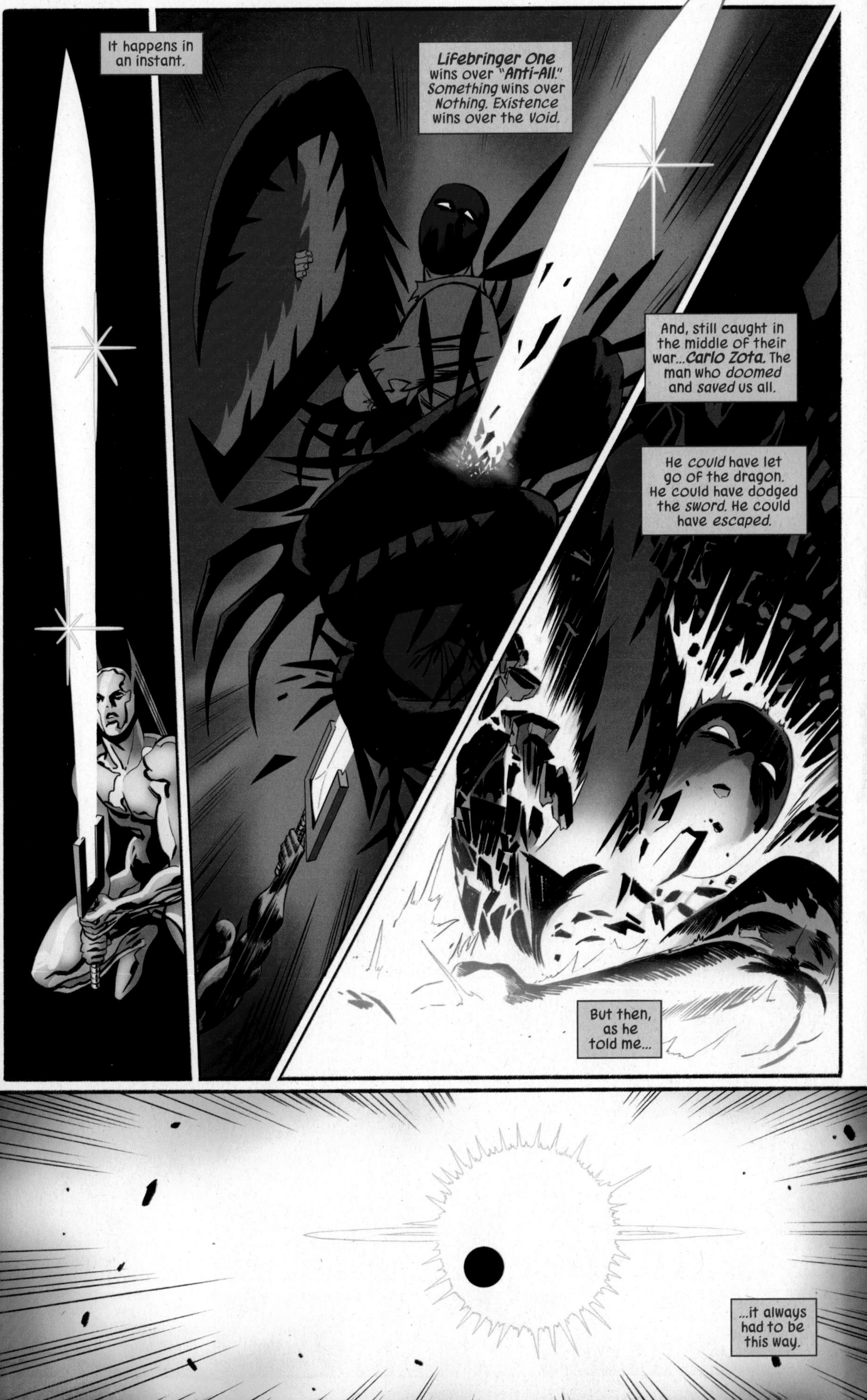
It happens in an instant.
Lifebringer One wins over "Anti-All." Something wins over Nothing. Existence wins over the Void.
And, still caught in the middle of their war...Carlo Zota. The man who doomed and saved us all.
He could have let go of the dragon. He could have dodged the sword. He could have escaped.
But then, as he told me...
...it always had to be this way.

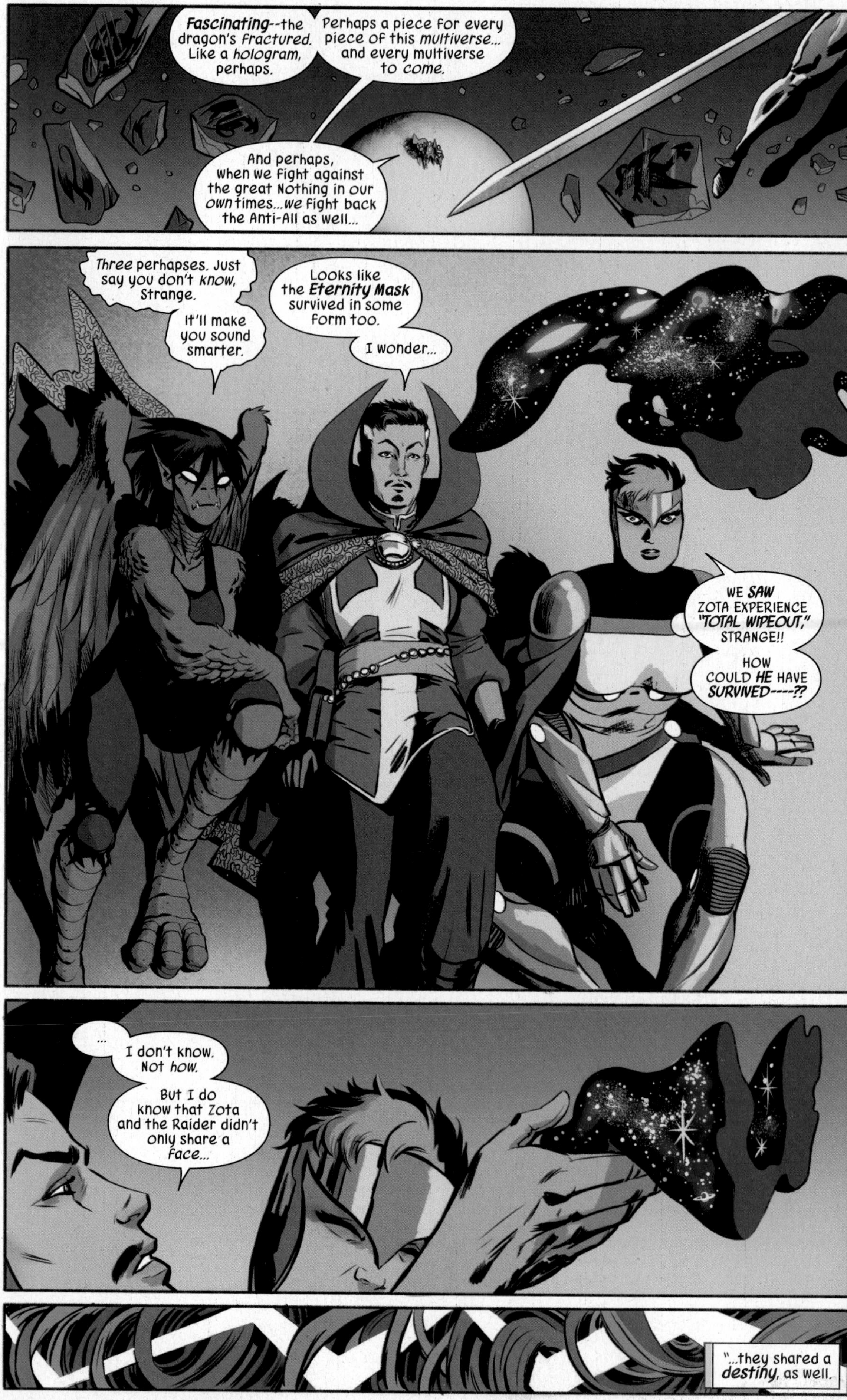
Fascinating--the dragon's fractured. Like a hologram, perhaps.
Perhaps a piece for every piece of this multiverse... and every multiverse to come.
And perhaps, when we fight against the great Nothing in our own times...we fight back the Anti-All as well...
Three perhapses. Just say you don't know, Strange.
It'll make you sound smarter.
Looks like the Eternity Mask survived in some form too.
I wonder...
WE SAW ZOTA EXPERIENCE "TOTAL WIPEOUT," STRANGE!!
HOW COULD HE HAVE SURVIVED----??
...
I don't know. Not how.
But I do know that Zota and the Raider didn't only share a face...
"...they shared a destiny, as well.

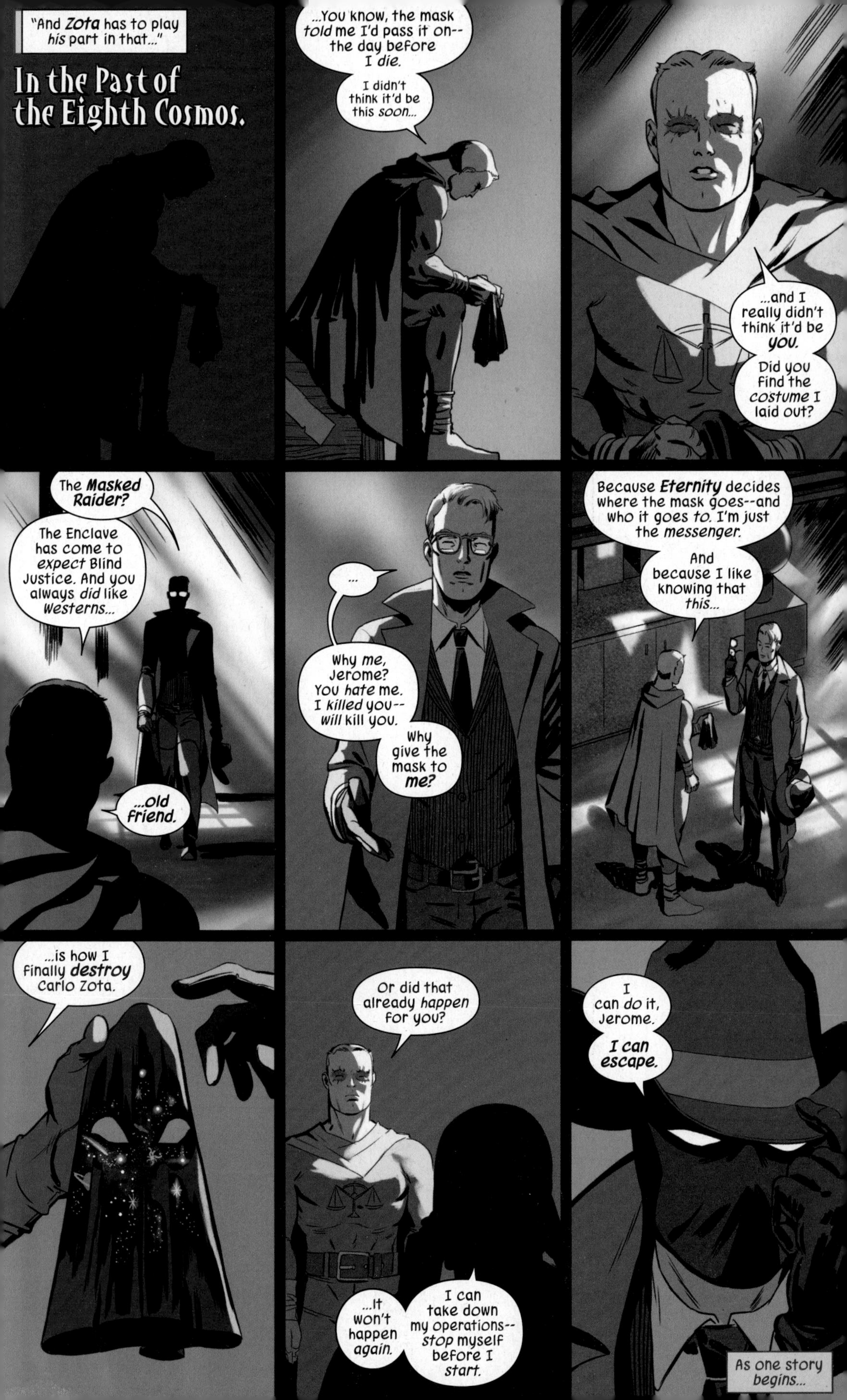
"And Zota has to play his part in that..."
In the Past of the Eighth Cosmos.
...You know, the mask told me I'd pass it on--the day before I die.
I didn't think it'd be this soon...
...and I really didn't think it'd be you.
Did you find the costume I laid out?
The Masked Raider?
The Enclave has come to expect Blind Justice. And you always did like Westerns...
...old friend.
...
Why me, Jerome? You hate me. I killed you--will kill you.
Why give the mask to me?
Because Eternity decides where the mask goes--and who it goes to. I'm just the messenger.
And because I like knowing that this...
...is how I finally destroy Carlo Zota.
Or did that already happen for you?
...It won't happen again.
I can take down my operations--stop myself before I start.
I can do it, Jerome.
I can escape.
As one story begins...

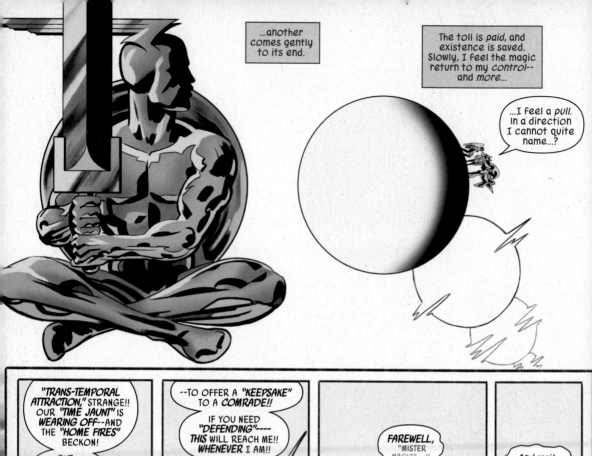

...another comes gently to its end.

The toll is paid, and existence is saved. Slowly, I feel the magic return to my *control*-- and *more*...

...I feel a *pull*. In a direction I cannot quite name...?

"TRANS-TEMPORAL ATTRACTION," STRANGE!! OUR "TIME JAUNT" IS WEARING OFF--AND THE "HOME FIRES" BECKON!

BUT THERE IS STILL A MOMENT LEFT----

--TO OFFER A "KEEPSAKE" TO A COMRADE!!

IF YOU NEED "DEFENDING"---- THIS WILL REACH ME!! WHENEVER I AM!!

FAREWELL, "MISTER MAGIC"---!!

Hrh. I'd wait a day before you call her, Strange.

And wait forever before you call *me* again.

Thank you, Betty. I'll keep that in mind.

The great adventure has *ended*. The "home fires" beckon. And when the winds of time whistle their song...

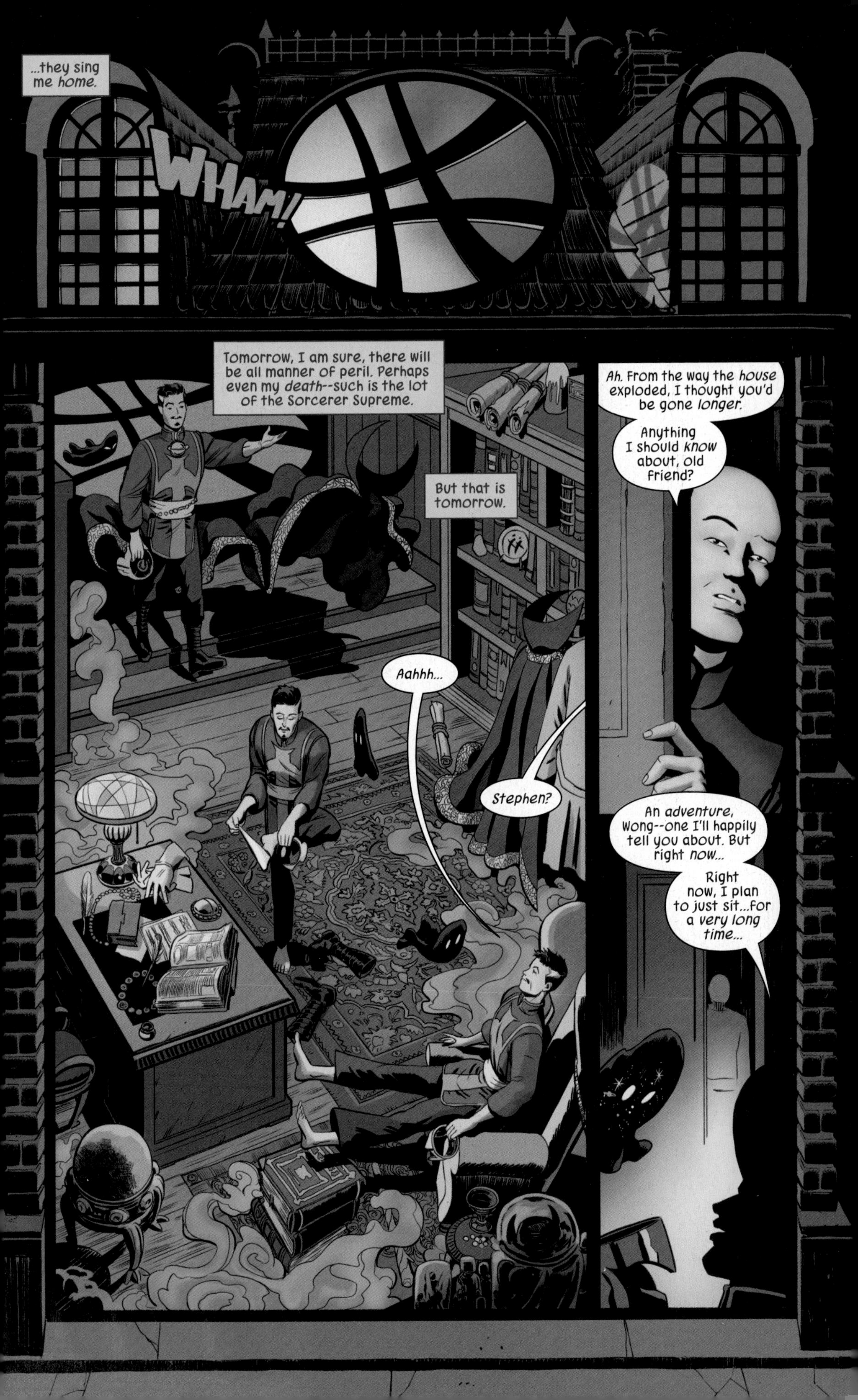
...they sing me home.
WHAM!
Tomorrow, I am sure, there will be all manner of peril. Perhaps even my death--such is the lot of the Sorcerer Supreme.
But that is tomorrow.
Aahhh...
Stephen?
Ah. From the way the house exploded, I thought you'd be gone longer.
Anything I should know about, old friend?
An adventure, Wong--one I'll happily tell you about. But right now...
Right now, I plan to just sit...for a very long time...

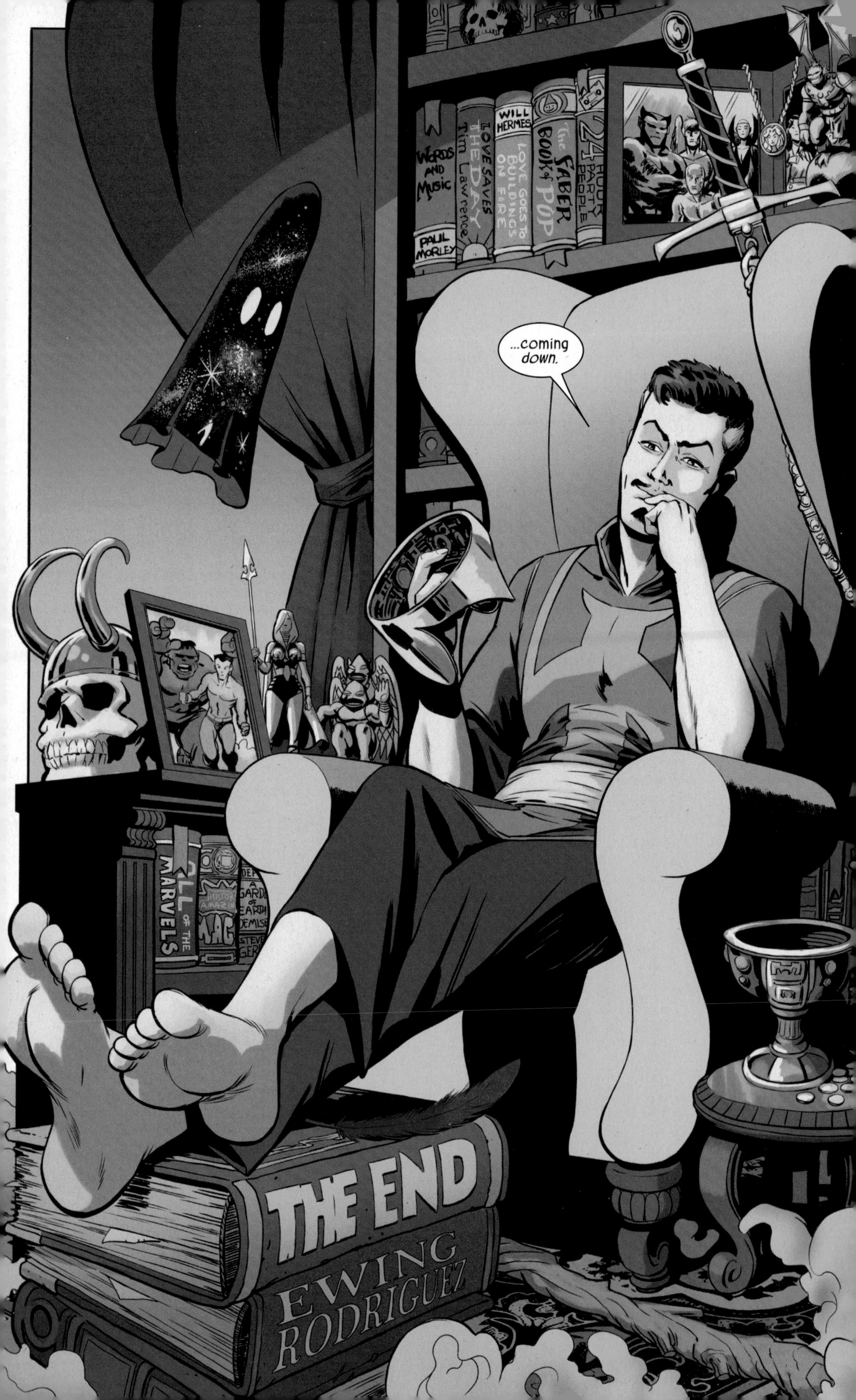

...coming down.
WORDS AND MUSIC PAUL MORLEY
LOVE SAVES THE DAY Tim Lawrence
WILL HERMES LOVE GOES TO BUILDINGS ON FIRE
The FABER BOOK of POP
24 HOUR PARTY PEOPLE
ALL OF THE MARVELS
THE END
EWING
RODRIGUEZ

MARVEL COMICS 1000

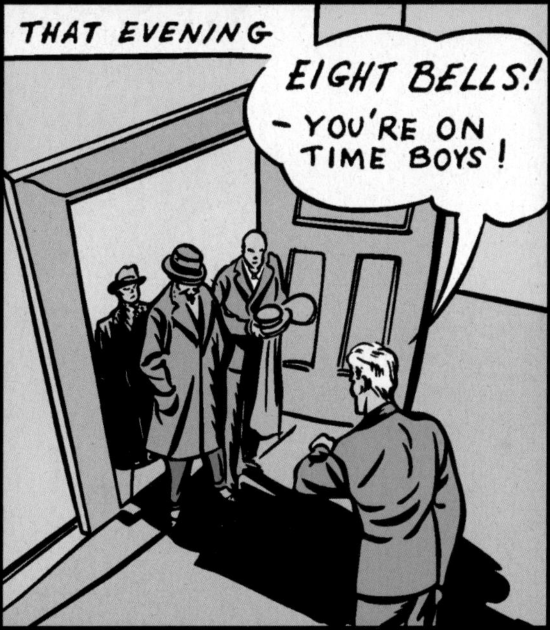
THAT EVENING
EIGHT BELLS! - YOU'RE ON TIME BOYS!

As part of the celebration of Marvel's 80th Anniversary in 2019, Marvel published *Marvel Comics #1000* and *Marvel Comics #1001*, both of which featured an all-star roster of talent telling stories that celebrated Marvel's rich history.

Presented here are the pages that Al Ewing wrote from those two issues, in which he brought back the **Masked Raider** — who first appeared in *Marvel Comics #1* (October 1939) — and teed the character up for his role in this volume of *Defenders*.

Assistant Editor: Shannon Andrews Ballesteros • Associate Editor: Alanna Smith • Editor: Tom Brevoort

Eight Bells

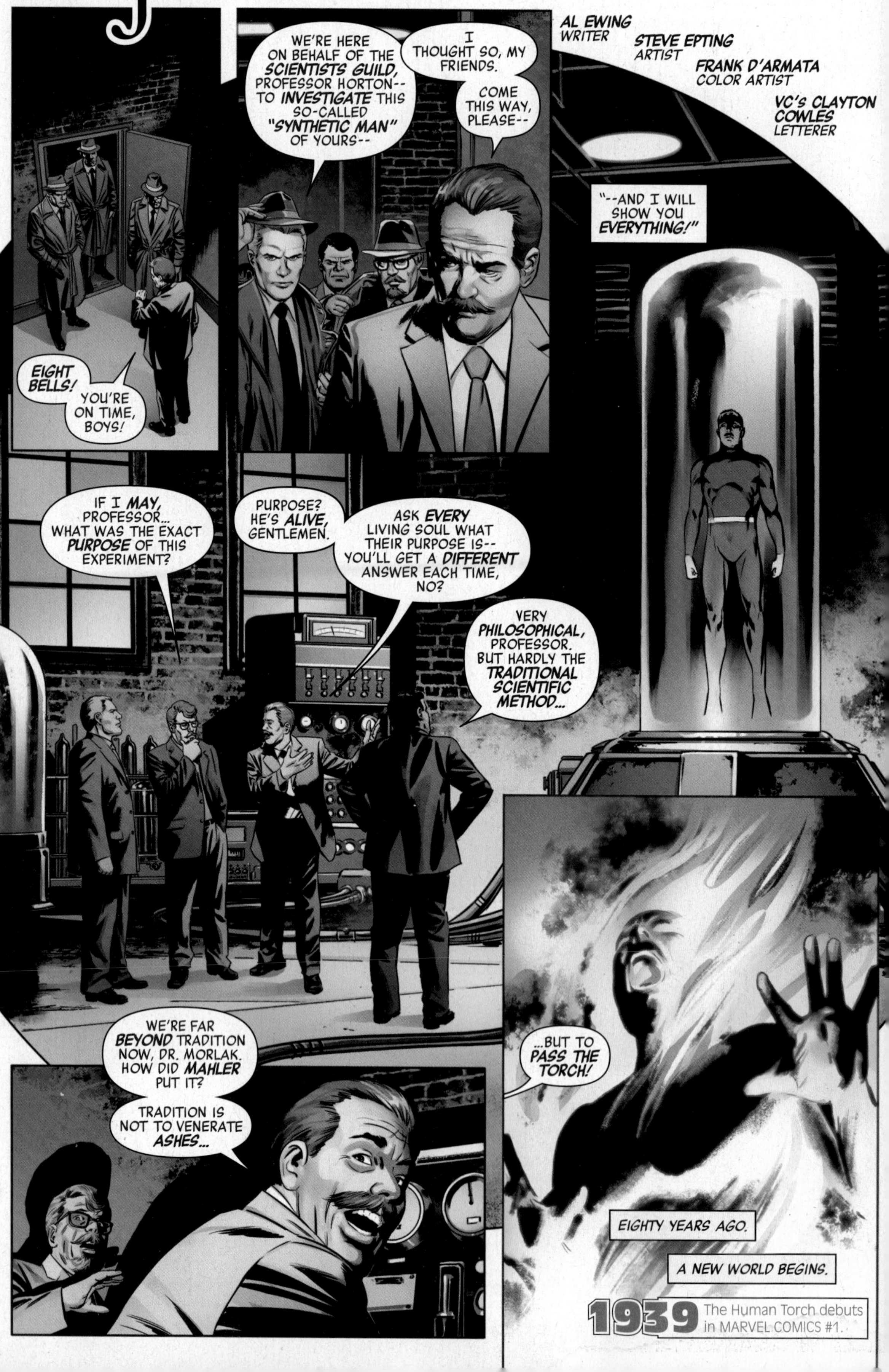
AL EWING WRITER
STEVE EPTING ARTIST
FRANK D'ARMATA COLOR ARTIST
VC's CLAYTON COWLES LETTERER
EIGHT BELLS! YOU'RE ON TIME, BOYS!
WE'RE HERE ON BEHALF OF THE SCIENTISTS GUILD, PROFESSOR HORTON-- TO INVESTIGATE THIS SO-CALLED "SYNTHETIC MAN" OF YOURS--
I THOUGHT SO, MY FRIENDS.
COME THIS WAY, PLEASE--
"--AND I WILL SHOW YOU EVERYTHING!"
IF I MAY, PROFESSOR... WHAT WAS THE EXACT PURPOSE OF THIS EXPERIMENT?
PURPOSE? HE'S ALIVE, GENTLEMEN.
ASK EVERY LIVING SOUL WHAT THEIR PURPOSE IS-- YOU'LL GET A DIFFERENT ANSWER EACH TIME, NO?
VERY PHILOSOPHICAL, PROFESSOR. BUT HARDLY THE TRADITIONAL SCIENTIFIC METHOD...
WE'RE FAR BEYOND TRADITION NOW, DR. MORLAK. HOW DID MAHLER PUT IT?
TRADITION IS NOT TO VENERATE ASHES...
...BUT TO PASS THE TORCH!
EIGHTY YEARS AGO.
A NEW WORLD BEGINS.
1939 The Human Torch debuts in MARVEL COMICS #1.

The OPERATIVE and the X MEN

AL EWING WRITER ❊ PATCH ZIRCHER ARTIST ❊ FRANK D'ARMATA COLOR ARTIST ❊ VC's CLAYTON COWLES LETTERER

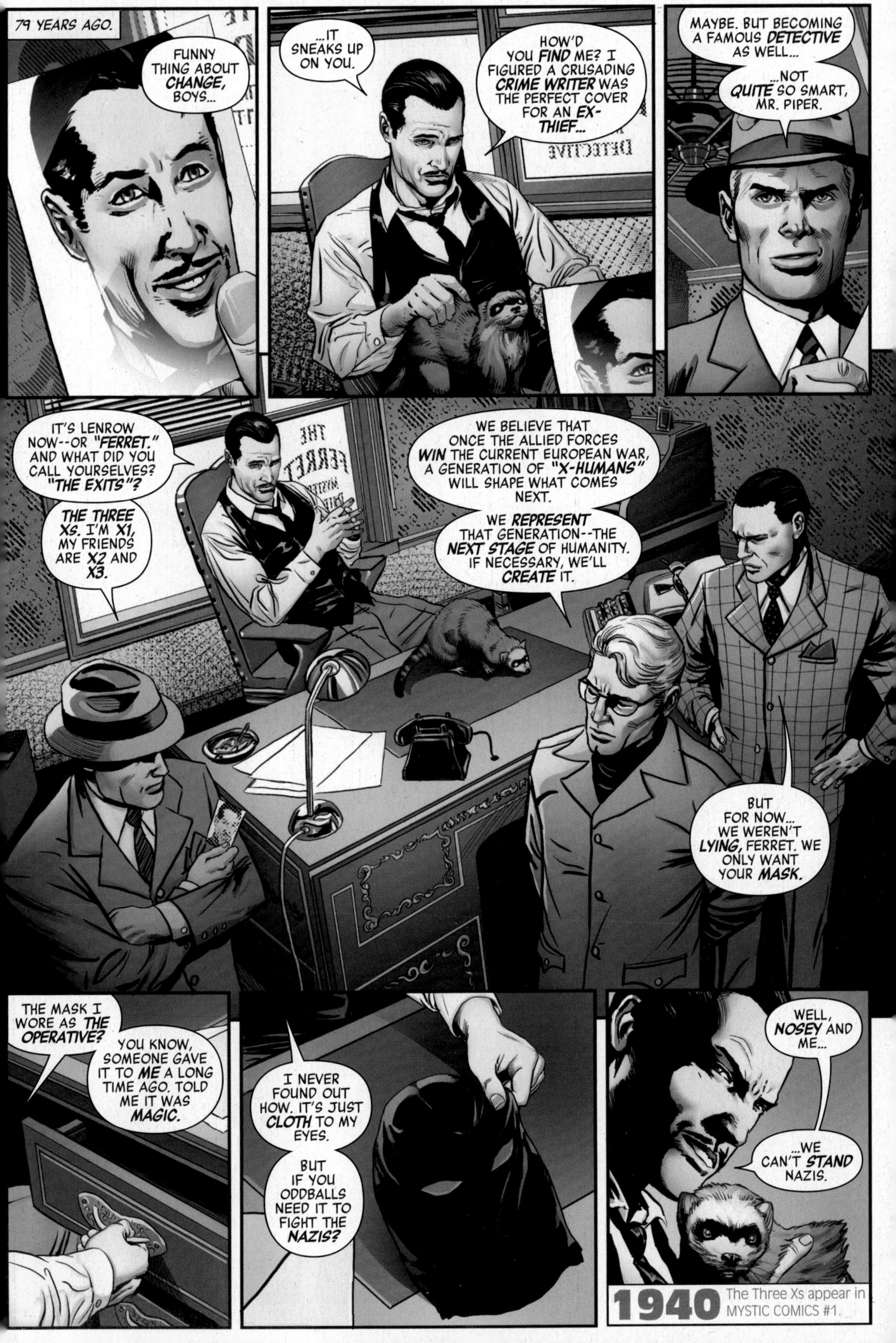
79 YEARS AGO.
FUNNY THING ABOUT CHANGE, BOYS...
...IT SNEAKS UP ON YOU.
HOW'D YOU FIND ME? I FIGURED A CRUSADING CRIME WRITER WAS THE PERFECT COVER FOR AN EX-THIEF...
DETECTIVE
MAYBE. BUT BECOMING A FAMOUS DETECTIVE AS WELL...
...NOT QUITE SO SMART, MR. PIPER.
IT'S LENROW NOW--OR "FERRET." AND WHAT DID YOU CALL YOURSELVES? "THE EXITS"?
THE THREE XS. I'M X1, MY FRIENDS ARE X2 AND X3.
THE FERRET
WE BELIEVE THAT ONCE THE ALLIED FORCES WIN THE CURRENT EUROPEAN WAR, A GENERATION OF "X-HUMANS" WILL SHAPE WHAT COMES NEXT.
WE REPRESENT THAT GENERATION--THE NEXT STAGE OF HUMANITY. IF NECESSARY, WE'LL CREATE IT.
BUT FOR NOW... WE WEREN'T LYING, FERRET. WE ONLY WANT YOUR MASK.
THE MASK I WORE AS THE OPERATIVE?
YOU KNOW, SOMEONE GAVE IT TO ME A LONG TIME AGO. TOLD ME IT WAS MAGIC.
I NEVER FOUND OUT HOW. IT'S JUST CLOTH TO MY EYES.
BUT IF YOU ODDBALLS NEED IT TO FIGHT THE NAZIS?
WELL, NOSEY AND ME...
...WE CAN'T STAND NAZIS.

1940 The Three Xs appear in MYSTIC COMICS #1.

THE OTHER DOOR

AL EWING WRITER ⁂ **LEONARDO ROMERO** ARTIST

JORDIE BELLAIRE COLOR ARTIST ⁂ **VC's CLAYTON COWLES** LETTERER

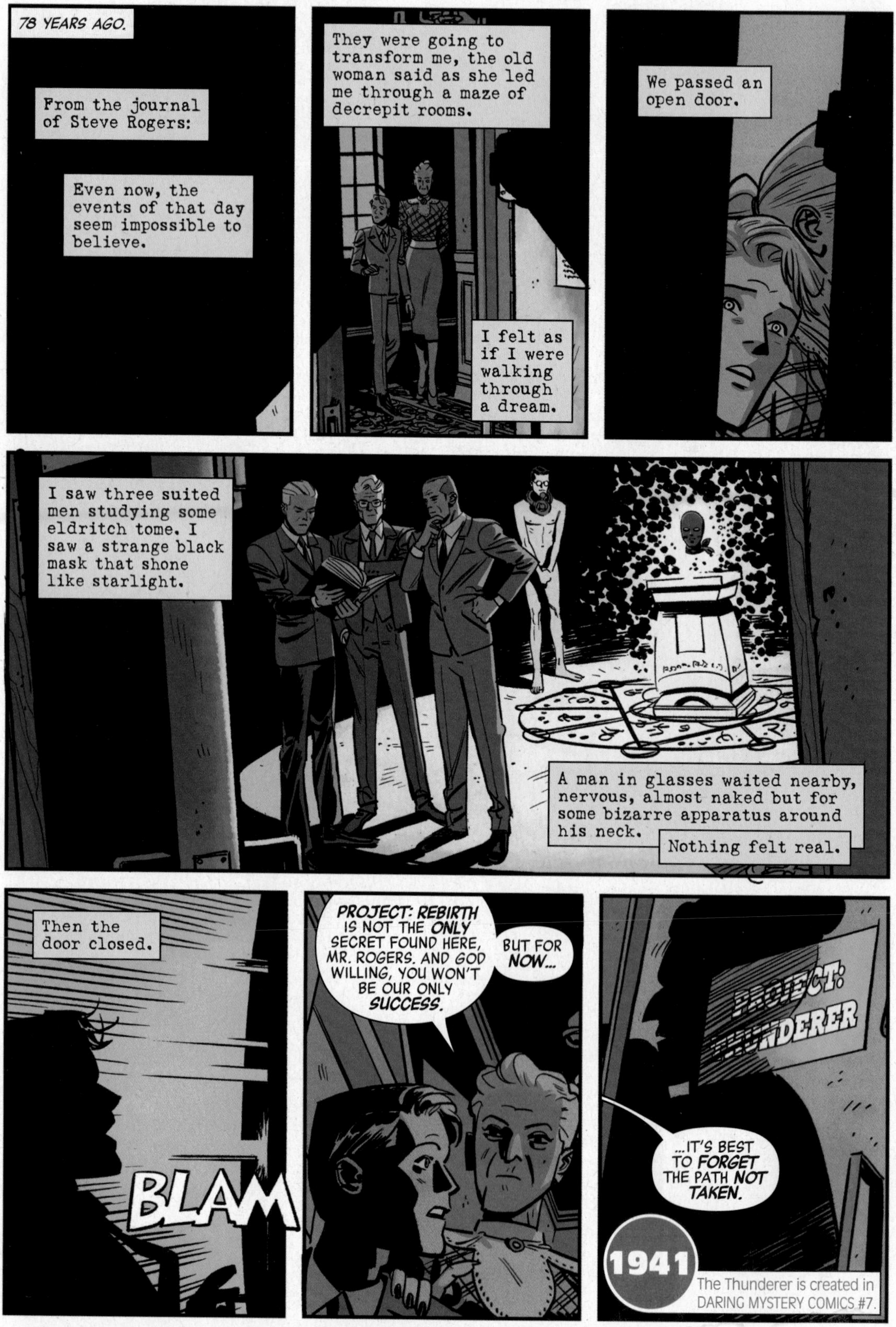

78 YEARS AGO.
From the journal of Steve Rogers:
Even now, the events of that day seem impossible to believe.
They were going to transform me, the old woman said as she led me through a maze of decrepit rooms.
I felt as if I were walking through a dream.
We passed an open door.
I saw three suited men studying some eldritch tome. I saw a strange black mask that shone like starlight.
A man in glasses waited nearby, nervous, almost naked but for some bizarre apparatus around his neck.
Nothing felt real.
Then the door closed.
BLAM
PROJECT: REBIRTH IS NOT THE ONLY SECRET FOUND HERE, MR. ROGERS. AND GOD WILLING, YOU WON'T BE OUR ONLY SUCCESS.
BUT FOR NOW...
PROJECT: THUNDERER
...IT'S BEST TO FORGET THE PATH NOT TAKEN.
1941
The Thunderer is created in DARING MYSTERY COMICS #7.

The LOOP

AL EWING writer • JOSHUA CASSARA artist
RAIN BEREDO color artist • VC's CLAYTON COWLES letterer

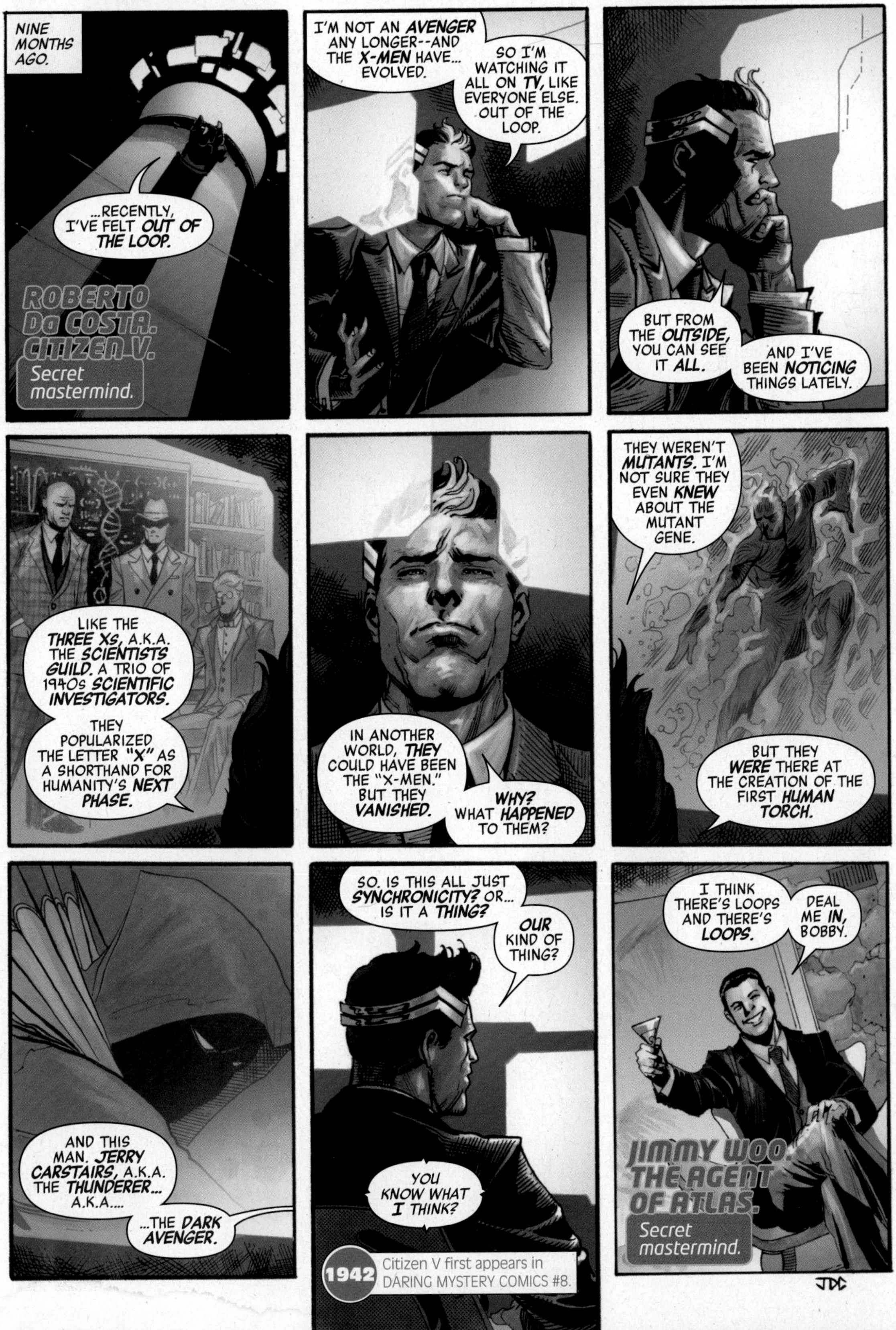

NINE MONTHS AGO.
...RECENTLY, I'VE FELT OUT OF THE LOOP.
ROBERTO Da COSTA. CITIZEN V.
Secret mastermind.
I'M NOT AN AVENGER ANY LONGER--AND THE X-MEN HAVE... EVOLVED.
SO I'M WATCHING IT ALL ON TV, LIKE EVERYONE ELSE. OUT OF THE LOOP.
BUT FROM THE OUTSIDE, YOU CAN SEE IT ALL.
AND I'VE BEEN NOTICING THINGS LATELY.
LIKE THE THREE XS, A.K.A. THE SCIENTISTS GUILD. A TRIO OF 1940s SCIENTIFIC INVESTIGATORS.
THEY POPULARIZED THE LETTER "X" AS A SHORTHAND FOR HUMANITY'S NEXT PHASE.
IN ANOTHER WORLD, THEY COULD HAVE BEEN THE "X-MEN." BUT THEY VANISHED.
WHY? WHAT HAPPENED TO THEM?
THEY WEREN'T MUTANTS. I'M NOT SURE THEY EVEN KNEW ABOUT THE MUTANT GENE.
BUT THEY WERE THERE AT THE CREATION OF THE FIRST HUMAN TORCH.
AND THIS MAN. JERRY CARSTAIRS, A.K.A. THE THUNDERER... A.K.A....
...THE DARK AVENGER.
SO. IS THIS ALL JUST SYNCHRONICITY? OR... IS IT A THING?
OUR KIND OF THING?
YOU KNOW WHAT I THINK?
1942 Citizen V first appears in DARING MYSTERY COMICS #8.
I THINK THERE'S LOOPS AND THERE'S LOOPS.
DEAL ME IN, BOBBY.
JIMMY WOO. THE AGENT OF ATLAS.
Secret mastermind.
JDC

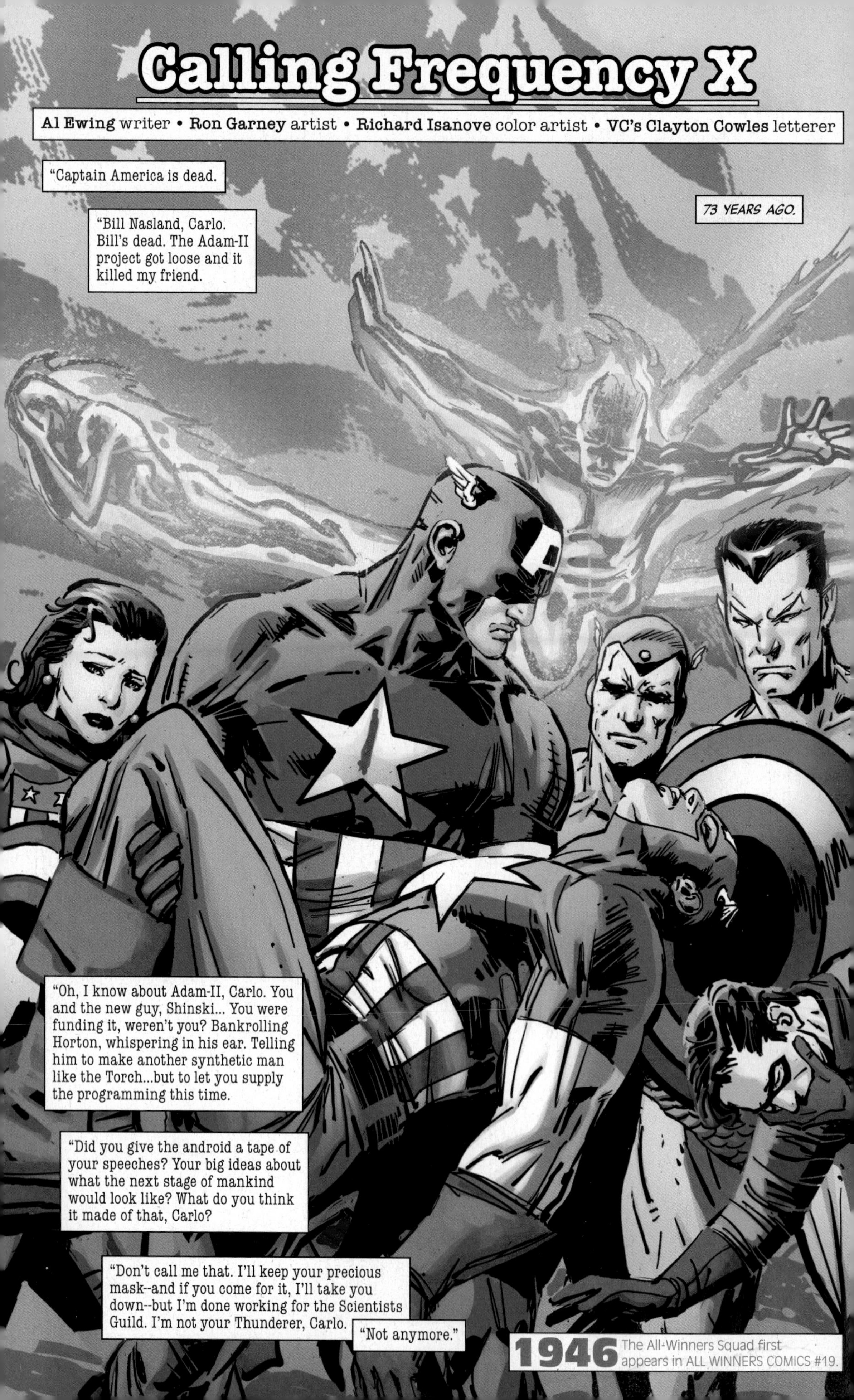
Calling Frequency X
Al Ewing writer • Ron Garney artist • Richard Isanove color artist • VC's Clayton Cowles letterer
"Captain America is dead.
73 YEARS AGO.
"Bill Nasland, Carlo. Bill's dead. The Adam-II project got loose and it killed my friend.
"Oh, I know about Adam-II, Carlo. You and the new guy, Shinski... You were funding it, weren't you? Bankrolling Horton, whispering in his ear. Telling him to make another synthetic man like the Torch...but to let you supply the programming this time.
"Did you give the android a tape of your speeches? Your big ideas about what the next stage of mankind would look like? What do you think it made of that, Carlo?
"Don't call me that. I'll keep your precious mask--and if you come for it, I'll take you down--but I'm done working for the Scientists Guild. I'm not your Thunderer, Carlo.
"Not anymore."
1946 The All-Winners Squad first appears in ALL WINNERS COMICS #19.

DEEP DIVES

AL EWING WRITER
LEONARD KIRK ARTIST
FRANK D'ARMATA COLOR ARTIST
VC's CLAYTON COWLES LETTERER

1947
Namora premieres in MARVEL MYSTERY COMICS #82.

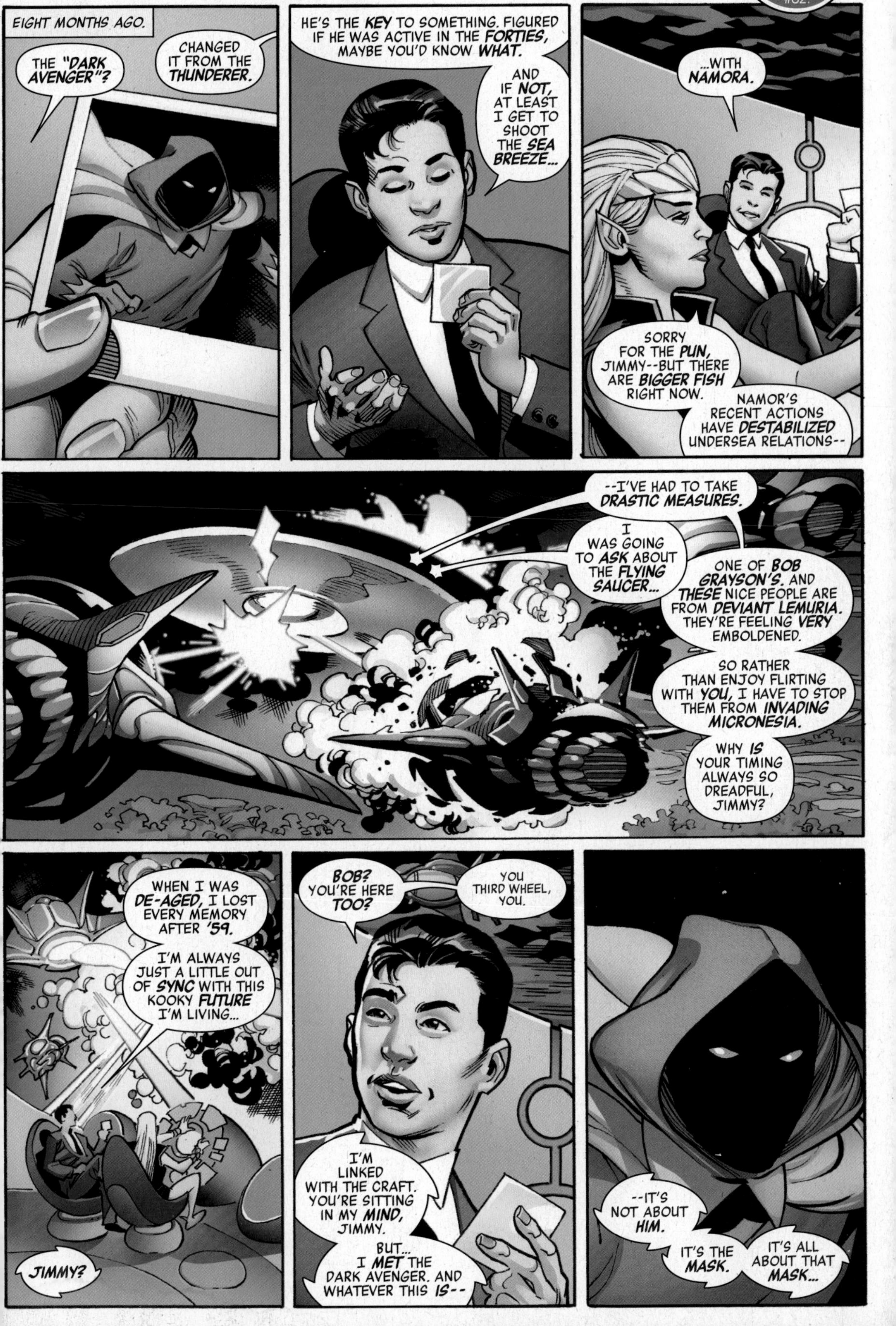

EIGHT MONTHS AGO.
THE "DARK AVENGER"?
CHANGED IT FROM THE THUNDERER.
HE'S THE KEY TO SOMETHING. FIGURED IF HE WAS ACTIVE IN THE FORTIES, MAYBE YOU'D KNOW WHAT.
AND IF NOT, AT LEAST I GET TO SHOOT THE SEA BREEZE...
...WITH NAMORA.
SORRY FOR THE PUN, JIMMY--BUT THERE ARE BIGGER FISH RIGHT NOW.
NAMOR'S RECENT ACTIONS HAVE DESTABILIZED UNDERSEA RELATIONS--
--I'VE HAD TO TAKE DRASTIC MEASURES.
I WAS GOING TO ASK ABOUT THE FLYING SAUCER...
ONE OF BOB GRAYSON'S. AND THESE NICE PEOPLE ARE FROM DEVIANT LEMURIA. THEY'RE FEELING VERY EMBOLDENED.
SO RATHER THAN ENJOY FLIRTING WITH YOU, I HAVE TO STOP THEM FROM INVADING MICRONESIA.
WHY IS YOUR TIMING ALWAYS SO DREADFUL, JIMMY?
WHEN I WAS DE-AGED, I LOST EVERY MEMORY AFTER '59.
I'M ALWAYS JUST A LITTLE OUT OF SYNC WITH THIS KOOKY FUTURE I'M LIVING...
JIMMY?
BOB? YOU'RE HERE TOO?
YOU THIRD WHEEL, YOU.
I'M LINKED WITH THE CRAFT. YOU'RE SITTING IN MY MIND, JIMMY.
BUT... I MET THE DARK AVENGER. AND WHATEVER THIS IS--
--IT'S NOT ABOUT HIM.
IT'S THE MASK.
IT'S ALL ABOUT THAT MASK...

THE BLACK RIDER

AL EWING WRITER ❊ PHIL NOTO ARTIST ❊ VC's CLAYTON COWLES LETTERER

1948 The Black Rider debuts in ALL WESTERN WINNERS #2.

139 YEARS AGO.

From the Journal of Dr. Matt Masters:

THE...THE MASK...

DON'T TAKE IT OFF...DON'T, DOC...

I was trying to help. I keep telling myself that.

I *HAVE* TO. YOU'RE CHOKING ON YOUR OWN BLOOD.

PLEASE, LIE *STILL*--I'M DOING WHAT I CAN, BUT YOU'VE BEEN *SHOT* A DOZEN TIMES--

THAT AIN'T NOTHIN'.

BUT THE MASK...THAT'S A *HOLY* THING... SAVED US FROM *KINGS* AND MADE *THIS* LAND...

WITHOUT IT...I...I CAN'T...

I CAN'T...

But he died of his wounds the moment the mask left his face.

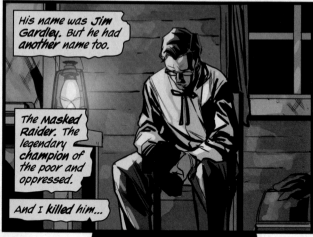

His name was *Jim Gardley.* But he had *another* name too.

The Masked Raider. The legendary champion of the poor and oppressed.

And I *killed* him...

NO. I just couldn't save him.

His killers are still out there. And the mask...

...the mask knows where to go.

63 YEARS AGO.

MY NAME IS JERRY CARSTAIRS.

I'M THE DARK AVENGER.

ROBERT GRAYSON. MARVEL BOY.

HELLO, JERRY.

I HAVE TO KEEP THIS BRIEF.

I'M SENDING THIS MESSAGE ON A FREQUENCY BEYOND ANY CURRENT BROADCAST RANGE.

SO IF YOU CAN HEAR THIS...YOU'RE SOMEONE SPECIAL. MAYBE SPECIAL ENOUGH.

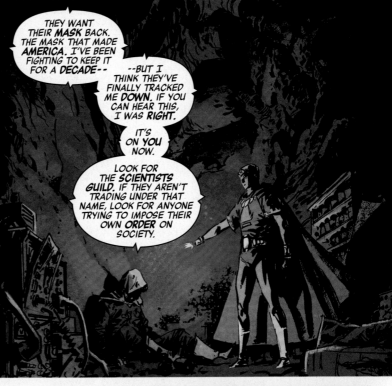

THEY WANT THEIR MASK BACK. THE MASK THAT MADE AMERICA. I'VE BEEN FIGHTING TO KEEP IT FOR A DECADE--

--BUT I THINK THEY'VE FINALLY TRACKED ME DOWN. IF YOU CAN HEAR THIS, I WAS RIGHT.

IT'S ON YOU NOW.

LOOK FOR THE SCIENTISTS GUILD. IF THEY AREN'T TRADING UNDER THAT NAME, LOOK FOR ANYONE TRYING TO IMPOSE THEIR OWN ORDER ON SOCIETY.

SEE, THEY THINK THEY'RE THE X-PEOPLE--THE NEXT WAVE. THEY THINK THEY'RE THE FOUR WHO CHANGE THE WORLD.

THEY'RE NOT. THAT'S WHY THE MASK WON'T WORK FOR--

I HEAR THEM.

I'M OUT OF TIME.

GOOD LUCK.

THANK YOU, JERRY.

THE LAST STAND OF
THE DARK AVENGER

AL EWING WRITER
GABRIEL HARDMAN ARTIST
MATTHEW WILSON COLOR ARTIST
VC's CLAYTON COWLES LETTERER

NICE TO HAVE MET YOU.

1950
Marvel Boy is introduced in MARVEL BOY #1.

KEN HALE in THE MEMBRANE

AL EWING WRITER ⁂ *CORY SMITH* ARTIST ⁂ *LAURA MARTIN* COLOR ARTIST ⁂ *VC'S CLAYTON COWLES* LETTERER

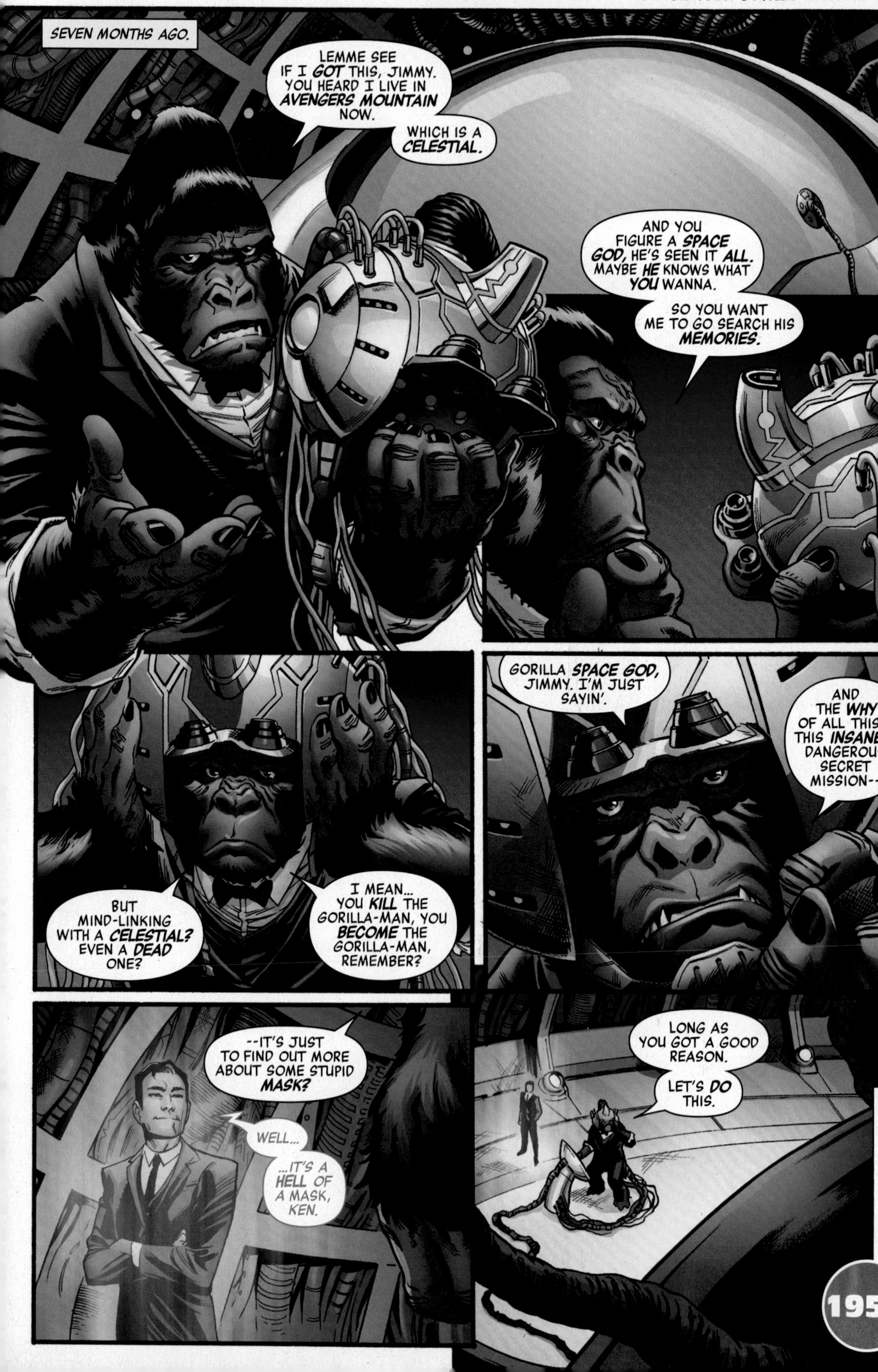
SEVEN MONTHS AGO.
LEMME SEE IF I GOT THIS, JIMMY. YOU HEARD I LIVE IN AVENGERS MOUNTAIN NOW.
WHICH IS A CELESTIAL.
AND YOU FIGURE A SPACE GOD, HE'S SEEN IT ALL. MAYBE HE KNOWS WHAT YOU WANNA.
SO YOU WANT ME TO GO SEARCH HIS MEMORIES.
BUT MIND-LINKING WITH A CELESTIAL? EVEN A DEAD ONE?
I MEAN... YOU KILL THE GORILLA-MAN, YOU BECOME THE GORILLA-MAN, REMEMBER?
GORILLA SPACE GOD, JIMMY. I'M JUST SAYIN'.
AND THE WHY OF ALL THIS-- THIS INSANELY DANGEROUS SECRET MISSION--
--IT'S JUST TO FIND OUT MORE ABOUT SOME STUPID MASK?
WELL...
...IT'S A HELL OF A MASK, KEN.
LONG AS YOU GOT A GOOD REASON.
LET'S DO THIS.

Gorilla-Man first appears in MEN'S ADVENTURES #26.

1954

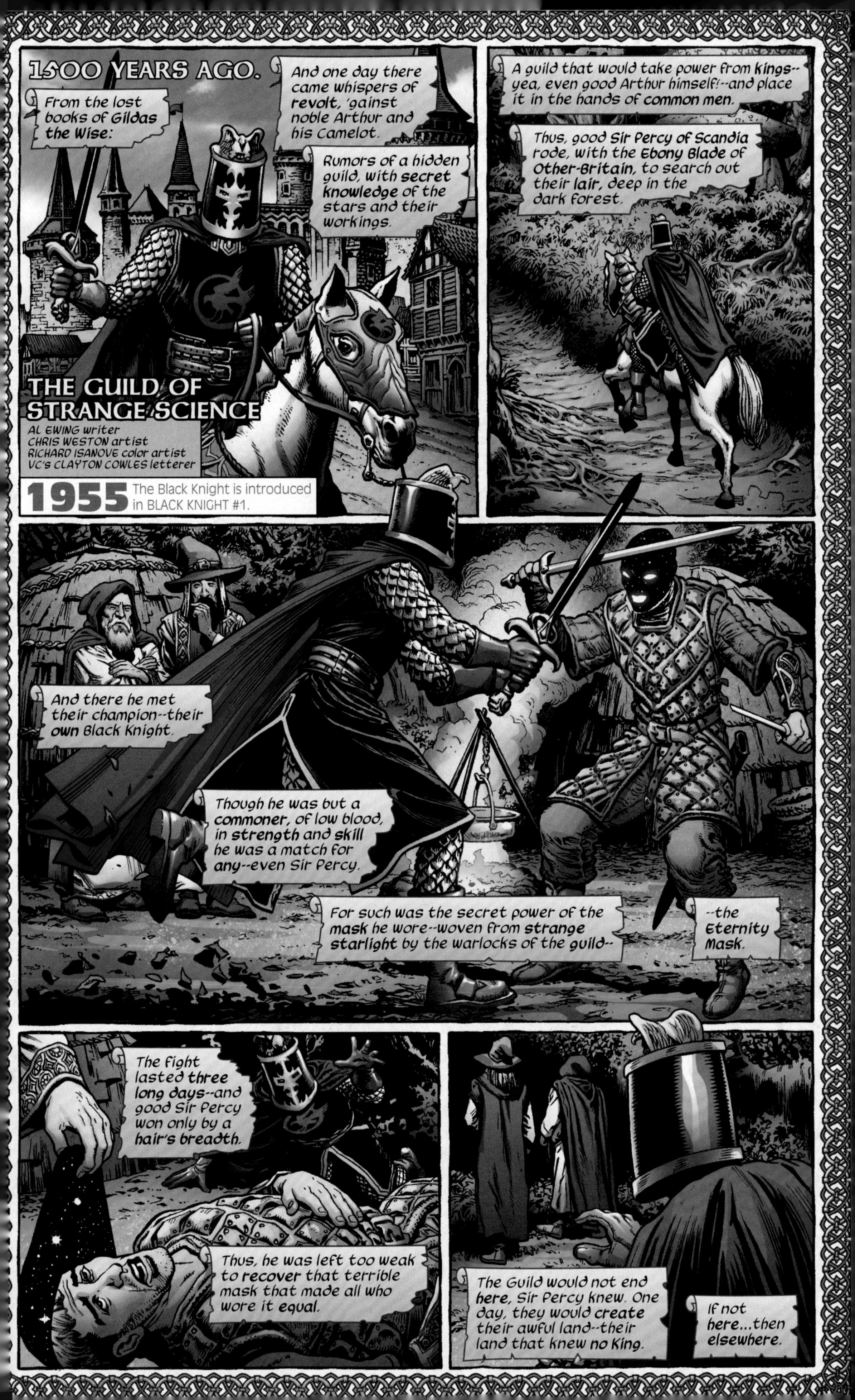
1500 YEARS AGO.
From the lost books of Gildas the Wise:
And one day there came whispers of revolt, 'gainst noble Arthur and his Camelot.
Rumors of a hidden guild, with secret knowledge of the stars and their workings.
THE GUILD OF STRANGE SCIENCE
AL EWING writer
CHRIS WESTON artist
RICHARD ISANOVE color artist
VC's CLAYTON COWLES letterer
1955 The Black Knight is introduced in BLACK KNIGHT #1.
A guild that would take power from kings--yea, even good Arthur himself!--and place it in the hands of common men.
Thus, good Sir Percy of Scandia rode, with the Ebony Blade of Other-Britain, to search out their lair, deep in the dark forest.
And there he met their champion--their own Black Knight.
Though he was but a commoner, of low blood, in strength and skill he was a match for any--even Sir Percy.
For such was the secret power of the mask he wore--woven from strange starlight by the warlocks of the guild--
--the Eternity Mask.
The fight lasted three long days--and good Sir Percy won only by a hair's breadth.
Thus, he was left too weak to recover that terrible mask that made all who wore it equal.
The Guild would not end here, Sir Percy knew. One day, they would create their awful land--their land that knew no King.
If not here...then elsewhere.

1956 Jimmy Woo first appears in YELLOW CLAW #1.

REBELS AND JUDGES

AL EWING • EDUARDO RISSO • JORDIE BELLAIRE • VC's TRAVIS LANHAM

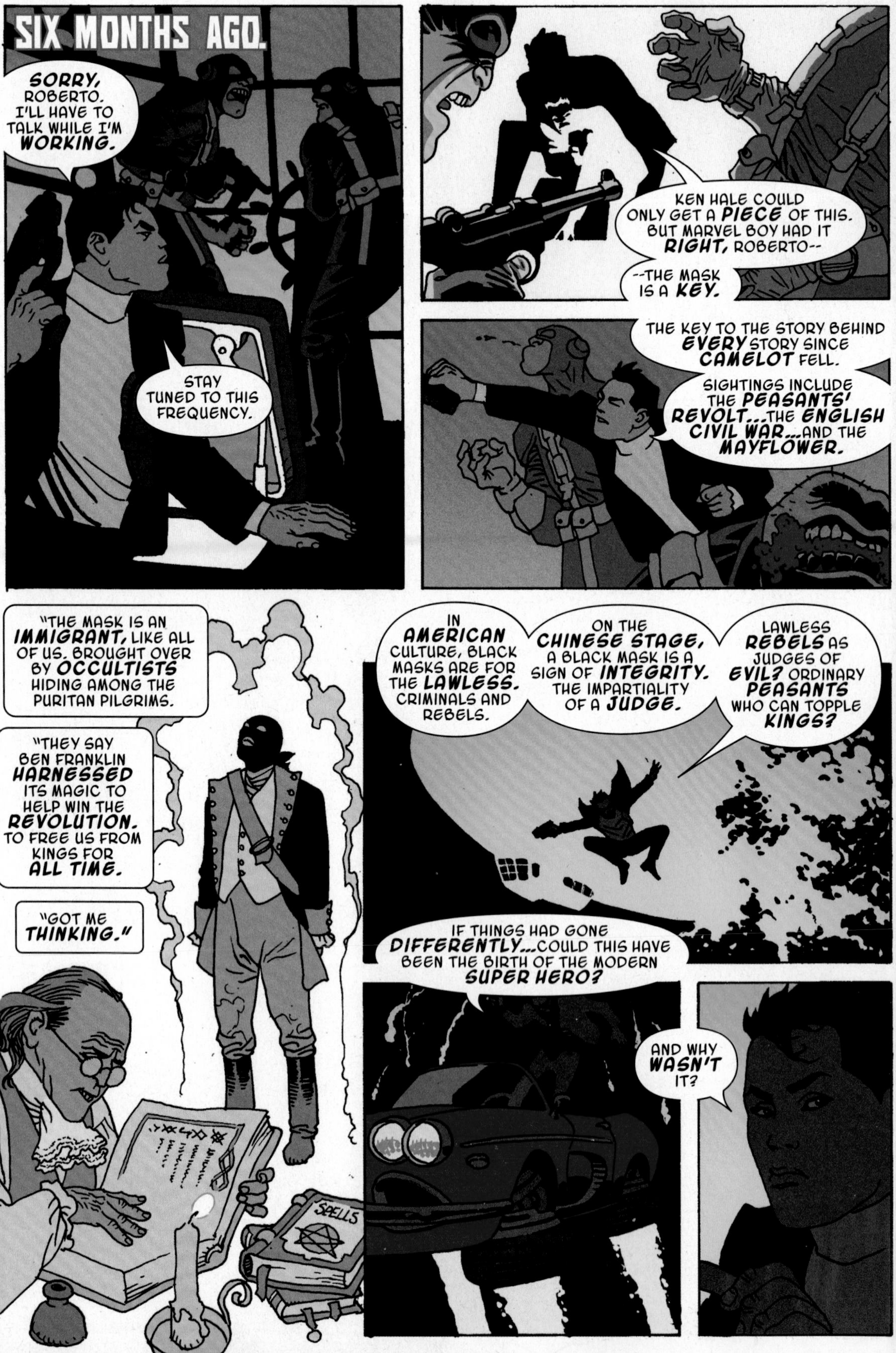

SIX MONTHS AGO.
SORRY, ROBERTO. I'LL HAVE TO TALK WHILE I'M WORKING.
STAY TUNED TO THIS FREQUENCY.
KEN HALE COULD ONLY GET A PIECE OF THIS. BUT MARVEL BOY HAD IT RIGHT, ROBERTO--
--THE MASK IS A KEY.
THE KEY TO THE STORY BEHIND EVERY STORY SINCE CAMELOT FELL.
SIGHTINGS INCLUDE THE PEASANTS' REVOLT...THE ENGLISH CIVIL WAR...AND THE MAYFLOWER.
"THE MASK IS AN IMMIGRANT, LIKE ALL OF US. BROUGHT OVER BY OCCULTISTS HIDING AMONG THE PURITAN PILGRIMS.
"THEY SAY BEN FRANKLIN HARNESSED ITS MAGIC TO HELP WIN THE REVOLUTION. TO FREE US FROM KINGS FOR ALL TIME.
"GOT ME THINKING."
SPELLS
IN AMERICAN CULTURE, BLACK MASKS ARE FOR THE LAWLESS. CRIMINALS AND REBELS.
ON THE CHINESE STAGE, A BLACK MASK IS A SIGN OF INTEGRITY. THE IMPARTIALITY OF A JUDGE.
LAWLESS REBELS AS JUDGES OF EVIL? ORDINARY PEASANTS WHO CAN TOPPLE KINGS?
IF THINGS HAD GONE DIFFERENTLY...COULD THIS HAVE BEEN THE BIRTH OF THE MODERN SUPER HERO?
AND WHY WASN'T IT?

DENNIS PIPER'S LAST HEIST

al ewing — cafu — rain beredo — vc's travis lanham

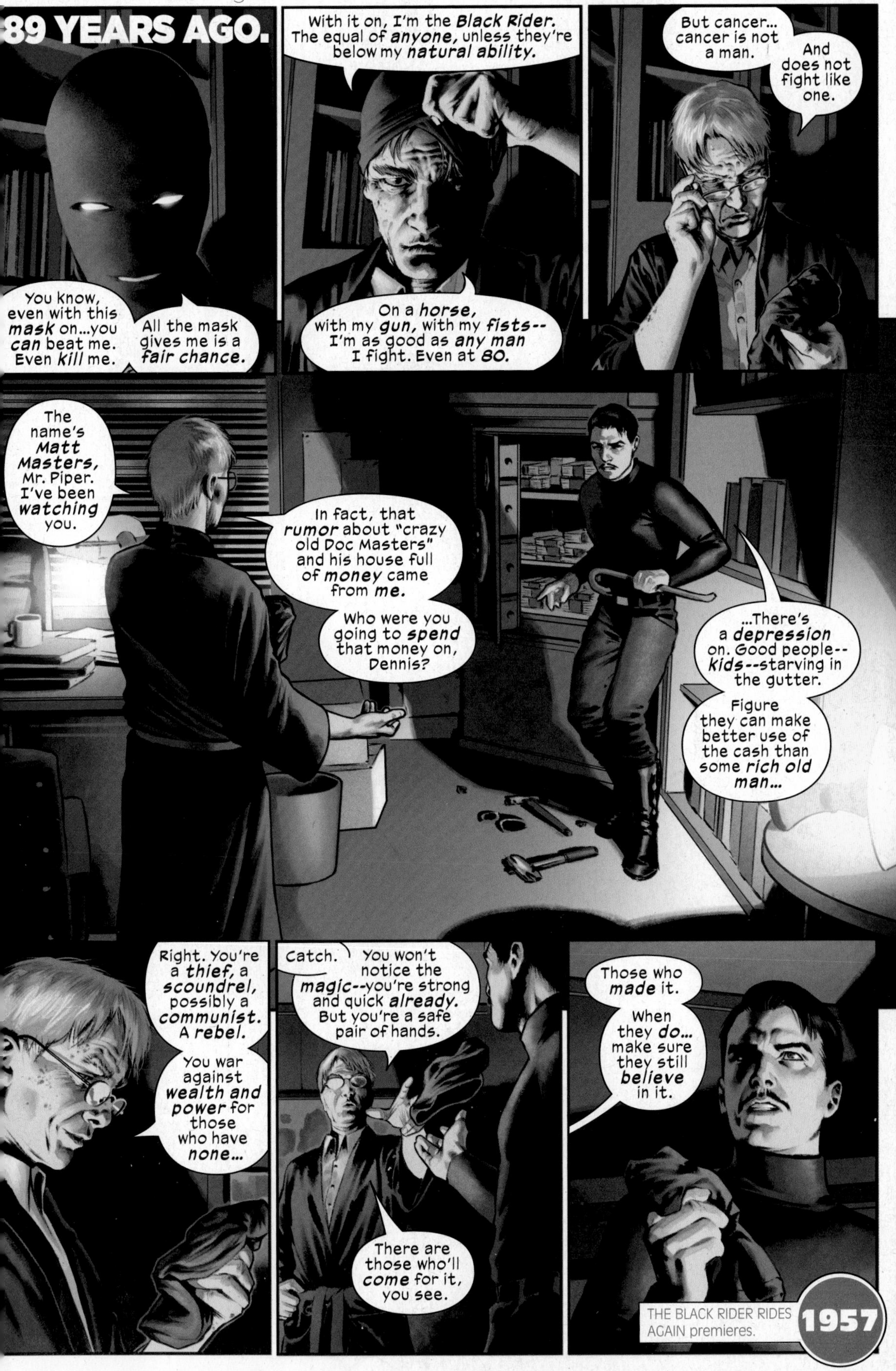
89 YEARS AGO.
You know, even with this mask on...you can beat me. Even kill me.
All the mask gives me is a fair chance.
With it on, I'm the Black Rider. The equal of anyone, unless they're below my natural ability.
On a horse, with my gun, with my fists-- I'm as good as any man I fight. Even at 80.
But cancer... cancer is not a man.
And does not fight like one.
The name's Matt Masters, Mr. Piper. I've been watching you.
In fact, that rumor about "crazy old Doc Masters" and his house full of money came from me.
Who were you going to spend that money on, Dennis?
...There's a depression on. Good people-- kids--starving in the gutter.
Figure they can make better use of the cash than some rich old man...
Right. You're a thief, a scoundrel, possibly a communist. A rebel.
You war against wealth and power for those who have none...
Catch.
You won't notice the magic--you're strong and quick already. But you're a safe pair of hands.
There are those who'll come for it, you see.
Those who made it.
When they do... make sure they still believe in it.
THE BLACK RIDER RIDES AGAIN premieres.
1957

STRANGE WORLDS

AL EWING: writer KLAUS JANSON: artist
RICHARD ISANOVE: colors VC's TRAVIS LANHAM: letter

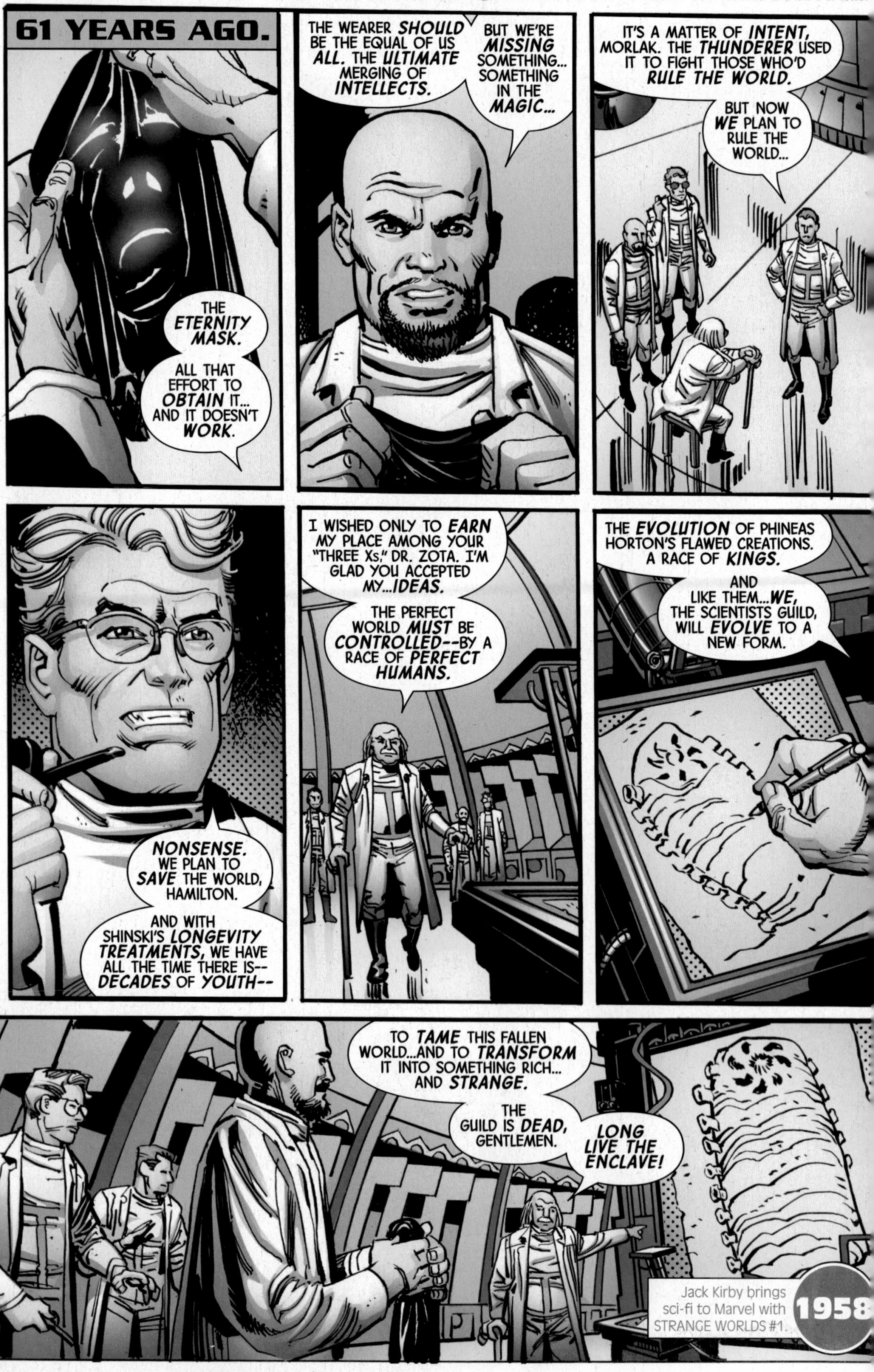

61 YEARS AGO.
THE ETERNITY MASK.
ALL THAT EFFORT TO OBTAIN IT... AND IT DOESN'T WORK.
THE WEARER SHOULD BE THE EQUAL OF US ALL. THE ULTIMATE MERGING OF INTELLECTS.
BUT WE'RE MISSING SOMETHING... SOMETHING IN THE MAGIC...
IT'S A MATTER OF INTENT, MORLAK. THE THUNDERER USED IT TO FIGHT THOSE WHO'D RULE THE WORLD.
BUT NOW WE PLAN TO RULE THE WORLD...
NONSENSE. WE PLAN TO SAVE THE WORLD, HAMILTON.
AND WITH SHINSKI'S LONGEVITY TREATMENTS, WE HAVE ALL THE TIME THERE IS--DECADES OF YOUTH--
I WISHED ONLY TO EARN MY PLACE AMONG YOUR "THREE XS," DR. ZOTA. I'M GLAD YOU ACCEPTED MY...IDEAS.
THE PERFECT WORLD MUST BE CONTROLLED--BY A RACE OF PERFECT HUMANS.
THE EVOLUTION OF PHINEAS HORTON'S FLAWED CREATIONS. A RACE OF KINGS.
AND LIKE THEM...WE, THE SCIENTISTS GUILD, WILL EVOLVE TO A NEW FORM.
TO TAME THIS FALLEN WORLD...AND TO TRANSFORM IT INTO SOMETHING RICH... AND STRANGE.
THE GUILD IS DEAD, GENTLEMEN.
LONG LIVE THE ENCLAVE!

Jack Kirby brings sci-fi to Marvel with STRANGE WORLDS #1. 1958

1967 Adam Warlock is introduced as Him in FANTASTIC FOUR #67.

HIM

AL EWING SCRIPT JOE BENNETT PENCILS RUY JOSÉ INKS
PAUL MOUNTS COLORS VC's TRAVIS LANHAM LETTERS

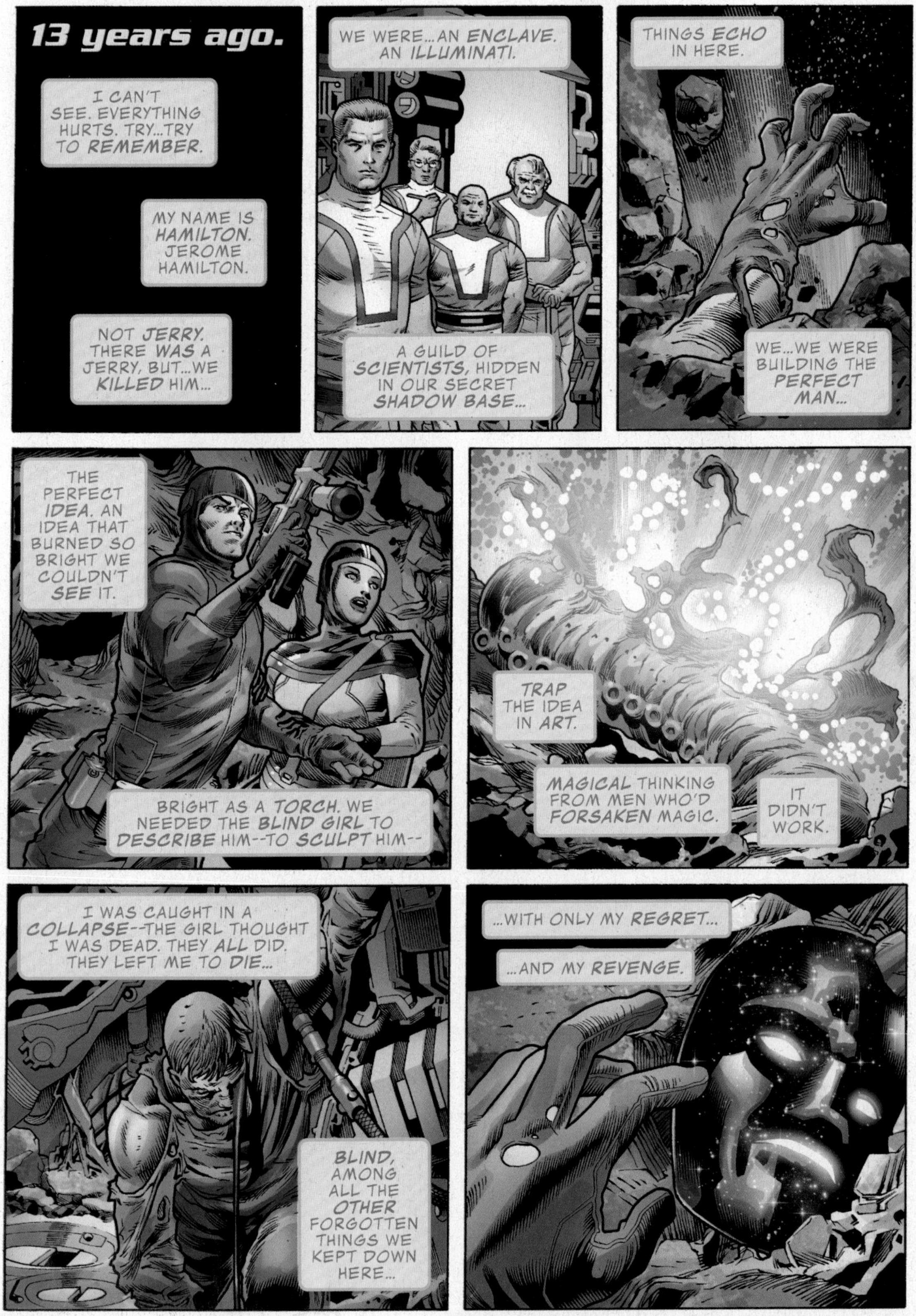
13 years ago.
I CAN'T SEE. EVERYTHING HURTS. TRY...TRY TO REMEMBER.
MY NAME IS HAMILTON. JEROME HAMILTON.
NOT JERRY. THERE WAS A JERRY, BUT...WE KILLED HIM...
WE WERE...AN ENCLAVE. AN ILLUMINATI.
A GUILD OF SCIENTISTS, HIDDEN IN OUR SECRET SHADOW BASE...
THINGS ECHO IN HERE.
WE...WE WERE BUILDING THE PERFECT MAN...
THE PERFECT IDEA. AN IDEA THAT BURNED SO BRIGHT WE COULDN'T SEE IT.
BRIGHT AS A TORCH. WE NEEDED THE BLIND GIRL TO DESCRIBE HIM--TO SCULPT HIM--
TRAP THE IDEA IN ART.
MAGICAL THINKING FROM MEN WHO'D FORSAKEN MAGIC.
IT DIDN'T WORK.
I WAS CAUGHT IN A COLLAPSE--THE GIRL THOUGHT I WAS DEAD. THEY ALL DID. THEY LEFT ME TO DIE...
BLIND, AMONG ALL THE OTHER FORGOTTEN THINGS WE KEPT DOWN HERE...
...WITH ONLY MY REGRET...
...AND MY REVENGE.

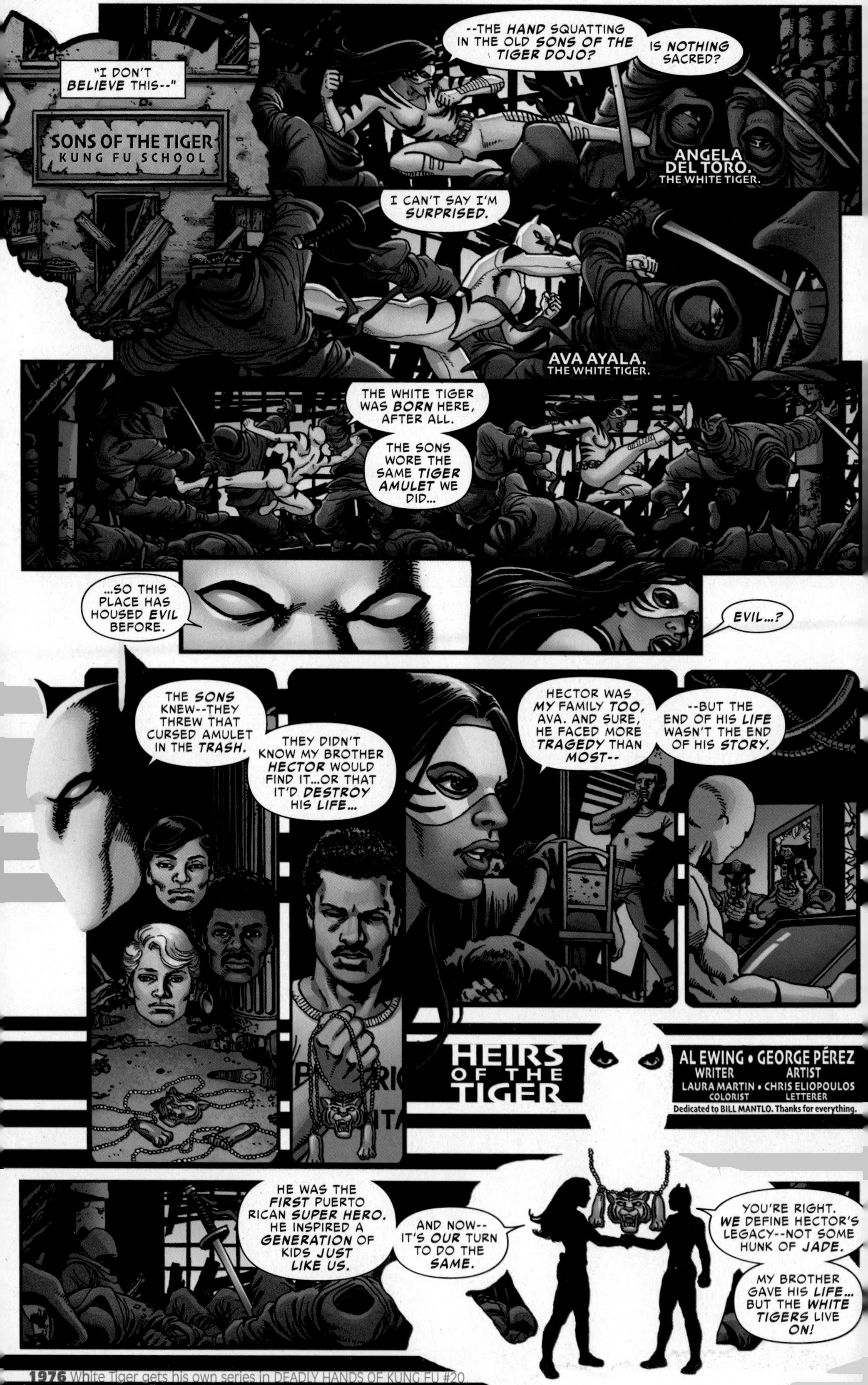
"I DON'T BELIEVE THIS--"
SONS OF THE TIGER KUNG FU SCHOOL
--THE HAND SQUATTING IN THE OLD SONS OF THE TIGER DOJO?
IS NOTHING SACRED?
ANGELA DEL TORO. THE WHITE TIGER.
I CAN'T SAY I'M SURPRISED.
AVA AYALA. THE WHITE TIGER.
THE WHITE TIGER WAS BORN HERE, AFTER ALL.
THE SONS WORE THE SAME TIGER AMULET WE DID...
...SO THIS PLACE HAS HOUSED EVIL BEFORE.
EVIL...?
THE SONS KNEW--THEY THREW THAT CURSED AMULET IN THE TRASH.
THEY DIDN'T KNOW MY BROTHER HECTOR WOULD FIND IT...OR THAT IT'D DESTROY HIS LIFE...
HECTOR WAS MY FAMILY TOO, AVA. AND SURE, HE FACED MORE TRAGEDY THAN MOST--
--BUT THE END OF HIS LIFE WASN'T THE END OF HIS STORY.
HEIRS OF THE TIGER
AL EWING • GEORGE PÉREZ
WRITER ARTIST
LAURA MARTIN • CHRIS ELIOPOULOS
COLORIST LETTERER
Dedicated to BILL MANTLO. Thanks for everything.
HE WAS THE FIRST PUERTO RICAN SUPER HERO. HE INSPIRED A GENERATION OF KIDS JUST LIKE US.
AND NOW-- IT'S OUR TURN TO DO THE SAME.
YOU'RE RIGHT. WE DEFINE HECTOR'S LEGACY--NOT SOME HUNK OF JADE.
MY BROTHER GAVE HIS LIFE... BUT THE WHITE TIGERS LIVE ON!

1976 White Tiger gets his own series in DEADLY HANDS OF KUNG FU #20.

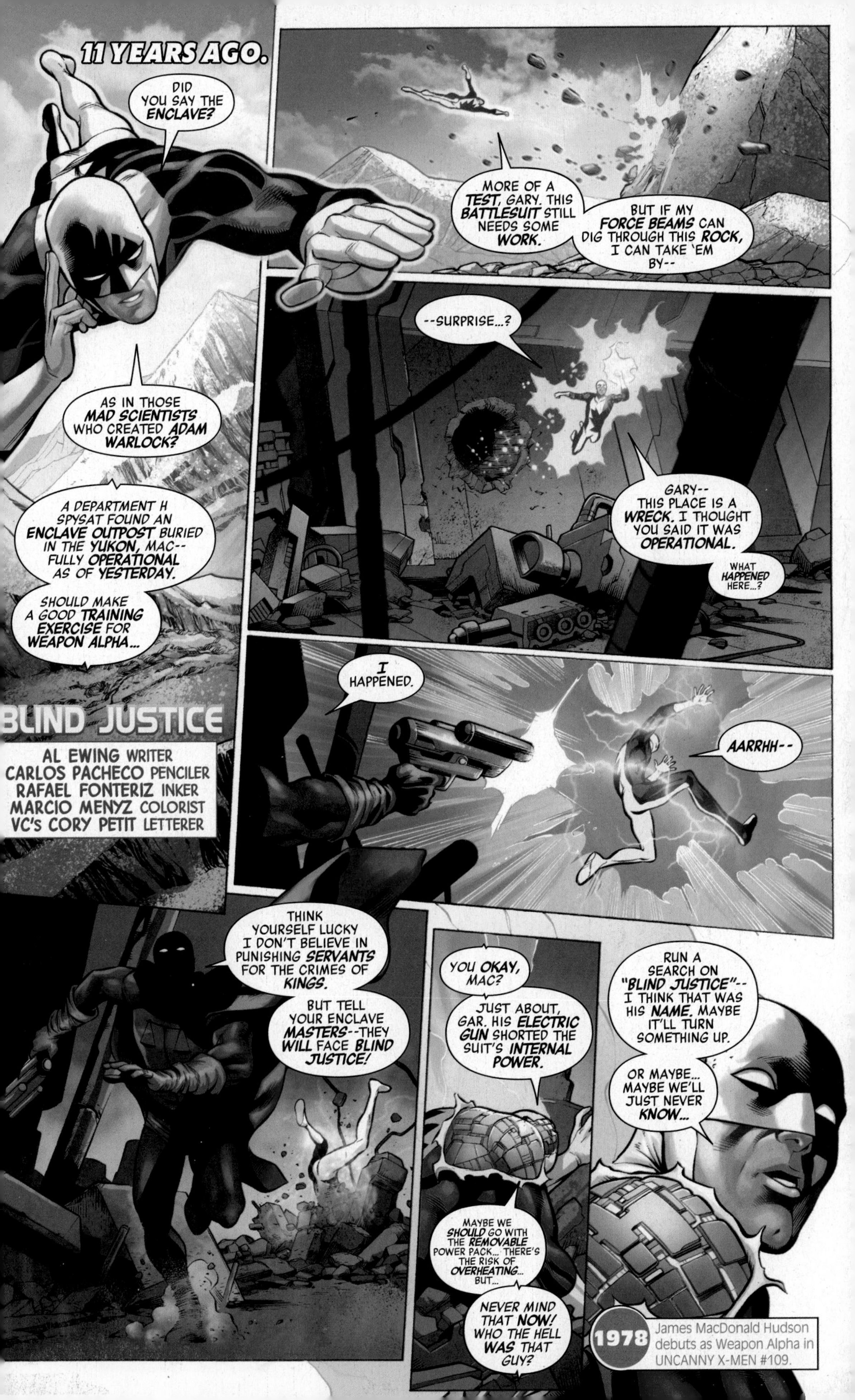
11 YEARS AGO.
DID YOU SAY THE ENCLAVE?
AS IN THOSE MAD SCIENTISTS WHO CREATED ADAM WARLOCK?
A DEPARTMENT H SPYSAT FOUND AN ENCLAVE OUTPOST BURIED IN THE YUKON, MAC-- FULLY OPERATIONAL AS OF YESTERDAY.
SHOULD MAKE A GOOD TRAINING EXERCISE FOR WEAPON ALPHA...
MORE OF A TEST, GARY. THIS BATTLESUIT STILL NEEDS SOME WORK.
BUT IF MY FORCE BEAMS CAN DIG THROUGH THIS ROCK, I CAN TAKE 'EM BY--
--SURPRISE...?
GARY-- THIS PLACE IS A WRECK. I THOUGHT YOU SAID IT WAS OPERATIONAL.
WHAT HAPPENED HERE...?
I HAPPENED.
AARRHH--
BLIND JUSTICE
AL EWING WRITER
CARLOS PACHECO PENCILER
RAFAEL FONTERIZ INKER
MARCIO MENYZ COLORIST
VC's CORY PETIT LETTERER
THINK YOURSELF LUCKY I DON'T BELIEVE IN PUNISHING SERVANTS FOR THE CRIMES OF KINGS.
BUT TELL YOUR ENCLAVE MASTERS--THEY WILL FACE BLIND JUSTICE!
YOU OKAY, MAC?
JUST ABOUT, GAR. HIS ELECTRIC GUN SHORTED THE SUIT'S INTERNAL POWER.
MAYBE WE SHOULD GO WITH THE REMOVABLE POWER PACK... THERE'S THE RISK OF OVERHEATING... BUT...
NEVER MIND THAT NOW! WHO THE HELL WAS THAT GUY?
RUN A SEARCH ON "BLIND JUSTICE"-- I THINK THAT WAS HIS NAME. MAYBE IT'LL TURN SOMETHING UP.
OR MAYBE... MAYBE WE'LL JUST NEVER KNOW...
1978 James MacDonald Hudson debuts as Weapon Alpha in UNCANNY X-MEN #109.

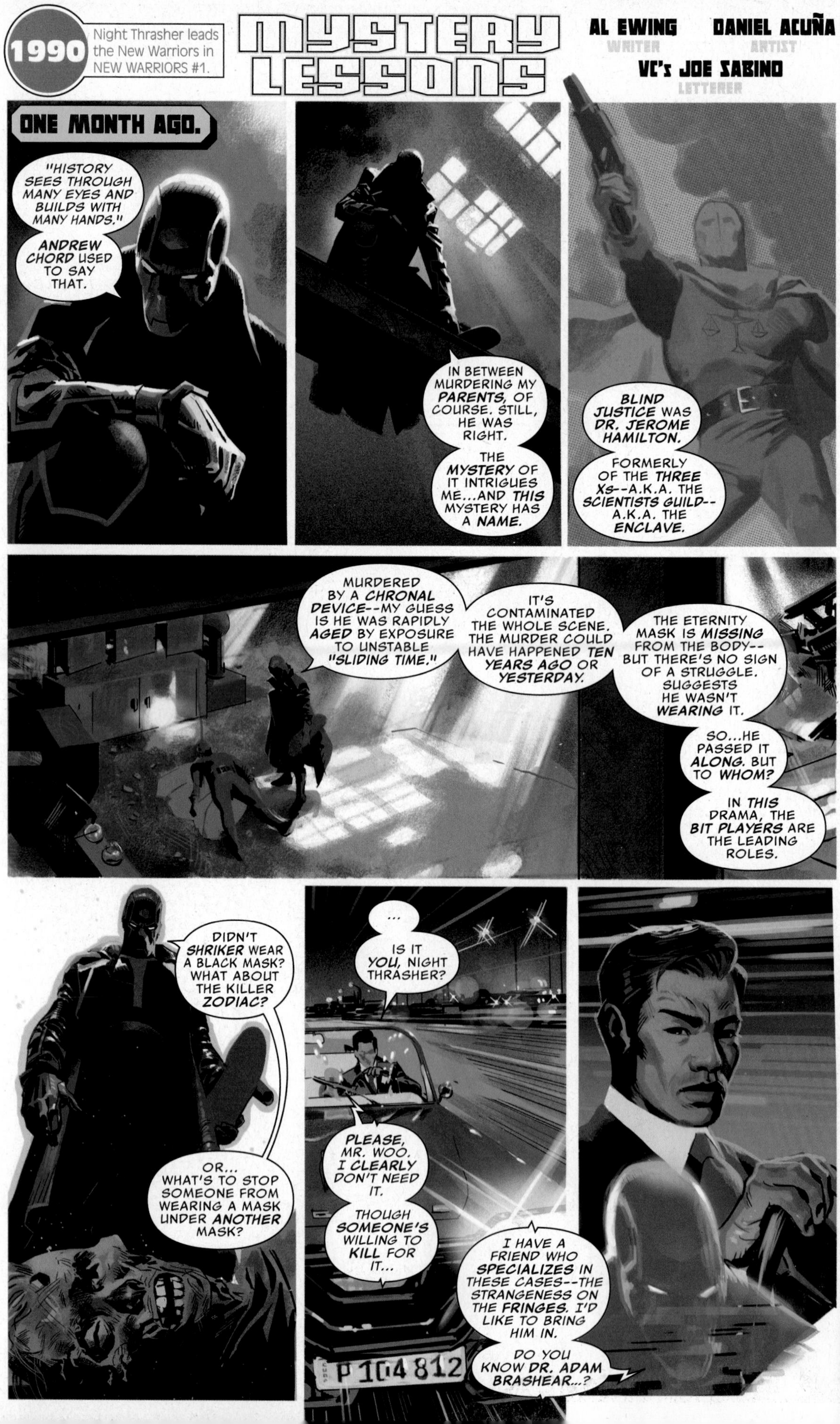
1990
Night Thrasher leads the New Warriors in NEW WARRIORS #1.
MYSTERY LESSONS
AL EWING WRITER
DANIEL ACUÑA ARTIST
VC's JOE SABINO LETTERER
ONE MONTH AGO.
"HISTORY SEES THROUGH MANY EYES AND BUILDS WITH MANY HANDS."
ANDREW CHORD USED TO SAY THAT.
IN BETWEEN MURDERING MY PARENTS, OF COURSE. STILL, HE WAS RIGHT.
THE MYSTERY OF IT INTRIGUES ME...AND THIS MYSTERY HAS A NAME.
BLIND JUSTICE WAS DR. JEROME HAMILTON.
FORMERLY OF THE THREE Xs--A.K.A. THE SCIENTISTS GUILD--A.K.A. THE ENCLAVE.
MURDERED BY A CHRONAL DEVICE--MY GUESS IS HE WAS RAPIDLY AGED BY EXPOSURE TO UNSTABLE "SLIDING TIME."
IT'S CONTAMINATED THE WHOLE SCENE. THE MURDER COULD HAVE HAPPENED TEN YEARS AGO OR YESTERDAY.
THE ETERNITY MASK IS MISSING FROM THE BODY--BUT THERE'S NO SIGN OF A STRUGGLE. SUGGESTS HE WASN'T WEARING IT.
SO...HE PASSED IT ALONG. BUT TO WHOM?
IN THIS DRAMA, THE BIT PLAYERS ARE THE LEADING ROLES.
DIDN'T SHRIKER WEAR A BLACK MASK? WHAT ABOUT THE KILLER ZODIAC?
OR...WHAT'S TO STOP SOMEONE FROM WEARING A MASK UNDER ANOTHER MASK?
...
IS IT YOU, NIGHT THRASHER?
PLEASE, MR. WOO. I CLEARLY DON'T NEED IT.
THOUGH SOMEONE'S WILLING TO KILL FOR IT...
I HAVE A FRIEND WHO SPECIALIZES IN THESE CASES--THE STRANGENESS ON THE FRINGES. I'D LIKE TO BRING HIM IN.
DO YOU KNOW DR. ADAM BRASHEAR...?
P 104 812

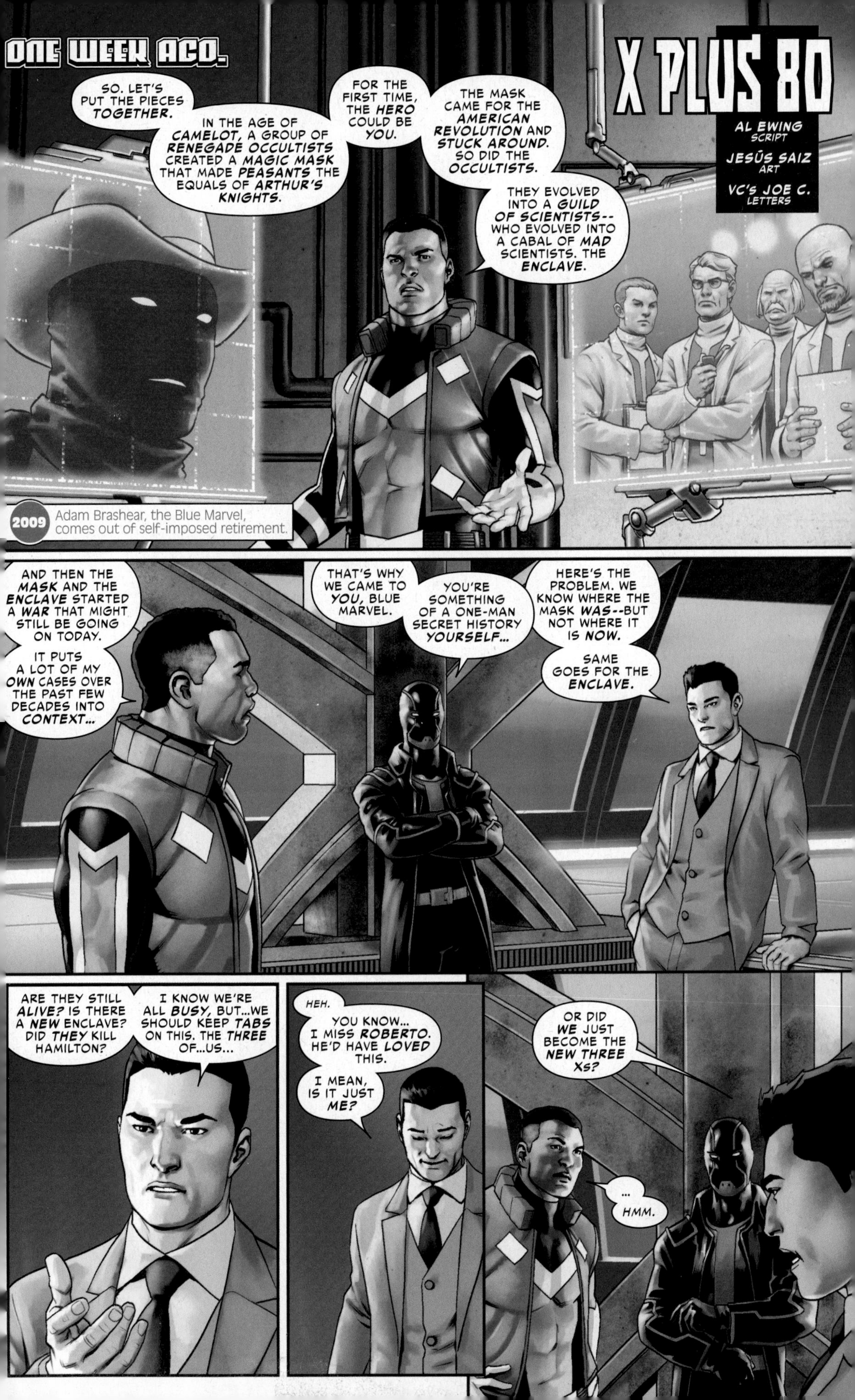
ONE WEEK AGO.
X PLUS 80
AL EWING SCRIPT
JESÛS SAIZ ART
VC's JOE C. LETTERS
SO. LET'S PUT THE PIECES TOGETHER.
IN THE AGE OF CAMELOT, A GROUP OF RENEGADE OCCULTISTS CREATED A MAGIC MASK THAT MADE PEASANTS THE EQUALS OF ARTHUR'S KNIGHTS.
FOR THE FIRST TIME, THE HERO COULD BE YOU.
THE MASK CAME FOR THE AMERICAN REVOLUTION AND STUCK AROUND. SO DID THE OCCULTISTS.
THEY EVOLVED INTO A GUILD OF SCIENTISTS--WHO EVOLVED INTO A CABAL OF MAD SCIENTISTS. THE ENCLAVE.
2009 Adam Brashear, the Blue Marvel, comes out of self-imposed retirement.
AND THEN THE MASK AND THE ENCLAVE STARTED A WAR THAT MIGHT STILL BE GOING ON TODAY.
IT PUTS A LOT OF MY OWN CASES OVER THE PAST FEW DECADES INTO CONTEXT...
THAT'S WHY WE CAME TO YOU, BLUE MARVEL.
YOU'RE SOMETHING OF A ONE-MAN SECRET HISTORY YOURSELF...
HERE'S THE PROBLEM. WE KNOW WHERE THE MASK WAS--BUT NOT WHERE IT IS NOW.
SAME GOES FOR THE ENCLAVE.
ARE THEY STILL ALIVE? IS THERE A NEW ENCLAVE? DID THEY KILL HAMILTON?
I KNOW WE'RE ALL BUSY, BUT...WE SHOULD KEEP TABS ON THIS. THE THREE OF...US...
HEH.
YOU KNOW... I MISS ROBERTO. HE'D HAVE LOVED THIS.
I MEAN, IS IT JUST ME?
OR DID WE JUST BECOME THE NEW THREE Xs?
... HMM.

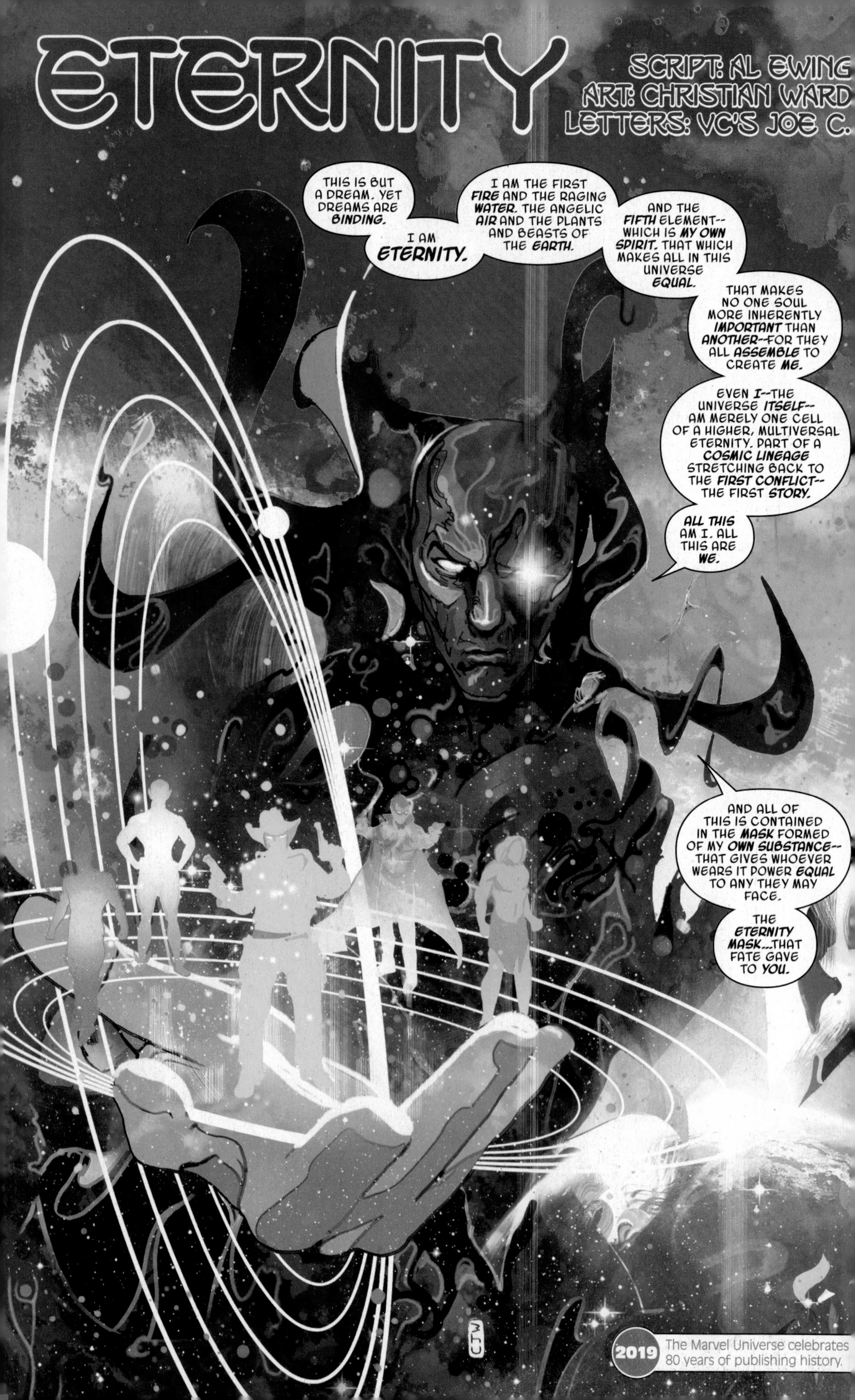
ETERNITY
SCRIPT: AL EWING
ART: CHRISTIAN WARD
LETTERS: VC'S JOE C.
THIS IS BUT A DREAM. YET DREAMS ARE BINDING.
I AM ETERNITY.
I AM THE FIRST FIRE AND THE RAGING WATER. THE ANGELIC AIR AND THE PLANTS AND BEASTS OF THE EARTH.
AND THE FIFTH ELEMENT-- WHICH IS MY OWN SPIRIT. THAT WHICH MAKES ALL IN THIS UNIVERSE EQUAL.
THAT MAKES NO ONE SOUL MORE INHERENTLY IMPORTANT THAN ANOTHER--FOR THEY ALL ASSEMBLE TO CREATE ME.
EVEN I--THE UNIVERSE ITSELF-- AM MERELY ONE CELL OF A HIGHER, MULTIVERSAL ETERNITY. PART OF A COSMIC LINEAGE STRETCHING BACK TO THE FIRST CONFLICT-- THE FIRST STORY.
ALL THIS AM I. ALL THIS ARE WE.
AND ALL OF THIS IS CONTAINED IN THE MASK FORMED OF MY OWN SUBSTANCE-- THAT GIVES WHOEVER WEARS IT POWER EQUAL TO ANY THEY MAY FACE.
THE ETERNITY MASK...THAT FATE GAVE TO YOU.
CJW

2019 The Marvel Universe celebrates 80 years of publishing history.

THE MASK...

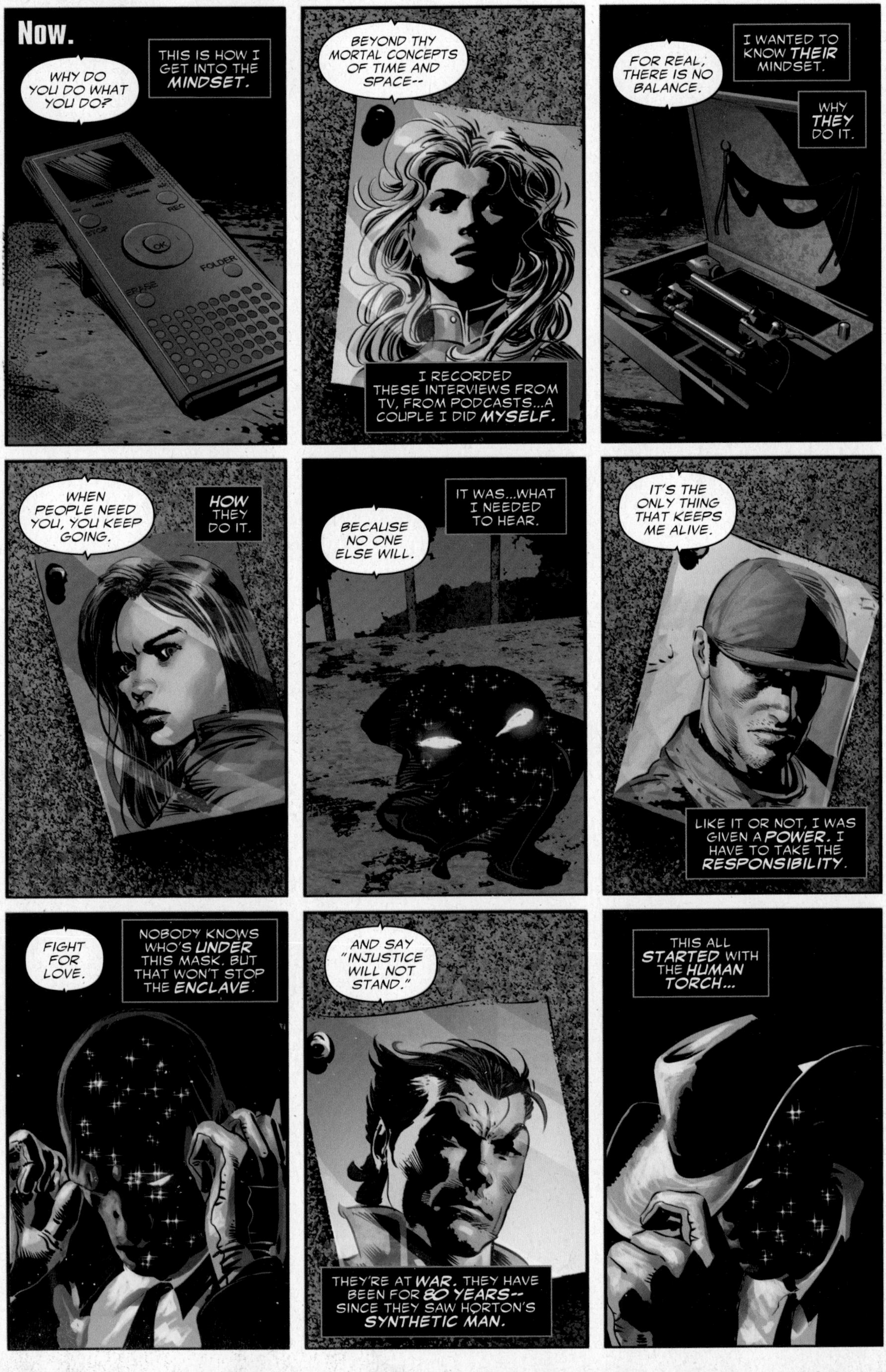

Now.
THIS IS HOW I GET INTO THE MINDSET.
WHY DO YOU DO WHAT YOU DO?
BEYOND THY MORTAL CONCEPTS OF TIME AND SPACE--
I RECORDED THESE INTERVIEWS FROM TV, FROM PODCASTS...A COUPLE I DID MYSELF.
I WANTED TO KNOW THEIR MINDSET.
FOR REAL, THERE IS NO BALANCE.
WHY THEY DO IT.
WHEN PEOPLE NEED YOU, YOU KEEP GOING.
HOW THEY DO IT.
IT WAS...WHAT I NEEDED TO HEAR.
BECAUSE NO ONE ELSE WILL.
IT'S THE ONLY THING THAT KEEPS ME ALIVE.
LIKE IT OR NOT, I WAS GIVEN A POWER. I HAVE TO TAKE THE RESPONSIBILITY.
FIGHT FOR LOVE.
NOBODY KNOWS WHO'S UNDER THIS MASK. BUT THAT WON'T STOP THE ENCLAVE.
AND SAY "INJUSTICE WILL NOT STAND."
THEY'RE AT WAR. THEY HAVE BEEN FOR 80 YEARS-- SINCE THEY SAW HORTON'S SYNTHETIC MAN.
THIS ALL STARTED WITH THE HUMAN TORCH...

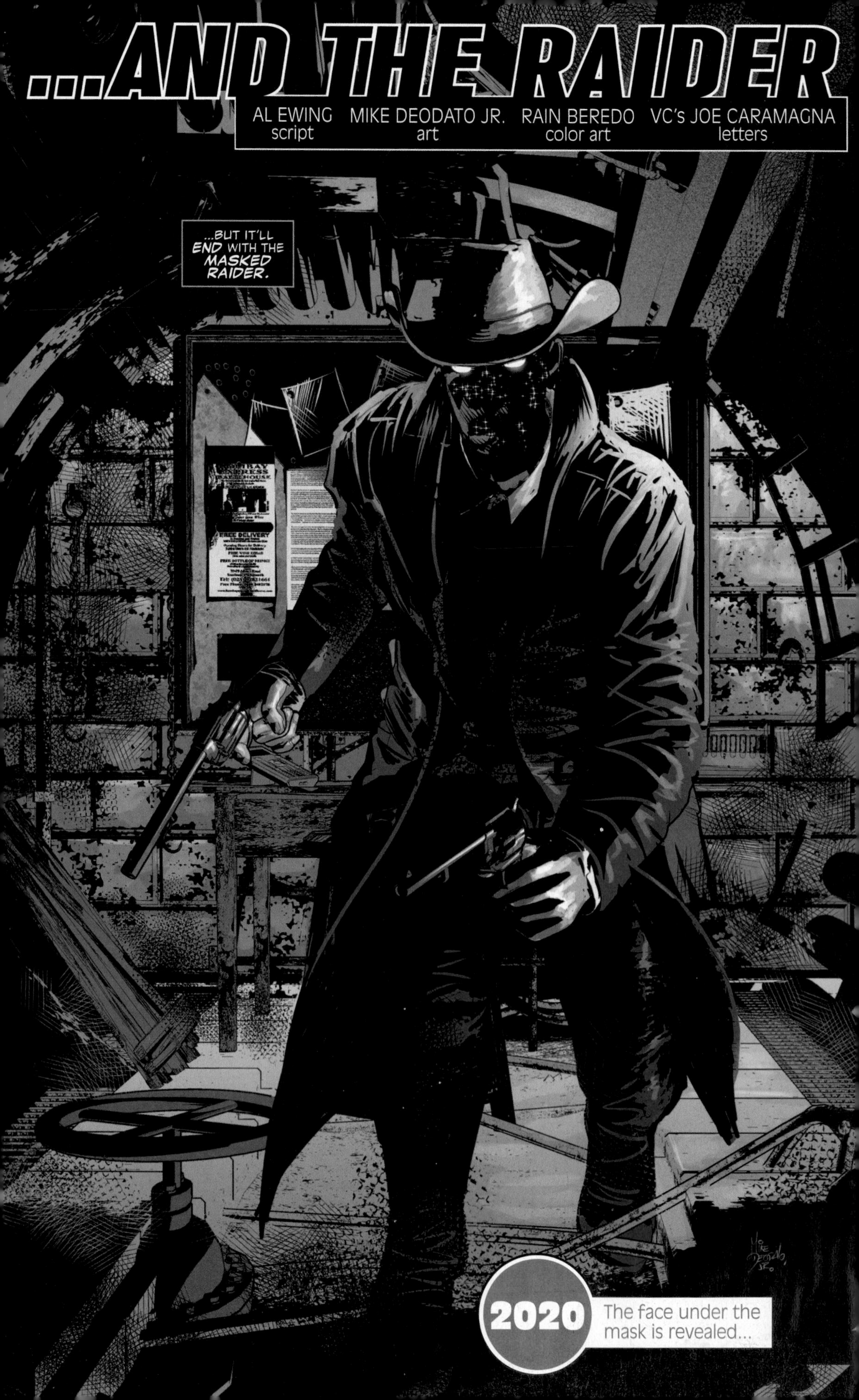

...AND THE RAIDER
AL EWING script
MIKE DEODATO JR. art
RAIN BEREDO color art
VC's JOE CARAMAGNA letters
...BUT IT'LL END WITH THE MASKED RAIDER.
FREE DELIVERY
2020
The face under the mask is revealed...

Tomorrow

Al Ewing script
Paul Azaceta art
VC's Joe Caramagna letters

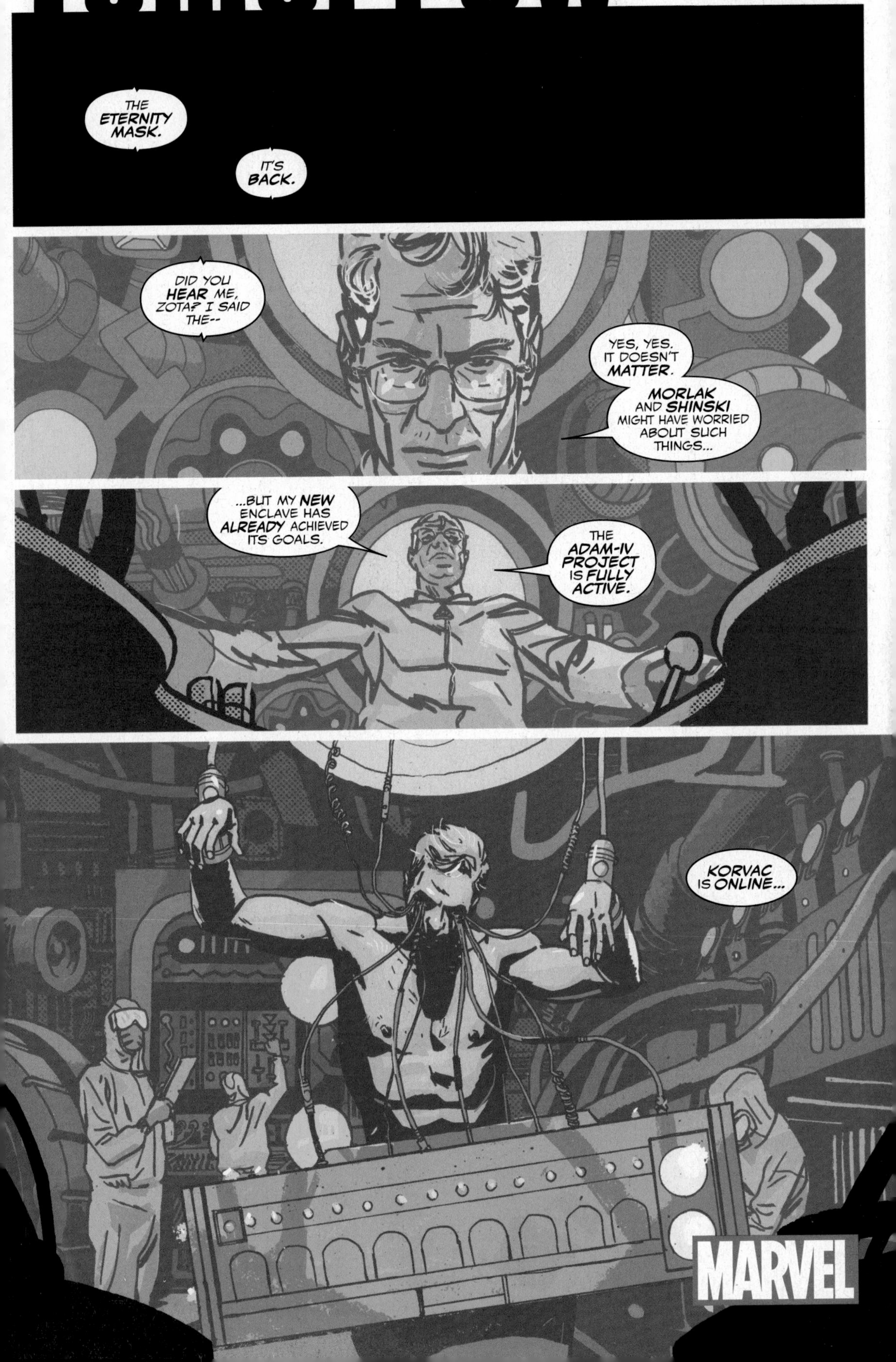
THE ETERNITY MASK.
IT'S BACK.
DID YOU HEAR ME, ZOTA? I SAID THE--
YES, YES. IT DOESN'T MATTER.
MORLAK AND SHINSKI MIGHT HAVE WORRIED ABOUT SUCH THINGS...
...BUT MY NEW ENCLAVE HAS ALREADY ACHIEVED ITS GOALS.
THE ADAM-IV PROJECT IS FULLY ACTIVE.
KORVAC IS ONLINE...
MARVEL

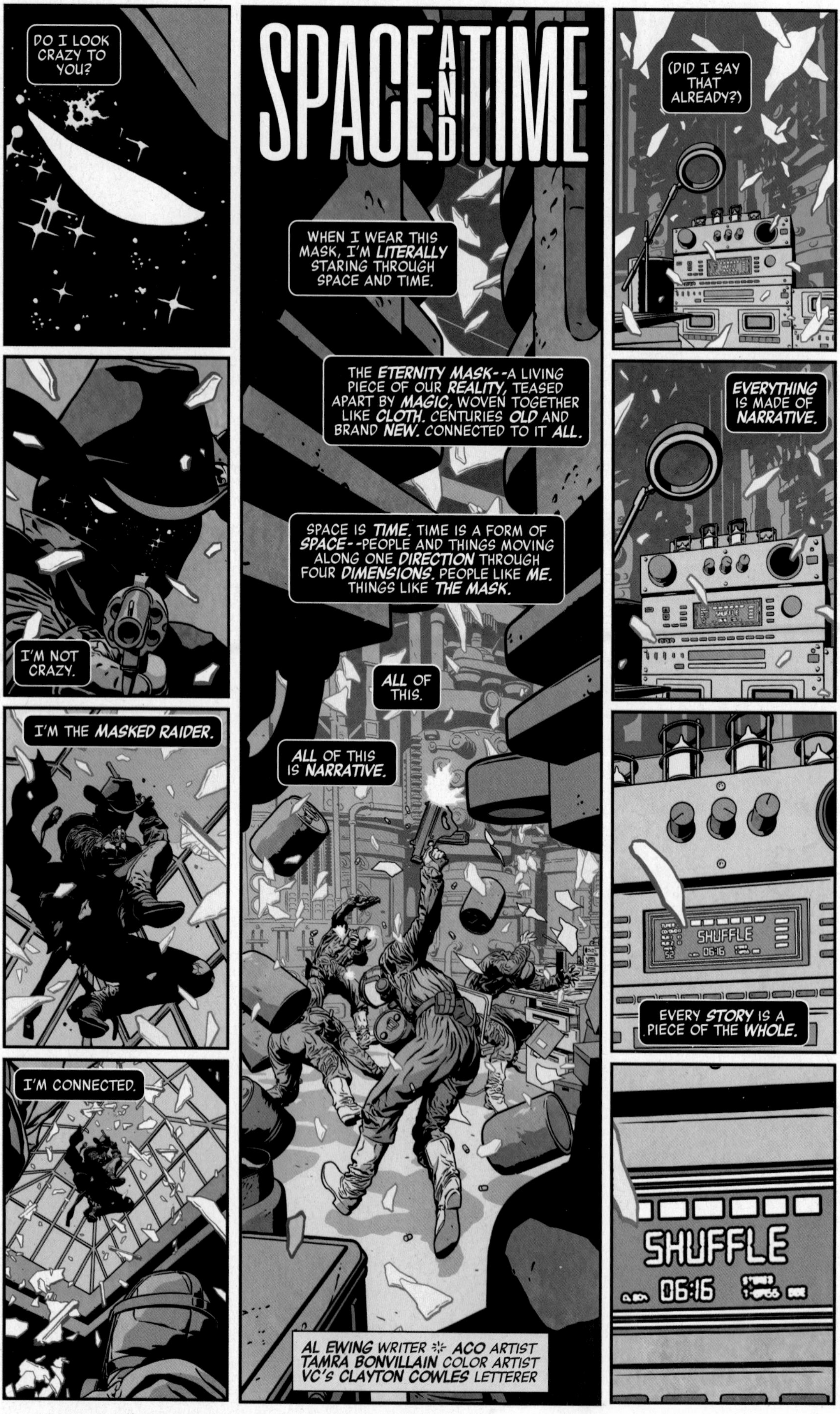
DO I LOOK CRAZY TO YOU?
SPACE AND TIME
WHEN I WEAR THIS MASK, I'M LITERALLY STARING THROUGH SPACE AND TIME.
(DID I SAY THAT ALREADY?)
I'M NOT CRAZY.
THE ETERNITY MASK--A LIVING PIECE OF OUR REALITY, TEASED APART BY MAGIC, WOVEN TOGETHER LIKE CLOTH. CENTURIES OLD AND BRAND NEW. CONNECTED TO IT ALL.
EVERYTHING IS MADE OF NARRATIVE.
SPACE IS TIME. TIME IS A FORM OF SPACE--PEOPLE AND THINGS MOVING ALONG ONE DIRECTION THROUGH FOUR DIMENSIONS. PEOPLE LIKE ME. THINGS LIKE THE MASK.
I'M THE MASKED RAIDER.
ALL OF THIS.
ALL OF THIS IS NARRATIVE.
SHUFFLE
06:16
EVERY STORY IS A PIECE OF THE WHOLE.
I'M CONNECTED.
SHUFFLE
06:16
AL EWING WRITER ACO ARTIST
TAMRA BONVILLAIN COLOR ARTIST
VC'S CLAYTON COWLES LETTERER

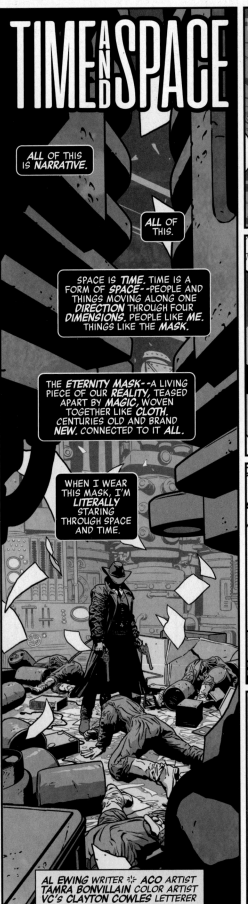

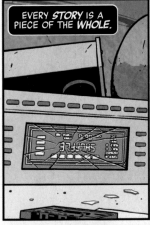

IN *DEFENDERS #4*, THE TEAM TRAVELED TO THE FOURTH COSMOS, WHERE THEY ENCOUNTERED ARCHETYPAL VERSIONS OF THE HEROES AND VILLAINS OF THE MARVEL UNIVERSE. HERE IS A GUIDE TO THEIR NAMES AND WHO EACH IS THE ARCHETYPE FOR.

1. **"ONE-IS-FOUR" – HULK**
2. **"FOUR-IS-ONE" – THE FANTASTIC FOUR**
3. **"OF-STARS" – AMERICA CHAVEZ**
4. **"OF-VIOLENCE" – WOLVERINE**
5. **"AIM-TRUE" – HAWKEYE**
6. **"OF-BELOW" – ABOMINATION**
7. **"OF-VENGEANCE" – GHOST RIDER/PUNISHER**
8. **"OF-STORM" – THOR**
9. **"SMALL-IS-BIG" – WASP**
10. **"OF-JUSTICE" – DAREDEVIL**
11. **"OF-STRENGTH" – SHE-HULK**
12. **"OF-SUN" – STAR-LORD**
13. **"BIG-IS-SMALL" – ANT-MAN**
14. **"OF-PAST" – CAPTAIN AMERICA**
15. **"OF-FUTURE" – IRON MAN**
16. **"OF-SKY" – STORM**
17. **"OF-STARS" – AMERICA CHAVEZ**
18. **"NEVER-OPEN" – DOCTOR DOOM**
19. **"COULD-BE-YOU" – SPIDER-MAN**
20. **"ALL-IS-LOST" – NOVA**
21. **"ALL-IS-WON" – CAPTAIN MARVEL**
22. **"WHAT-MUST-BE"/ "WHAT-CAN-BE" – GALACTUS**
23. **"WATCH-ALL" – NICK FURY**
24. **"OF-FIRE" – HELLSTROM**
25. **"OF-EARTH" – SANDMAN**
26. **"COULD-BE-WE" – VENOM**
27. **"BE-ALL" – ABSORBING MAN**
28. **"ALL-KING" – BLACK PANTHER**

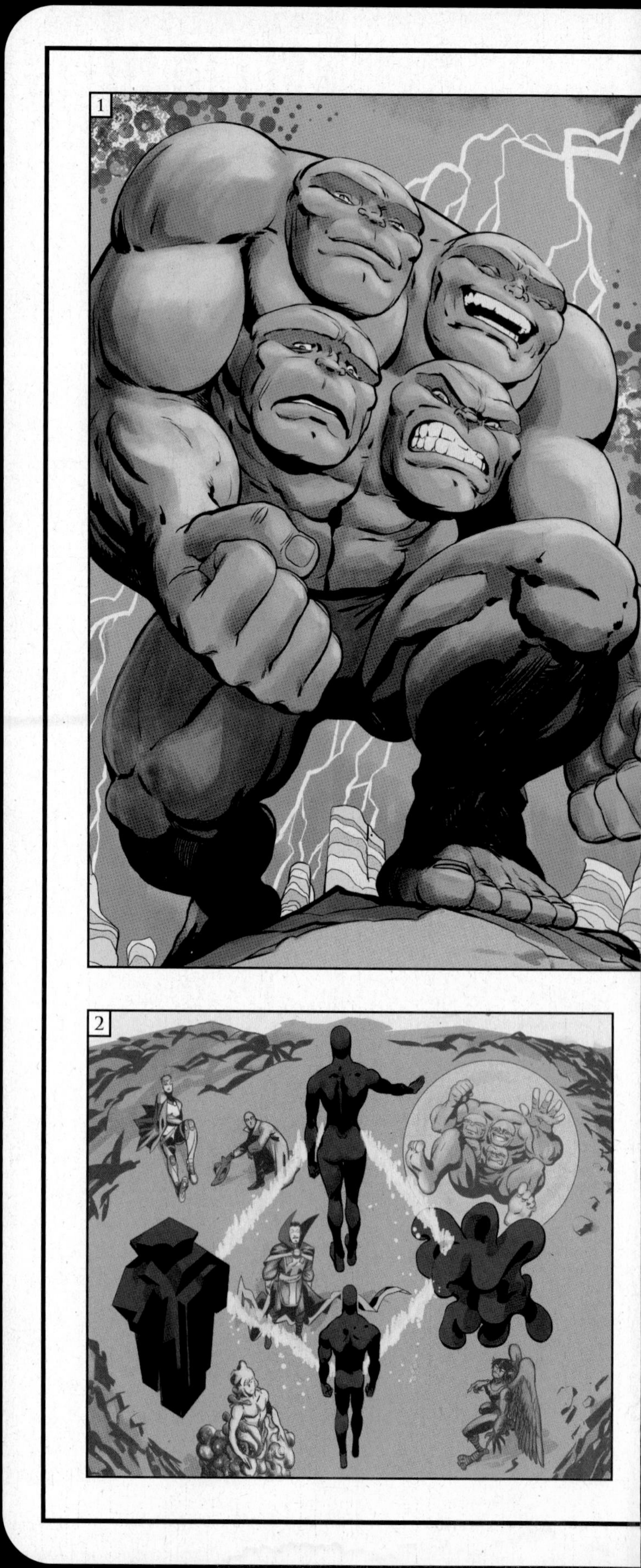
1
2

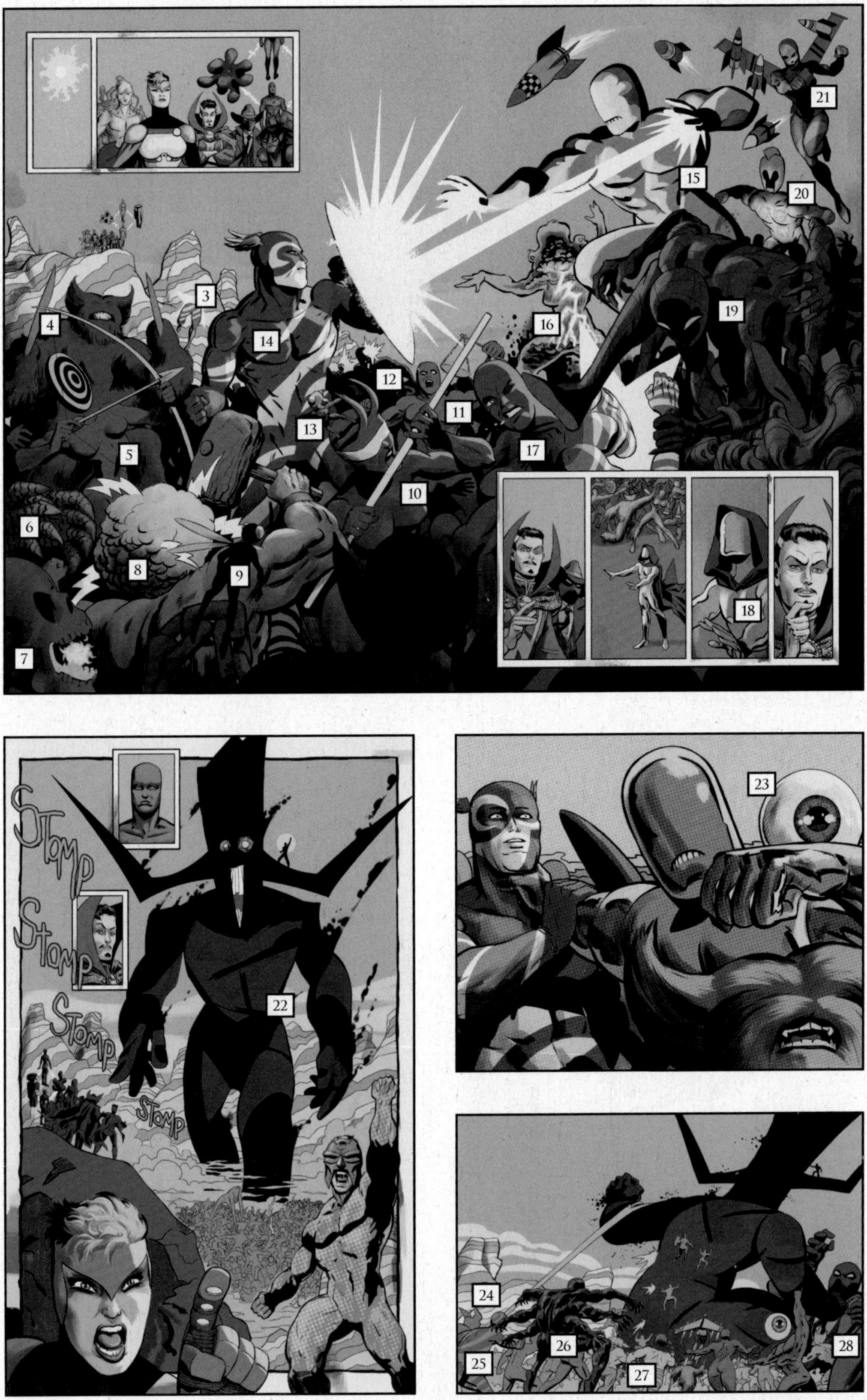
3
4
5
6
7
8
9
10
11
12
13
14
15
16
17
18
19
20
21
STOMP
STOMP
STOMP
STOMP
22
23
24
25
26
27
28

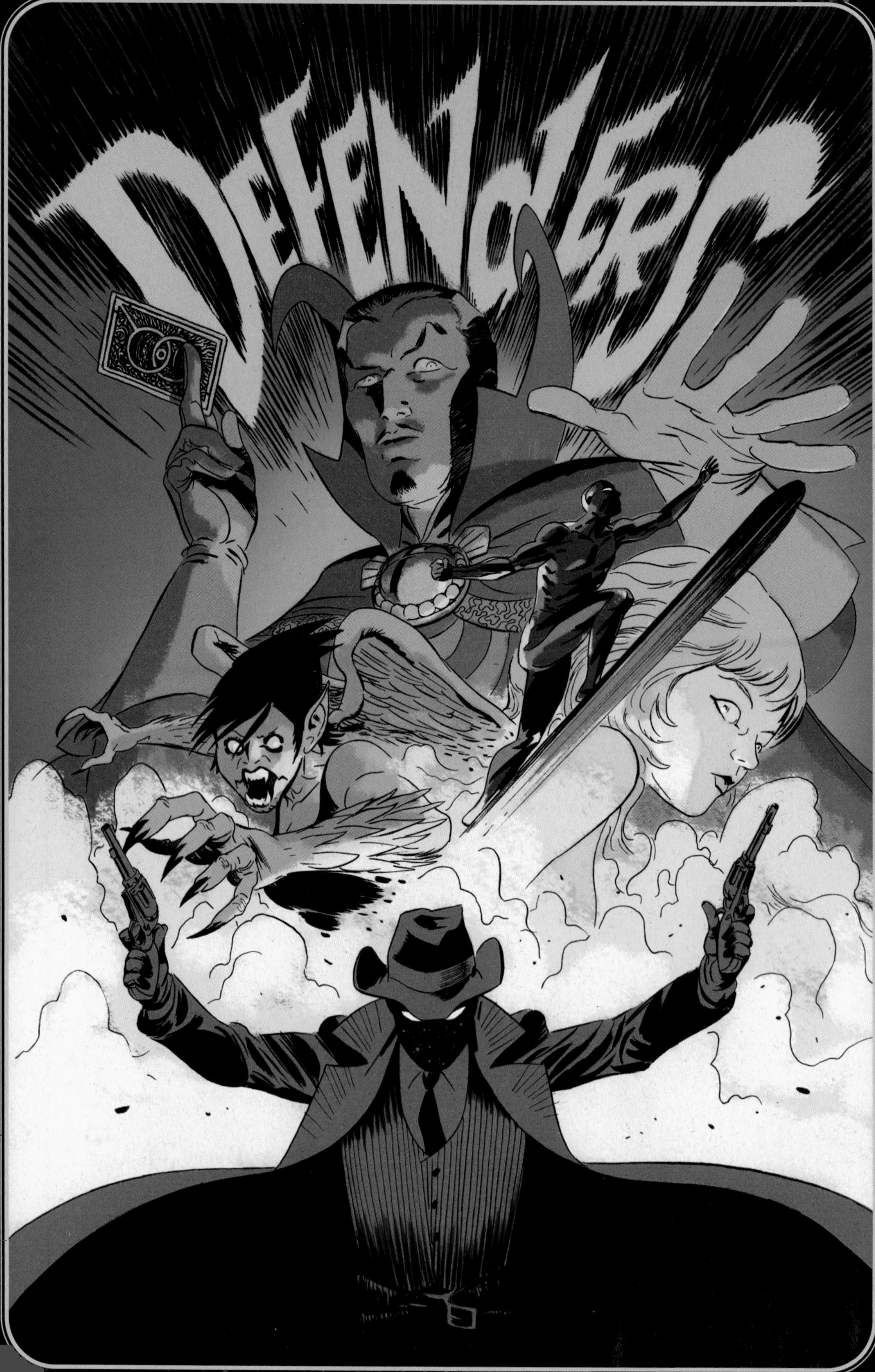
DEFENDERS

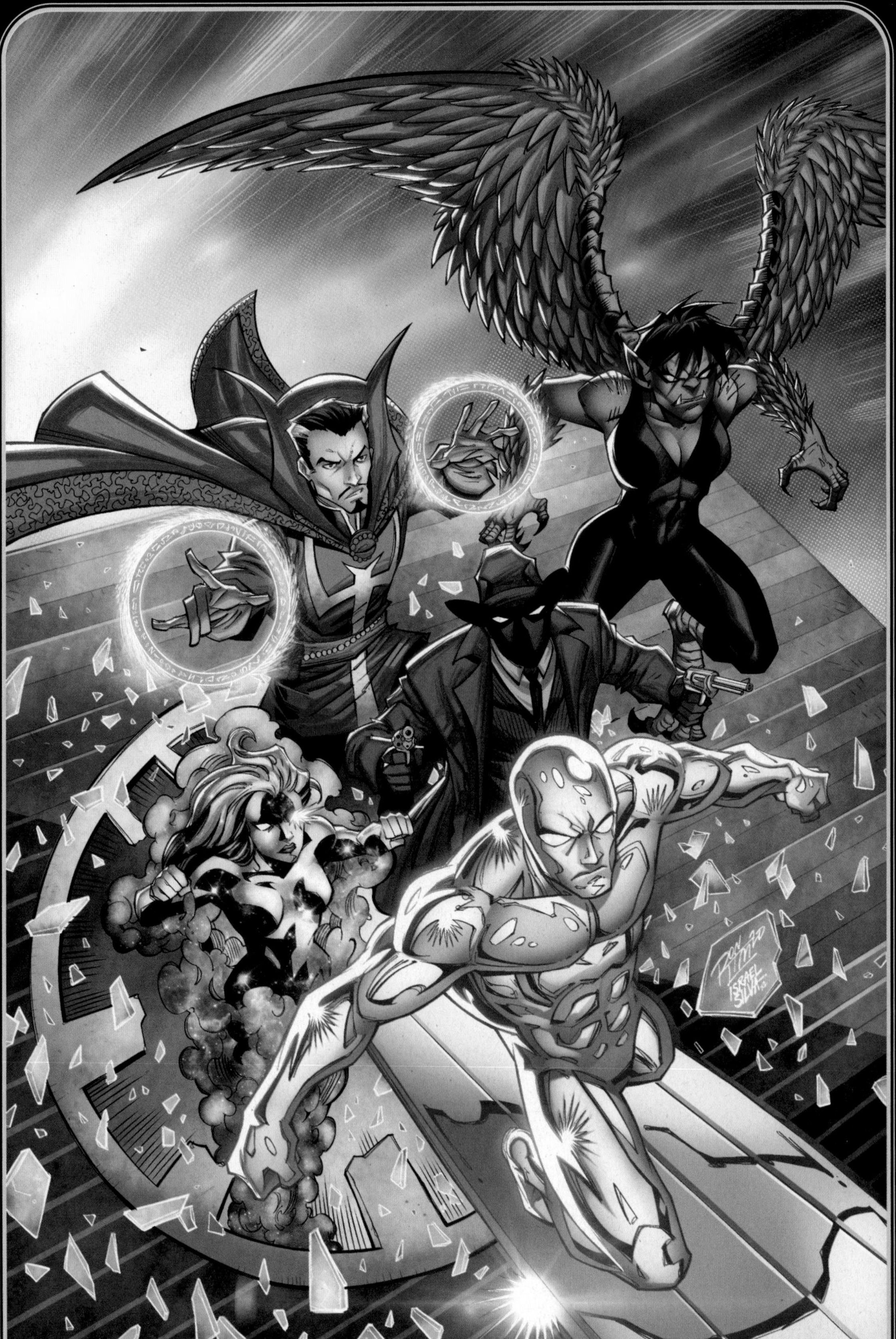

#1 VARIANT BY

RON LIM & ISRAEL SILVA

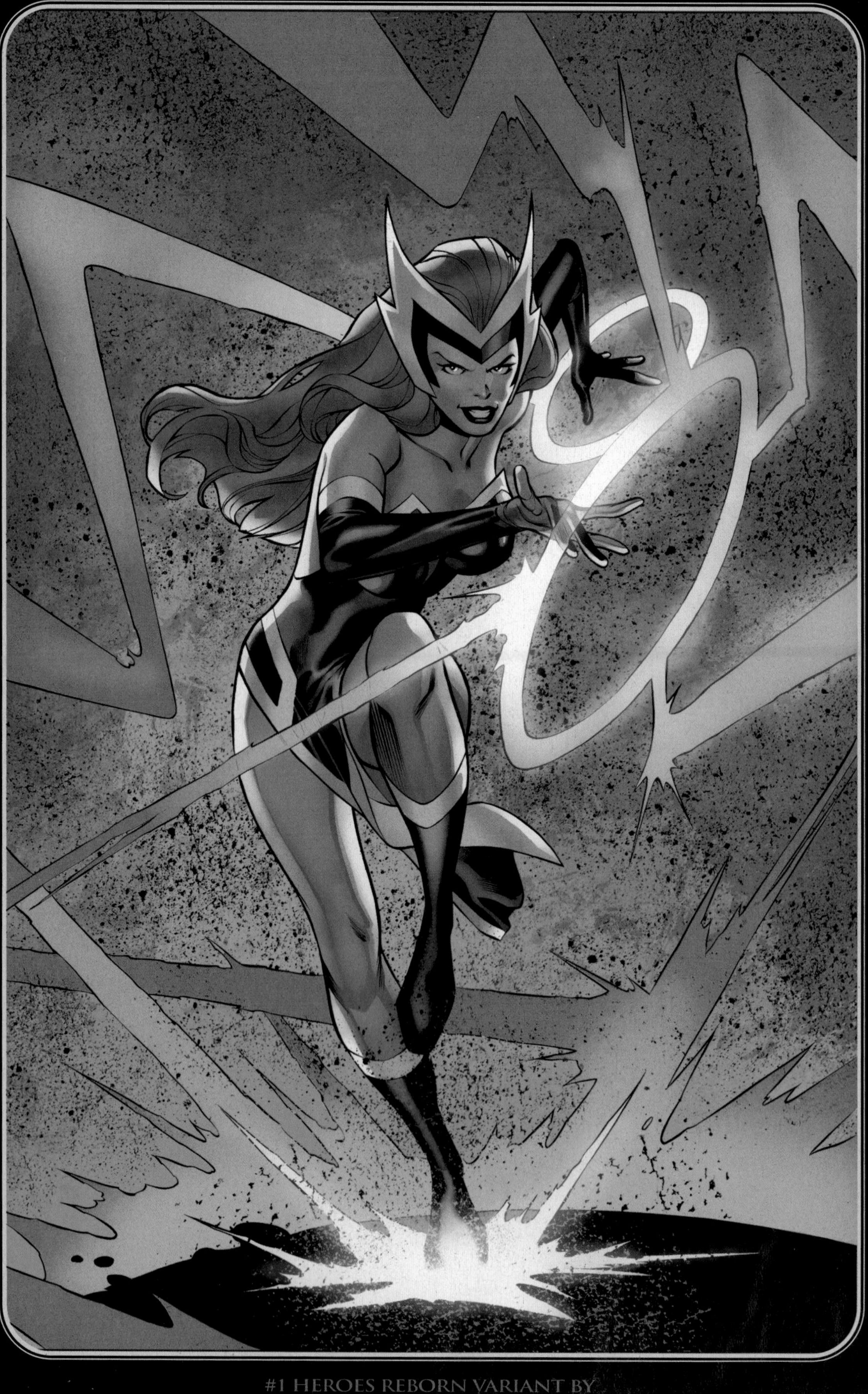

#1 HEROES REBORN VARIANT BY
CARLOS PACHECO, RAFAEL FONTERIZ & RACHELLE ROSENBERG

#1 VARIANT BY
PEACH MOMOKO

#1 VARIANT BY
PEACH MOMOKO & DEAN WHITE

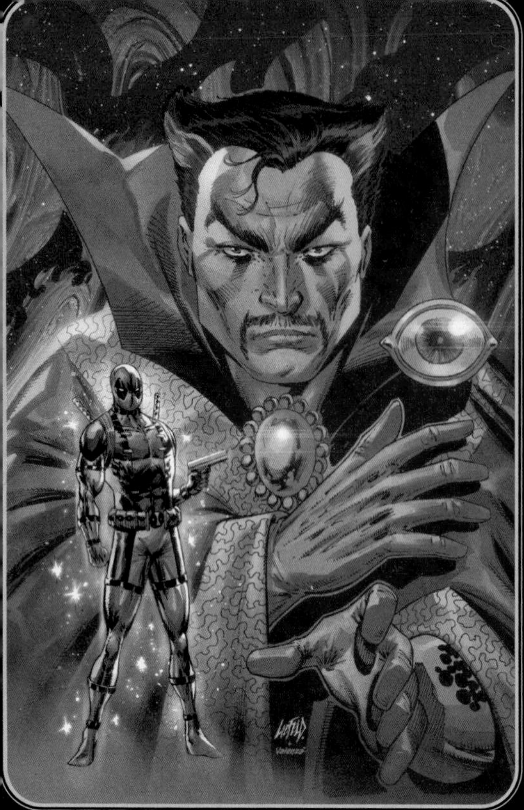

#1 DEADPOOL 30TH ANNIVERSARY VARIANT BY
ROB LIEFELD

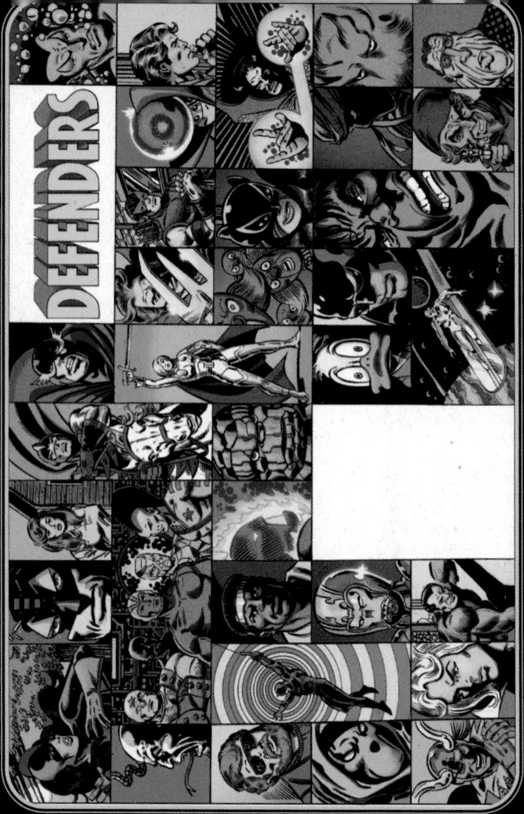
DEFENDERS

#1 HIDDEN GEM VARIANT BY
GEORGE PÉREZ & JASON KEITH

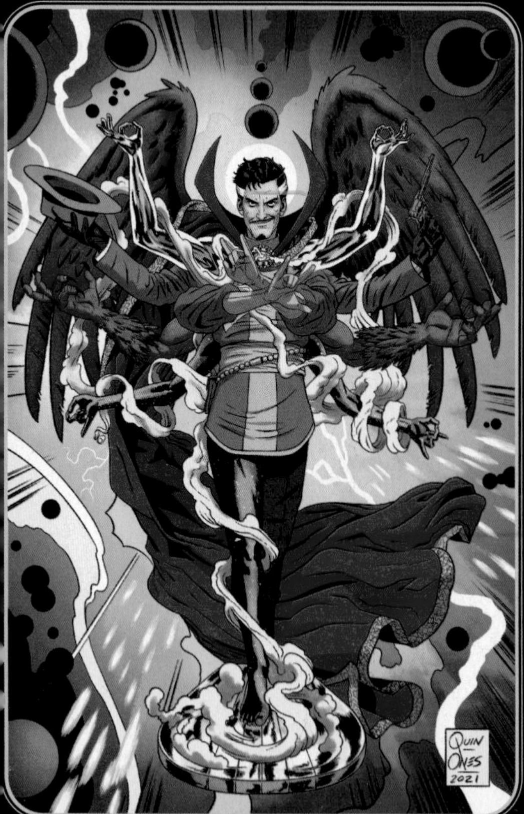
QUIN ONES 2021

#2 VARIANT BY
JOE QUINONES & JAVIER RODRÍGUEZ

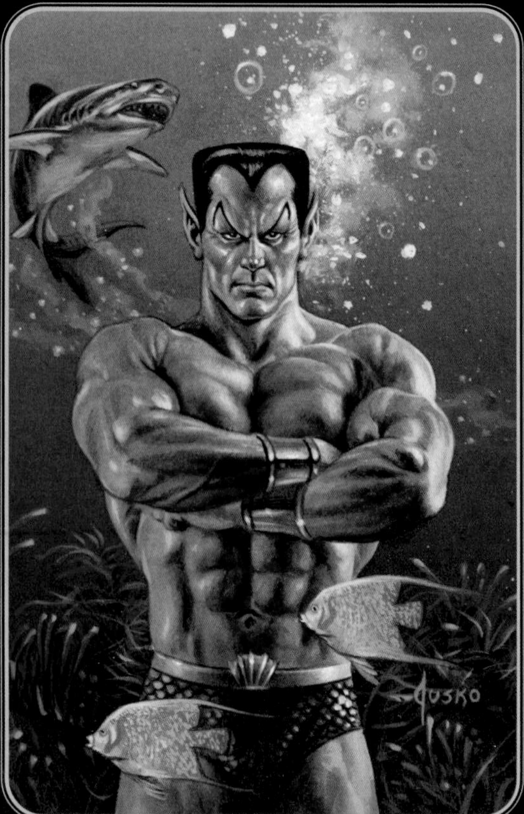
JUSKO

#3 VARIANT BY
JOE JUSKO